Carol Costa and C. Wesley Addison, CPA

Alpha
Teach Yourself

Accounting

in **24** hours

ALPHA

A Pearson Education Company

Alpha Teach Yourself Accounting in 24 Hours

International Standard Book Number: 0-02-864158-2
Library of Congress Catalog Card Number: 2001088753

Printed in the United States of America

First printing: 2001

03   02   4

Note: This publication contains the opinions and ideas of its authors. It is intended to provide helpful and informative material on the subject matter covered. It is sold with the understanding that the authors and publisher are not engaged in rendering professional services in the book. If the reader requires personal assistance or advice, a competent professional should be consulted.

ACQUISITIONS EDITOR
Mike Sanders

DEVELOPMENT EDITOR
Nancy D. Warner

PRODUCTION EDITOR
Billy Fields

COPY EDITOR
Krista Hansing

INDEXER
Amy Lawrance

PRODUCTION
Angela Calvert
John Etchison
Mary Hunt
Gloria Schurick

COVER DESIGNER
Alan Clements

BOOK DESIGNER
Gary Adair

PUBLISHER
Marie Butler-Knight

PRODUCT MANAGER
Phil Kitchel

MANAGING EDITOR
Jennifer Chisholm

Overview

Contents

Appendixes

Introduction

The goal of this book is to teach the reader the basic principles of the monthly accounting process, from the first step of developing a Chart of Accounts to the last step of issuing financial statements and tax reports.

Although accounting software programs are widely used, they are only as good as the information that is being entered into the computer. True, these programs are time savers in that so many functions are done automatically. However, that very element of automatic postings and reports may cause problems for users who do not understand essential accounting procedures. Even the simplest programs have the potential to produce erroneous reports if the entries are not properly prepared and entered into the system.

If you have already purchased an accounting software program, you know that the first thing it requires you to do is set up a Chart of Accounts for your business. That challenge may be daunting enough to cause many people to shut down the program and abandon the thought of doing their own account-ing. Yet, even if you hire someone else to do the accounting for your business, it is prudent for you to understand how the system works.

Bank loans, credit ratings, and major inventory purchases are often determined by financial reports. At the very least, you must know how to read those reports and use the information to keep your business running successfully.

There is an old adage that the first step is always the hardest. The underlying thought is that if you can get past the first step, it gets easier to accomplish your task.

This book is designed to guide you through that first difficult step and then keep you from missing any other important steps along the way.

If you are willing to commit 24 hours of your time to the lessons in this book, you can acquire the knowledge necessary to set up and manage an accurate accounting system.

The processing of financial data within the accounting system is accom-plished through the use of journals that flow into the General Ledger, allow-ing the information for the financial statements to flow out.

Cash Receipts and Cash Disbursements>>>>GENERAL
LEDGER>>>>Balance Sheet and Profit and Loss Statement

You will learn how to develop and maintain these journals, and how to enter the data into the General Ledger so that the financial statements can be issued.

The key to a smooth running accounting system is organization. You will learn how to structure a basic system that can be expanded to include more features and reports as needed.

There will be some slight variances in procedures and account structures depending on the type of business that is being serviced, but the fundamentals of accounting do not change. Once you have learned the basics, you will find that they apply to almost any business or personal enterprise.

You don't need exceptional math skills. Accounting is mostly addition and subtraction. An inexpensive calculator will work nicely. You don't have to be computer-literate. A set of books can be kept manually with paper and pencil.

GO TO ▶
This sidebar gives you a cross-references to another chapter or section in the book to learn more about a particular topic.

A good accounting system will provide all the reports and information needed to run a successful business. It will enable you to monitor transactions, inventory, cash flow, and profits. It will also keep track of income and deductions for tax purposes.

Whether you want to set up an accounting system for your own business or you simply want to gain knowledge to enhance your qualifications for the job market, you can teach yourself accounting in the next 24 hours.

Last but not least, this book has a lot of miscellaneous cross-references, tips, shortcuts, and warning sidebar boxes. Here's how they stack up:

JUST A MINUTE

 This sidebar offers advice or teaches an easier way to do something.

TIME SAVER

 Here you'll find information on a faster way to do something.

PROCEED WITH CAUTION

These are warnings that caution you about potential problems and help you steer clear of trouble.

 These are quick references to direct you toward furtherreading and examples in other sources.

STRICTLY DEFINED

These boxes offer definitions of terms you may not know.

About the Authors

Carol Costa is a professional writer with a business background in accounting and real estate. She specializes in articles on accounting, taxes, and real estate investment. Her features have been published in numerous magazines and newspapers in the United States and Canada. Costa has owned and managed a bookkeeping and tax service, worked as a staff accountant at a CPA firm, and managed accounting systems for a variety of small and large businesses. In 1978, Costa completed courses in Corporate Tax Accounting and Creative Writing at the University of Arizona. From 1983 to 1985 she worked as a correspondent for the *Phoenix Business Journal* and the *Tucson Business Chronicle*. She has also worked as a newspaper editor and a theater critic. Carol Costa is based in Tucson, Arizona.

C. Wesley Addison is a Certified Public Accountant and the senior partner in the public accounting firm of Addison & Gadea P.C. After earning a degree in accounting at the University of California San Diego in 1975, he went on to obtain a Master's degree in accounting at the University of Arizona in 1978. Addison specializes in HUD accounting and income tax for corporations, partnerships, and individuals. A member of AICPA and the Arizona Society of Certified Public Accountants, Addison has twenty-two years of experience in all aspects of accounting and taxes. C. Wesley Addison is based in Tucson, Arizona.

Acknowledgments

Thanks to our families, who are a constant source of encouragement and support.

Thanks to our agent, Andree Abecassis of Ann Elmo Agency, for her friendship and expert representation.

Thanks to Mike Sanders, Nancy Warner, Billy Fields, and the staff of Pearson Education who contributed their expertise to this book.

PART I

The Chart of Accounts, How it Relates to the General Ledger and the Financial Statements

HOUR 1

The Chart of Accounts/Balance Sheet Accounts

CHAPTER SUMMARY

LESSON PLAN:

In this hour you will learn about ...

- The purpose of the Chart of Accounts
- Its function in the accounting system
- The development of the General Ledger
- The Balance Sheet Accounts: Assets, Liabilities, and Equity

A Chart of Accounts is the blueprint used to build an accounting system. It is both functional and flexible. Simply stated, the Chart of Accounts is an index or a listing of the files or sections in the accounting system used to store financial records.

Creating the Chart of Accounts will provide valuable insight into the internal structure of an accounting system and the way it should work.

Certain accounts are used by every business and are therefore always included in the Chart of Accounts. Other accounts may or not be used, depending on the type of business that is being operated.

For example, a retail business needs inventory, so that account would be added to the store's Chart of Accounts. On the other hand, a service business, such as a law firm, does not sell tangible products, so an inventory account would not be needed.

In other words, the Chart of Accounts is customized to fit the needs of the business or individual that will use the accounting system. It should also be prepared with future growth in mind.

GO TO ▶
Refer to Hour 7, "Cost of Sales or Services," for a detailed explanation of inventory and the records that it necessitates.

Many businesses start out as a one-person operation and quickly expand into companies with multiple locations and employees. It is wise to study and develop a system that will adequately handle all aspects of accounting, such as payroll and taxes. You want these features set up and ready to go as soon as the need arises. In the long run, this will save you time and money.

Your accounting system can be set up in one of two ways: on an *accrual* basis or a *cash* basis.

STRICTLY DEFINED

> In an accounting system, the **accrual** method allows a business to record revenue that is forthcoming from sales or services. At the same time, the business can record expenses that are pending against that income, even if they have not actually been paid out. If you operate your business on a **cash** basis, you recognize and report income at the time you receive it. Expenses are also recorded in the accounting system at the time they are paid.

Setting up your books on an accrual basis provides a better view of your financial condition because it allows you to more accurately track revenue and expenses. Income is recognized and recorded in the accounting system at the time the sale or service transpires. On the other side, purchases and expenses are recorded as they are made, rather than when the costs are truly disbursed.

Most businesses offer their customers the option of using cash or credit to purchase products or services. The business owner purchases goods and supplies on credit also. Accounting systems that are set up on an accrual basis allow credit sales and purchases to be easily handled and recorded.

GO TO ▶
Refer to Hour 3, "Chart of Accounts Becomes the General Ledger," for specific instructions on setting up the accounts and posting opening balances to the accounting system.

In today's world of instant credit, "buy now and pay later" is the normal way business transactions are handled. It follows that accounting systems should be set up to keep the records that these transactions necessitate in good, reportable order.

INTRODUCTION TO THE GENERAL LEDGER

After the Chart of Accounts is developed, those accounts become the General Ledger.

All financial transactions eventually end up in the General Ledger. This is the heart of the accounting system, where accounts can be examined and adjusted before being transferred to the financial statements.

On a financial statement, the accounts are categorized into a Balance Sheet and a Profit and Loss Statement. These reports provide an in-depth look at the business and the information required for banks, vendors, management decisions, and tax reports.

The Balance Sheet is made up of Assets, Liabilities, and Equity accounts. The Profit and Loss Statement contains Income, Cost of Sales, and Expenses.

When the Chart of Accounts is being developed, the accounts are categorized and arranged for their final appearance on the financial statements. While the financial statements are the last step or the final result of the accounting process, the Chart of Accounts is the first step toward reaching that end.

THE BALANCE SHEET ACCOUNTS

Many companies view the Balance Sheet as the most important of the financial reports because the Balance Sheet reflects the net worth of the company. Crucial financial decisions on bank loans and credit ratings are often determined by the Balance Sheet alone.

The accounts that you will learn about in this hour are listed in the order they appear on the Balance Sheet. This will help to familiarize you with the various accounts, their importance, and their usual placement in the General Ledger.

You will create a chart that can be used for either a sales or a service business. Each account will have its own name and will be assigned a number that designates the order in which it will appear in the General Ledger and on the financial statements.

Each category of accounts has a particular range of numbers that can be assigned to it as well. As each account is named and assigned a number, its purpose in the accounting system will be briefly explained.

FYI Although numbering accounts is not new, it was a step that could be skipped when setting up a manual accounting system. However, computer software programs require that the accounts be assigned four-digit numbers because those numbers allow the computer programs to sort the accounting files and produce the reports.

Even if you are not initially planning to use a computerized accounting program, it is a good idea to assign numbers to each account so that they are ready to be computerized at a later date.

ASSETS

Assets are things of value that belong to a business. In a computer software program, the numerical range assigned to assets is 1000 to 1999.

Under this heading, you list accounts in this category that are common to most businesses. As the accounts are created and placed in the asset section, consideration is given to whether the asset will be *current* or *long-term*.

STRICTLY DEFINED

A **current asset** is one that is readily available for use or liquidation. A **long-term asset** is one that may not be available for immediate use.

Current assets are listed first in the Chart of Accounts and then appear at the beginning of the Balance Sheet. Cash is a current asset, and the cash accounts are always listed first.

Cash in Checking (Account 1000) reflects the amount of money in the operating account or the account that is used to deposit revenue and pay expenses.

Most businesses also have a savings account, and the next account listed should be Cash in Savings (Account 1010). You may or may not use this account during the year; this is usually a depository account where surplus cash or profits are kept. This could be another checking account, but it is more likely to be a savings account so that the funds in it can earn interest.

GO TO ▶
Refer to Hour 6, "Daily Sales Transactions," for instructions on recording credit sales and setting up files for individual customers.

Cash on Hand (Account 1020) is used to keep track of the change fund needed for the cash register of a retail business. It can also be a fund used for small cash expenditures and is sometimes called the Petty Cash account.

The next one to be listed on the Chart is Accounts Receivable (Account 1100). This is an account necessary to keep books on an accrual basis; it will be used to record credit sales.

Keeping in mind that this Chart of Accounts can be used for either a sales or a service business, the next account is Inventory (Account 1200).

As merchandise is purchased, the cost is added to the Inventory account. As merchandise is sold, the cost is deducted from this account. This keeps a running total of the goods available for sale.

On a monthly or yearly basis, depending on the size of the business, a physical inventory is taken. Every piece of merchandise is counted and evaluated to make sure that the balance in the Inventory account agrees with the merchandise or actual products on hand.

PROCEED WITH CAUTION

Keeping track of inventory is a time-consuming task, but it is essential to running a successful retail business. For a small business, a physical count should be taken each month, and the balance in the inventory account should be adjusted accordingly. This will alert the owner to shortages resulting from theft or damage before they become too costly.

Next on the Chart of Accounts are the accounts that report the value of the tangible assets of the business. Most of these are depreciable assets, and the cost of these assets is written off over a period of time. Assets classified as depreciable are those that begin to lose their value over the years from use, aging, and normal wear and tear.

If the company occupies its own building, an account should be set up for the land on which the building is located. The cost of the land is recorded in Land (Account 1300). The value of the land is always deducted from the total cost of the improvements, such as buildings or other structures. Unlike the next assets that you will list, land is not depreciated.

In general, the next asset accounts to be set up are used to record the cost of items of significant value used in the operation of the business. As a rule, items expected to have a year or more of useful life that cost more than $500 are posted to these accounts. Items of lesser cost or useful life are written off as expenses.

Since you have already set up an account for land, the next account is Building (Account 1350). A building is a depreciable asset; therefore, an account to record the amount of the depreciation month to month and year to year will also be set up. It is Accumulated Depreciation–Building (Account 1351). Note that the account number for the depreciation account places it immediately after the Building account.

If values were recorded in these two accounts, they would appear on the Balance Sheet as follows:

Building	$ 100,000
Accumulated Depreciation–Building	–10,000

Anyone looking at the Balance Sheet can make a quick calculation and see that the depreciated value of the building is currently $90,000. The depreciation account for each asset directly follows the asset that it refers to, making the financial information easier to interpret.

GO TO ▶
Refer to Hour 4, "Depreciable Assets, Prepaid Expenses, and Other Accounts," to learn about the types of assets that are depreciated, the different types of depreciation, and how the entries are made.

Often business property is leased. However, if you lease an empty warehouse or retail space in a shopping center, you usually have to pay for the improvements done to accommodate your business needs. The cost of these improvements is a depreciable asset. You set up an account called Leasehold Improvements (Account 1400), and you add Accumulated Depreciation–Leasehold Improvements (Account 1401) as well.

Automobiles and trucks are used in many businesses, so this account appears on most charts as Vehicles (Account 1450). The value of the vehicle at the time it was put into service for business use is recorded in this account. This is followed by Accumulated Depreciation–Vehicles (Account 1451).

Furniture and Fixtures (Account 1500) encompasses store fixtures, chairs, and desks. The depreciation for these items is recorded in Accumulated Depreciation-Furniture and Fixtures (Account 1501).

The cost of computers, cash registers, and the like can be recorded in Equipment (Account 1550). You also add Accumulated Depreciation–Equipment (Account 1551). A computer is an asset that clearly demonstrates the need for depreciation—sleeker, faster, and more efficient models are constantly being developed. Computers need to be replaced on a regular basis just to keep up with current technology.

A variety of costs are associated with setting up a brand new business. Because some of these expenses are substantial, they should be recorded in Organization Costs (Account 1570). Organization costs can be written off over a period of time. However, because the amounts recorded in this account are cash expenditures for intangible things such as license fees, rather than objects, it is called *amortization*. The end result is the same. Each year the amount of the asset is reduced.

The account that is set up to record the decrease in the value of this asset is called Amortization–Organization Costs (Account 1571).

JUST A MINUTE

Depreciating assets provides valuable managerial information. The decreasing value of the asset reported on the Balance Sheet allows the owner to see how much useful life remains in the business property and also provides the opportunity to budget and plan for replacements and repairs. "Depreciating assets" is a function and it is singular.

Deposits (Account 1580) is set up for cash deposits paid on rental property, or deposits required by utility companies. At the end of a specified time period, the deposits in this account are returned to the business. This account retains the dollar amount of the deposits until they are returned to one of the cash accounts. This is a good example of a long-term asset because the value of it may not be available to the business for an extended period of time.

Other Assets (Account 1600) is used to record miscellaneous items of significant value that will not depreciate over time. One example of the type of asset recorded in this account might be a U.S. Patent, which is more likely to increase in value than decrease.

Before you move on to the Liability section of the Balance Sheet, remember that as you progress through the hours of this book, you will be learning about other accounts. As these accounts are introduced and explained, you will be adding them to the Chart of Accounts and the General Ledger.

LIABILITIES

Liabilities are the debts incurred by a business. They can include bank loans, personal loans, credit card purchases, and taxes payable to federal or state governments. In a computerized system, Liabilities are assigned numbers in the range of 2000 to 2999.

Accounts Payable (Account 2000) is usually the first account to be listed in the Liabilities section of the Balance Sheet. This account contains the combined balances owed to vendors for merchandise, supplies, or services for the business.

Liabilities are usually classified as short-term or long-term. This is simply a way of noting which debts will affect the business over the long haul.

GO TO ▶
Refer to Hour 7 for detailed instructions on recording credit purchases of inventory and supplies, as well as setting up individual vendor accounts.

GO TO ▶
Refer to Hour 10, "The Importance of Work Papers, Receipts, and Other Records," to learn how to keep sales tax records, complete the reports, and pay the tax in a timely manner.

Long-term Liabilities are the principal amounts on installment loans on which payments are made on a monthly basis for an extended period of time. For example, an auto loan is a long-term liability.

Short-term or current liabilities are debts that must be paid within a month or two, usually no longer than one year. That is why Accounts Payable is listed first. Everything recorded in that account is expected to be paid out within 30 days or so.

Just as current assets are found at the beginning of that section of the Balance Sheet, short-term liabilities are arranged in the Chart of Accounts to appear first under the Liability section in the Balance Sheet.

The sales tax account will not be needed by all businesses, but it applies to most. This tax is governed by the state or states in which business is conducted. Sales Tax Collected (Account 2100) is used to record the tax collected on sales of merchandise. It is usually reported and paid on a monthly basis.

GO TO ▶
Refer to Hour 12, "Payroll Taxes: Employee/Employer," for in-depth explanations of the taxes associated with payroll and employees.

Accrued Payroll Taxes (Account 2300) can be set up to accumulate the various taxes associated with employees. Even if a new business does not yet have employees, it is a good idea to set up this account. Many accounting systems divide the payroll tax account into the types of taxes, such as Social Security tax, Medicare tax, and federal withholding tax—this will be explained in detail in Hour 12. Payroll taxes are reported and paid on a monthly or quarterly basis, so, like sales tax, they are considered to be a short-term or current liability.

Loans Payable are generally long-term debts and should be specifically titled to include the name of the payee, for example, Loan Payable–First National Bank (Account 2400) and Loan Payable–John Doe (Account 2450). This enables the accounting system to keep track of individual debts, and it provides a record of payments and current balances.

Credit Cards Payable can be either a short-term or long-term debt, depending on how quickly or slowly they will be paid in full. Again, the specific name of the creditor should be included in these account titles, as in Credit Card Payable–VISA (Account 2460). Note that from the placement and the account number assigned, you are assuming that the credit card bill will be paid over a longer period of time.

It is a good idea to include a catchall account where any miscellaneous debts can be recorded, titled Accrued Expenses (Account 2500). This account may not be used on a regular basis, but it is there if needed.

EQUITY ACCOUNTS

Equity is the value of a business or property that remains after claims or expenses have been deducted. In accounting terms, the total value of the assets minus the total amount of the liabilities equals equity.

This brings you to the final section of the Balance Sheet where the equity accounts appear. They are listed right after the liabilities. In a computerized system, the equity account numbers begin with 3000 and end with 3999.

If the business is a corporation with stock and stockholders, Common Stock (Account 3010) is listed on the Chart of Accounts. The number of shares issued to stockholders is multiplied by the value of each share and is recorded in this account.

Perhaps the most important account in the Chart of Accounts is Retained Earnings (Account 3040). This is where the net profit or loss of the business is recorded and accumulated over the months or years. This may be the first account that someone looks at when viewing the Balance Sheet because it reflects the success or failure of the day-to-day business operations.

Capital (Account 3210) is the Equity account that reflects the amount of the initial investment put into the business to get it started. Most of the time that investment is cash, but other things of value, such as the cost of equipment or vehicles designated for use in the business, could be considered capital and should be recorded in this account.

If the business has a number of partners, a capital account can be set up for each partner. This would enable the accounting system to keep track of the exact amount that each partner contributed to the business.

Drawing (Account 3220) is used to record withdrawals by business owners. Again, if there are partners, a separate drawing account should be set up for each one to monitor the amounts that they take out of the business.

When the Balance Sheet accounts are put into use, they have either debit or credit totals. Generally, asset accounts carry debit balances; liability and equity accounts carry credit balances.

The Balance Sheet is the first accounting report to be generated for a new business. Even if the business has not yet begun to operate or process any other financial transactions, it will most likely have assets, liabilities, and equity.

GO TO ▶
Refer to Hour 3 to learn about opening entries for the accounting system, explanations of which accounts carry debit balances and which accounts carry credit balances, and how they offset each other.

This is the Chart of Accounts that was created in this hour. You can see that the accounts are listed in the same order as they were named in the preceding text. You also can see that each account listing is identified based on where it would appear on the Balance Sheet.

Chart of Accounts Setup Report	Balance Sheet Section
1000 Cash in Checking	Asset
1010 Cash in Savings	Asset
1020 Cash on Hand	Asset
1100 Accounts Receivable	Asset
1200 Inventory	Asset
1300 Land	Asset
1350 Building	Asset
1351 Accumulated Depreciation–Building	Asset
1400 Leasehold Improvements	Asset
1401 Accumulated Depreciation–Leasehold Improvements	Asset
1450 Vehicles	Asset
1451 Accumulated Depreciation–Vehicles	Asset
1500 Furniture & Fixtures	Asset
1501 Accumulated Depreciation–Furniture & Fixtures	Asset
1550 Equipment	Asset
1551 Accumulated Depreciation–Equipment	Asset
1570 Organization Costs	Asset
1571 Amortization–Organization Costs	Asset
1580 Deposits	Asset
1600 Other Assets	Asset
2000 Accounts Payable	Liability
2100 Sales Tax Collected	Liability
2300 Accrued Payroll Taxes	Liability
2400 Loan Payable–First National Bank	Liability
2450 Loan Payable–John Doe	Liability
2460 Credit Card Payable–VISA	Liability
2500 Accrued Expenses	Liability
3010 Common Stock	Equity

Chart of Accounts Setup Report	Balance Sheet Section
3040 Retained Earnings	Equity
3210 Capital	Equity
3220 Drawing	Equity

You now have the basic accounts needed to produce the Balance Sheet. You will find a sample of a Balance Sheet in Appendix B, "Sample Forms."

HOUR'S UP!

In this hour, you were given a good deal of information about the Chart of Accounts and the Balance Sheet. Try to answer the following questions without referring back to the text.

1. What are the three sections that make up a Balance Sheet?

   a. Income, Expenses, Equity

   b. Assets, Liabilities, Equity

   c. Assets, Depreciation, Profits

2. Crucial financial decisions may be determined by a company's Balance Sheet.

   a. True

   b. False

3. All Liabilities listed on the Balance Sheet are long-term.

   a. True

   b. False

4. Organization Costs are written off by:

   a. Deletion

   b. Amortization

   c. Depreciation

5. What is a Chart of Accounts?

   a. A blueprint used to build an accounting system

   b. A listing of files used to store financial information

   c. The first step in producing financial statements

   d. All of the above

6. The Capital account can be found in what section of the Balance Sheet?

    a. Equity

    b. Asset

    c. Liability

7. Most businesses use a cash basis accounting system.

    a. True

    b. False

8. Furniture & Fixtures can be found in what section of the Balance Sheet?

    a. Liabilities

    b. Assets

    c. Equity

9. Land is a depreciable asset.

    a. True

    b. False

10. A retail store needs an Inventory account.

    a. True

    b. False

QUIZ

HOUR 2

Profit and Loss Statement Accounts

LESSON PLAN:

In this hour you will learn about …

- The Profit and Loss Statement
- The accounts needed to record income
- The Cost of Sales accounts
- Accounts for recording General Expenses
- How the Profit and Loss Statement evolves from these accounts

The Profit and Loss Statement is the second half of the financial statements. This statement lists all the income and expenses of the business for a specified period of time. It is longer and more detailed than the Balance Sheet.

The structuring and selection of the information that will ultimately be included on the Profit and Loss Statement is determined by the things it is used for:

- It provides a recap or summation of all the financial transactions the business has conducted during the month.

- It determines whether the business is operating at a profit or a loss.

- It generates information that the business owner can use to manage the business.

- It includes the information needed to prepare federal and state tax returns.

As stated in Hour 1, "The Chart of Accounts/Balance Sheet Accounts," certain accounts appear on the Profit and Loss Statement of any business. Other accounts are only needed by a particular type of business. For example, an account to record delivery charges would be used by an auto parts dealer but would not be needed for a fast food restaurant. However, the Chart of Accounts that you will create for the Profit and Loss Statement will be one that can be used by a variety of business enterprises, so you will include some extra accounts that might not be needed for some companies.

GO TO ▶
Refer to Hour 22, "End-of-the-Year Payroll Reports and Other Tax Reports," to learn what tax reports must be filed and how to file them.

You will follow the same procedure used in Hour 1 for the Balance Sheet accounts. As each account is titled and listed, a brief explanation of its use or the reason for its inclusion will be presented.

INCOME ACCOUNTS

Everyone in business wants to make money, so the first accounts listed for the Profit and Loss Section of the financial statements are the income accounts.

In a computerized system, the income accounts are assigned numbers ranging from 4000 to 4299. Again, the way the accounts will eventually appear on the financial statements in a computerized system is determined by their numerical order in the system.

As the title implies, Sale of Goods or Services (Account 4000) can be used for most types of businesses. This account is used to record the company's primary income from sales or services.

Sales Discounts (Account 4010) is created to keep track of reductions allowed on merchandise sold at special prices.

A certain percentage of the goods and services sold will be deemed unsatisfactory to the customer for one reason or another. The account needed to record refunds and credits on prior sales is titled Sales Returns and Allowances (Account 4020).

GO TO ▶
Refer to Hour 8, "Discounts, Allowances, and Other Adjustments," to learn how to handle the various adjustments that are a part of the daily business operations.

Although Sales Discounts and Returns and Allowances are actually expenses to the business, the accounts are included in the income section of the Chart of Accounts because they are directly related to the initial income received from a sale. Like the depreciation accounts, they are placed in this position on the Chart of Accounts and the Profit and Loss Statement to point out a reduction in value of the income account.

Other Income (Account 4100) should be established for times when income cannot be classified as an ordinary business transaction or sale. This account can be used for any of those miscellaneous income amounts, such as the cash received for recycling damaged boxes or other containers.

Since you are assuming that the business will be profitable and have a bank account or two, the next account listed is Interest Income (Account 4150). The bank will provide statements on a monthly or quarterly basis to show the interest earned on the bank accounts; that interest can be recorded in this account.

One more account that should be included in this section of the Chart of Accounts may or may not be used: Sale of Fixed Assets (Account 4200). If one of the assets is sold during the year, the proceeds should be recorded in this account. It is important that the revenue realized from the sale of an asset, especially one that has been depreciated, be properly recorded for use in preparing the tax return.

GO TO ▶
Refer to Hour 4, "Depreciable Assets, Prepaid Expenses, and Other Accounts," for information on the disposition of depreciable assets.

COST OF SALES ACCOUNTS

The accounts that are set up to reflect the direct costs associated with a company's sales or services are aptly called Cost of Sales accounts. On the Profit and Loss Statement, these accounts are listed right after the income accounts.

The Profit and Loss Statement lists the income and the cost of sales, and then shows the difference between them as the *Gross Profit*. As you learn about the accounts in this section of the Chart of Accounts, you should be able to see the importance of the Gross Profit.

The general expenses associated with a business stay pretty well within a certain amount each month. Things such as rent, utilities, and salaries will not fluctuate much, so the owner knows how much will be expended for those items.

It's the direct cost expenditures, such as inventory purchases, that must be closely monitored. A comparison of the Gross Profit figure from one month to another serves as a guideline. If the Gross Profit is down, it may mean that the cost of merchandise purchased for sale has risen. This would then necessitate an increase in the sales price of the goods to avoid a loss for the following month.

JUST A MINUTE

You may think that the Gross Profit and Cost of Sales apply only to a business that sells merchandise. However, many service businesses are structured to use these accounts. A law firm, for instance, is a service business, but costs such as court fees or outside investigators are directly related to the income received from clients.

The Cost of Sales accounts in a computerized system, like the income accounts, are in the 4000 range, signifying their relationship to one another.

Purchases (Account 4300) is the account where the cost of goods intended to be resold is recorded. This account is directly related to the Balance Sheet Asset Inventory.

GO TO ▶
Refer to Hour 7, "Cost of Sales or Services," to learn how to keep an accurate record of purchases and determine the amount of inventory available for sale each month.

Purchase Discounts (Account 4310) is used to keep track of discounts related to purchases. Some vendors allow a discount if their billing statement is paid within 10 days; that discount would be recorded in this account.

Just as the consumer is allowed to return items sold to them, the company can also return products to its vendors and receive a refund or a credit. For these transactions, you establish an account called Purchase Returns and Allowances (Account 4330).

Like the accounts discussed for sales returns and credits, these last two accounts are established to show the decreases in the goods purchased for resale.

Another account that can be created for a business that purchases merchandise is Freight Charges (Account 4350). Placing this account in the cost of sales section is a good way to track the costs that vendors pass on to purchasers for shipping inventory to them.

To make this chart useful to a business that does not sell merchandise, you can establish an account titled Other Costs (Account 4400). This is another one of those catch-all accounts that is used for a variety of costs directly related to the income accounts. If desired, this account could be divided into different categories of the costs relevant to a particular type of business.

All the accounts that you have created in the 4000–4500 numerical range will be used to report the Gross Profit on the Profit and Loss Statement. Gross Profit, however, is not an account, but a total generated by the accounting system that reflects the difference between the total income and the total cost of sales. Remember that the Gross Profit is a significant part of the information required for good management.

EXPENSE ACCOUNTS

General expenses are totaled and deducted from the Gross Profit to determine the *Net Profit* on the financial statements. These expenses are varied, and the list can be extensive.

STRICTLY DEFINED

The **Net Profit** is the amount of income that remains after the General Expenses have been deducted from the Gross Profit. Income less Cost of Sales equals the Gross Profit. Gross Profit less Expenses equals the Net Profit.

To simplify things, you will create this portion of the Chart of Accounts with some groupings that encompass categories of related disbursements. That is, instead of having a separate account for gasoline, vehicle repairs, and license fees, you will create one account called Auto Expenses that will take in all of these expenditures.

Depending on the needs of the individual business, these items may need to be separated into different accounts, but once you understand how these expense accounts are created, you can easily do that on your own.

These expense accounts are created in the Chart of Accounts and are then transferred to the General Ledger.

Earlier in this hour, you learned that one of the determining factors in setting up the Chart of Accounts for the Profit and Loss Statement is for tax reporting. Generally, the expense accounts that you will create all have one thing in common: They are deductible on a business tax return.

A few expenses have been restricted by the Internal Revenue Service code in recent years. Those will be pointed out and explained as you move along. In a computerized accounting system, the numerical assignment range is 5000 to 6999 for general and administrative expense accounts.

General Expenses are sometimes arranged with the accounts that are expected to carry the largest balances listed first. Other accountants like to list the expenses alphabetically. Either way is fine, although it is not always easy to maintain the original order because accounts may be added or eliminated as time goes on. The expense accounts here will be listed in random order because their placement in the Profit and Loss Statement does not have to follow any particular format.

GO TO ▶
Refer to Hour 16, "Cash Disbursements Journal," to learn about the various disbursements and how they are posted to the expense accounts in the General Ledger.

With that said, you can start with Advertising (Account 5100). This account can encompass anything that relates to business promotions: radio and television ads, printed sales flyers mailed to customers, and special promotional expenses such as participation in craft fairs or other events.

Auto Expenses (Account 5150) is created as a general account for expenses involving the use of company vehicles, or reimbursement for the use of a personal auto for business.

The same rule applies to the expense accounts that were discussed in the preceding Hour for the Balance Sheet accounts. Even if a business has no employees, accounts should be set up and ready in the event that employees are hired at a later date. For this reason, Salaries and Wages (Account 6000) should be added to your Chart of Accounts.

GO TO ▶
Refer to Hour 4 to learn what assets are subject to Depreciation and how to write them off on a monthly or yearly basis.

Bank Service Charges (Account 6120) will be used to record all the fees that the bank deducts for its services.

Hour 1 introduced you to Accumulated Depreciation for assets. Now in the expense section, you need to set up an account titled Depreciation Expense (Account 6160). This account gathers all the depreciation for all assets so that it can be written off as an expense.

Since the Balance Sheet section also contains an Accumulated Amortization account, the expense section should have Amortization Expense (Account 6170).

Many businesses belong to merchant organizations or other groups that offer help and advice. They also subscribe to publications that keep them abreast of legal issues and market trends. An account titled Dues and Subscriptions (Account 6180) is used to record the expense associated with organizations and publications.

Equipment Rental (Account 6200) is set up for leases on copy machines, computers, and other equipment needed for business purposes.

For recording the payments for electricity, gas, water, or trash services, Utilities (Account 6220) is established.

Expenses for insurance premiums are usually divided into three categories, with a separate account for each one. Insurance–Employee Group (Account 6230) is for medical benefits. Insurance–General (Account 6240) is used to record premiums for business policies, such as fire, liability, and loss of income. The third insurance account is Insurance–Officers Life (Account 6250).

Interest Expense (Account 6260) is used to record interest that is paid on bank loans and other debts. All interest incurred on business indebtedness is deductible.

Fees paid for legal advice or tax services should be recorded in the account titled Legal and Accounting (Account 6270).

Miscellaneous Expense (Account 6280) is set up for small expenditures that don't fit into another account category.

Most companies have a separate account to track mailing costs—that is Postage (Account 6290). Everything else from paper to paper clips can be recorded in Office Expense (Account 6300).

Many companies rent their business space, and those rents are recorded in Rent Expense (Account 6360).

The next account to set up is Repairs and Maintenance (Account 6380). This account can be used to record payments to cleaning services or for repairs to business property.

Payroll Taxes (Account 6490), Other Taxes (Account 6500), and Income Tax (Account 6510) are accounts which can be used to record tax expenses for employees and business tax returns.

Penalties (Account 6520) is set up with the resolution that it will not be used. This account is for recording tax penalties that might be assessed on unpaid taxes.

Although there are other accounts where expenses for supplies can be recorded, companies that buy large quantities of particular items used on a regular basis might want to set up an individual account for this. Keep track of these expenditures in an account simply called Supplies (Account 6520).

Telephone bills can be a major expense, especially if business is conducted in other locales. A separate account is usually set up for this expense, titled Telephone (Account 6530). All phone charges, including those for portable phones and pagers, can be recorded in this account.

Travel (Account 6540) holds expenses for business travel.

A separate account should be set up for Meals (Account 6550), which can be used to record the cost of entertaining clients.

GO TO ▶
Refer to Hour 14, "Payroll Tax Reports," for an explanation of all the various taxes that a business may be responsible for paying, and instructions on forms and filings.

PROCEED WITH CAUTION

Tax deductions for entertainment have come under a lot of scrutiny from the IRS in recent years. Meticulous records must be kept detailing the purpose of the expense, exact dates, and the names of the business people present. Even then, all of the expenses may not be allowed. To avoid problems and penalties, consult a tax professional for advice.

You have now created a Chart of Accounts that can be used by a variety of businesses. You have also learned the order and placement of certain accounts. This precise order will be carried over from the Chart of Accounts to the General Ledger and finally to the financial statements.

Like the Balance Sheet accounts that you created in Hour 1, this Chart of Accounts for the Profit and Loss Statement can be expanded or customized to fit the needs of other businesses. As you work your way through the next steps of managing an accounting system, you will be introduced to a variety of companies that may require additional accounts and special procedures. However, for the initial transactions you will be learning, you will use the accounts now in place.

The following is the Chart of Accounts created for the Profit and Loss Statement in this hour. It also identifies what section of the Profit and Loss Statement each account belongs in.

Chart of Accounts Setup Report	Profit and Loss Section
4000 Sales of Goods or Services	Income
4010 Sales Discounts	Income
4020 Sales Returns and Allowances	Income
4100 Other Income	Income
4150 Interest Income	Income
4200 Sale of Fixed Assets	Income
4300 Purchases	Cost of Sales
4310 Purchase Discounts	Cost of Sales
4330 Purchase Returns and Allowances	Cost of Sales
4350 Freight Charges	Cost of Sales
4400 Other Costs	Cost of Sales
5100 Advertising	Expense
5150 Auto Expenses	Expense
6000 Salaries and Wages	Expense
6120 Bank Service Charges	Expense
6160 Depreciation Expense	Expense
6170 Amortization Expense	Expense
6180 Dues and Subscriptions	Expense
6200 Equipment Rental	Expense
6220 Utilities	Expense
6230 Insurance–Employees Group	Expense
6240 Insurance–General	Expense
6250 Insurance–Officers Life	Expense
6260 Interest Expense	Expense
6270 Legal and Accounting	Expense
6280 Miscellaneous Expense	Expense

Chart of Accounts Setup Report	Profit and Loss Section
6290 Postage	Expense
6300 Office Expense	Expense
6360 Rent Expense	Expense
6380 Repairs and Maintenance	Expense
6490 Payroll Taxes	Expense
6500 Other Taxes	Expense
6510 Income Taxes	Expense
6520 Penalties	Expense
6520 Supplies	Expense
6530 Telephone Expense	Expense
6540 Travel	Expense
6550 Meals	Expense

You now have the basic accounts needed to produce the Profit and Loss Statement. You will find a sample Profit and Loss Statement in Appendix B, "Sample Forms."

HOUR'S UP!

These questions deal with the additional accounts that you added to the Chart of Accounts to be used for the Profit and Loss Statement. Try to answer them without going back to the text.

1. Dues and Subscriptions is an Income Account.
    a. True
    b. False
2. How is the Gross Profit determined?
    a. Assets less Liabilities
    b. Income less Expenses
    c. Income less Cost of Sales
3. What items will be recorded in the Auto Expenses account?
    a. Gasoline
    b. Oil Changes
    c. Auto Repairs
    d. All of the above

QUIZ

4. The Profit and Loss Statement provides information needed to prepare tax returns.

   a. True

   b. False

5. What are the three categories of Insurance Expense accounts?

   a. Home Owners, Fire, and Health

   b. Group Health, Officers Life, and General

   c. Auto, Life, and General

6. How is Net Profit determined?

   a. Income less Cost of Sales less Expenses

   b. Income plus Expenses less Cost of Sales

   c. Assets less Liabilities

7. The cost of cellular phones and pagers is recorded in Telephone Expense.

   a. True

   b. False

8. Which of the following expenses will be recorded as an Office Expense?

   a. Electricity

   b. Legal Fees

   C. Paper

9. Tax deductions for Meals (Entertainment Expenses) are restricted by Internal Revenue Service.

   a. True

   b. False

10. Sales Discounts appear in what section of the Profit and Loss Statement?

    a. Income

    b. Cost of Sales

    c. Expenses

QUIZ

HOUR 3

Chart of Accounts Becomes the General Ledger

CHAPTER SUMMARY

LESSON PLAN:

In this hour you will learn about ...

- How the Chart of Accounts becomes the General Ledger
- Setting up the accounting periods
- Preparing opening entries
- Posting debits and credits

You have already been given some information about the General Ledger: It is the basic structure of the accounting system. It is the place where accounts can be examined and adjusted. At the end of each month, the balances in the General Ledger accounts are transferred to the Balance Sheet and the Profit and Loss Statement.

Perhaps the most important thing to remember about the General Ledger is this: The General Ledger must always be kept in balance. That means that the debits will always offset the credits, and vice versa.

Initially, the Chart of Accounts is placed into the General Ledger as it was created. It remains in the same order. Each account is listed on a separate page in the General Ledger, and that page has columns or spaces for the transactions that will be posted during the month and the year.

Each General Ledger account will be set up with the following column headings:

- **Date.** This column is used to record the date.
- **Reference No.** This column is used to record the entry numbers posted to that account. During the month, numerous entries are posted to the General Ledger. Usually these are numbered so that if a question arises, the entry can be more easily identified and located.
- **Description.** This is a brief explanation of the entry that has been posted.

GO TO ▶
Refer to Hour 6, "Daily Sales Transactions," to learn how to post these transactions to the General Ledger.

- **Debit or Credit.** The amount of the transaction will be recorded in either the Debit or the Credit column. The ending balance of the account will also appear in either the Debit or the Credit column, depending on the balance of the account when it is being reviewed.

Pads of columned ledger paper can be purchased at any office supply store to help you set up your General Ledger pages.

Here is a sample of how the cash accounts will look when they are transferred to the General Ledger:

Date	Ref. No.	Description	Debit	Credit
1000	Cash in Checking	Beginning Balance	0.00	
		Ending Balance	0.00	
1010	Cash in Savings	Beginning Balance	0.00	
		Ending Balance	0.00	

All the accounts in the Chart of Accounts will be set up in exactly the same way. Since no transactions have been posted, there are no entries in the Date or Reference No. columns, and the balances of the accounts are still at zero. However, the account balance will change each time an entry is posted to the account.

ACCOUNTING PERIODS

Once the General Ledger is set up, you must establish the accounting periods that will be used. Most businesses operate on a calendar year; the year begins on January 1 and ends on December 31 each year.

However, some businesses use a *fiscal year.* A fiscal year is a 12-month period that does not begin and end in the same year. For example, a fiscal year that begins on April 1, 2000, ends on March 31, 2001. A company that does a large amount of business during the summer months might chose a fiscal year that begins when its sales are the strongest. The fiscal year for such a company would begin June 1st and end May 31st.

STRICTLY DEFINED

Only corporations and partnerships operate on a **fiscal year** because the end of the accounting year determines when the federal tax return is due. A small business transfers its profit or loss to the individual owner at the end of the year, to be reported on a personal tax return that is always due April 15 of the following year.

For the purposes of this book, you will assume a 12-month accounting period that begins January 1 and ends December 31. That is not to say that a business cannot begin in the middle of the year. It can, but even if it begins in September, for accounting and tax purposes it will still end on December 31. In that case, your General Ledger for the first year would only have entries for four months, but those four months would constitute an entire year on the owner's personal tax return.

OPENING ENTRIES

Assume it is January 1 and you are setting up an accounting system for a new business. You have created the Chart of Accounts and have used them to set up your General Ledger. The next step is the opening entries.

Opening entries are made for everything that the business acquired in order to open its doors, make that first sale, or service that first client. A bookshop, for instance, might have the following things in place: a bank account, retail space in a mall, furniture, fixtures, equipment, and inventory.

Assume that the owner had $15,000 to begin this business venture and borrowed an additional $5,000 from the bank. This gives the owner a total of $20,000.

The owner then made the following expenditures: desk and chair, $200; store fixtures, $1,300; books, $8,000; cash register, $600; first month's rent on retail space, $500. The total cost of these items is $10,600, which leaves the owner $9,400 in his bank account.

Here is a recap of all the financial activity that will be part of the opening entry for this business:

Cash in Bank	$9,400.00
Inventory	8,000.00
Furniture & Fixtures	1,300.00
Equipment	600.00
Loan Payable–First National Bank	5,000.00
Capital	5,000.00
Office Expense	200.00
Rent Expense	500.00

This represents everything the business has as of January 1, and this information must be entered into the accounting system. However, before an entry can be made, you must remember that the General Ledger must always be kept in balance. Debits must always equal credits, and vice versa.

DEBIT AND CREDIT ACCOUNTS

A debit is a positive number. A credit is a negative number. Sometimes these numbers are referred to as black or red. Years ago, bookkeepers recorded debits with black ink and credits with red ink. When a business was said to "be in the red," it meant that it had too many negative numbers and was in a loss situation.

Accounting ledgers at that time were done manually. The term "in the red" is still used occasionally with regard to bank accounts, but accounting systems no longer use the term or that distinction.

In modern accounting systems, a negative number has a minus sign in front of it or is shown in parentheses, for example, –200.00 or (200.00). This alerts you to the fact that the number is a credit rather than a debit. This does not mean that the account is registering a loss; a credit balance today simply means that it is an offset to a debit.

GO TO ▶
Refer to Hour 19, "The Trial Balance," to see how the General Ledger retains its zero balance status as every debit account is offset by a credit account.

Every account in the General Ledger has either a debit or a credit balance. When these are all added together, the end result should be zero because they are meant to offset each other.

Some accounts normally carry a debit balance. On the other side, some accounts normally carry a credit balance. Before you post the opening entry for the bookstore, you must determine which of the listed amounts will be credited to the designated General Ledger account and which will be debited.

The following chart lists the accounts in the General Ledger and indicates whether it normally carries a debit or a credit balance.

Debit Accounts	Credit Accounts
Cash in Checking	Accumulated Depreciation
Cash in Savings	Accumulated Amortization
Accounts Receivable	Accounts Payable
Inventory	Loan Payable–FNB
Deposits	Loan Payable–John Doe
Land	Credit Card Payable–VISA
Building	Accrued Payroll Taxes

Debit Accounts	Credit Accounts
Leasehold Improvements	Sales Tax Collected
Vehicles	Accrued Expenses
Furniture & Fixtures	Common Stock
Equipment	Retained Earnings
Organization Costs	Capital
Other Assets	Sales of Goods/Services
Sales Discounts	Other Income
Sales Returns & Allowances	Interest Income
Drawing	Purchase Discounts
Purchases	Purchase Returns
Freight Charges	
Other Costs	
Advertising	
Auto Expenses	
Salaries & Wages	
Bank Service Charges	
Depreciation Expense	
Amortization Expense	
Dues & Subscriptions	
Equipment Rental	
Utilities	
Insurance–Employees Group	
Insurance–General	
Insurance–Officers Life	
Interest Expense	
Legal & Accounting	
Miscellaneous Expense	
Postage	
Office Expense	
Rent Expense	
Payroll Taxes	
Other Taxes	
Income Tax	

continues

continued

Debit Accounts	Credit Accounts
Penalties	
Supplies	
Telephone Expense	
Travel	
Meals	

Notice that there are more debit accounts than credit accounts in the list of accounts in the General Ledger. This is only because there are so many categories of expenses that are recorded in separate accounts, and all expenses are considered to be debit accounts.

JUST A MINUTE

A number of accumulated depreciation accounts exist in your General Ledger, one for each depreciable asset. All of those accumulated depreciation accounts carry a credit balance and are offset by the debit account Depreciation Expense.

POSTING TO THE GENERAL LEDGER

Every debit that is posted will have a credit posted to offset it. In most cases, there are related accounts that work together to achieve this balance. Some of them, such as Accumulated Amortization in the asset section and Amortization Expense in the expense section, are obvious because they have similar titles. The same holds true for Accrued Payroll Taxes in the liabilities section and Payroll Taxes in the expense section.

Study the next chart to familiarize yourself with the offsetting debit and credit accounts in the General Ledger. You will see that the Cash account is the one account that is used over and over again as an offsetting account. When revenue is received, cash is debited; when an expense is paid, cash is credited.

Debit Account	Offsetting Credit Account
Cash in Checking	Sale of Goods or Services
Rent Expense	Cash in Checking
Loan Payable–John Doe	Cash in Checking
Cash in Checking	Purchase Returns
Inventory	Cash in Checking

Debit Account	Offsetting Credit Account
Sales Returns and Allowances	Cash in Checking
Insurance–General	Cash in Checking
Cash in Checking	Capital
Cash in Savings	Interest Income
Bank Charges	Cash in Checking
Deposits	Cash in Checking
Cash in Checking	Other Income
Drawing	Cash in Checking

This brings you back to the opening entry that still needs to be posted to the General Ledger.

You have already seen a recap of this financial activity. It could be posted as one entry, and that's how it would ordinarily be done. However, because you are just learning about debits and credits and how they offset each other, taking each part of the activity separately and posting it that way first will be more helpful.

The owner had $15,000 to begin his business venture. That would be posted as follows:

Cash in Checking	15,000.00 debit
Capital	(15,000.00) credit

The owner's cash was deposited into the checking account. It was added to the account, so the dollar amount is a debit to that account. To offset this debit, the Capital account that was set up to record the amounts invested in the business is credited for the same amount.

The owner then borrowed an additional $5,000 from First National Bank:

Cash in Checking	5,000.00 debit
Loan Payable–First National Bank	(5,000.00) credit

The proceeds from this loan were also deposited in the checking account, another debit to that account. The offset is a credit to the liability account that resulted from the loan because the money will have to be paid back to the bank.

The owner made the following expenditures: desk and chair, $200.00:

Cash in Checking	(200.00) credit
Office Expense	200.00 debit

A check for $200 was written to pay for the desk and chair. Since money was taken out of the bank, the checking account is credited. The other side of that is the debit to the expense account to record the expense to the business.

GO TO ▶
Refer to Hour 1, "The Chart of Accounts/Balance Sheet Accounts," to learn why assets costing less than $500 should be written off as an expense.

The owner purchased store fixtures at a cost of $1,300:

Cash in Checking	(1,300.00) credit
Furniture & Fixtures	1,300.00 debit

Another check was written to cover the cost of the fixtures, so again the checking account is credited. This is a major purchase, so the cost of the fixtures should be added or debited to the asset account Furniture & Fixtures.

Inventory (books) was obtained at a cost of $8,000:

Cash in Checking	(8,000.00) credit
Inventory	8,000.00 debit

More money came out of the bank account to pay for the books, so the checking account receives another credit. The books will be sold to customers and as merchandise for resale, so the cost of them is added or debited to the Inventory account.

A cash register was purchased for $600:

Cash in Checking	(600.00) credit
Equipment	600.00 debit

The checking account is credited once again to record the cost of the cash register. The register can be classified as equipment, and because it is also a major purchase, the cost of it is added or debited to the Equipment account.

The first month's rent on the retail space was paid in the amount of $500:

Cash in Checking	(500.00) credit
Rent Expense	500.00 debit

The last expenditure is for rent on the retail space, resulting in a credit to the checking account. The offset is a debit for the same amount to the expense account Rent.

Notice how many times the cash account was used to offset the other entries. Also take note that every entry has a debit and a credit that, when added together, result in zero.

The following is how the General Ledger accounts will look as a result of these postings.

Date	Ref. No.	Description	Debit	Credit
1000 Cash in Checking				
		Beginning Balance	0.00	
1-1-00		Opening Entry	15,000.00	
1-1-00		Opening Entry	5,000.00	
1-1-00		Opening Entry		200.00
1-1-00		Opening Entry		1,300.00
1-1-00		Opening Entry		8,000.00
1-1-00		Opening Entry		600.00
1-1-00		Opening Entry		500.00
		Ending Balance	9,400.00	
1200 Inventory				
		Beginning Balance	0.00	
1-1-00		Opening Entry	8,000.00	
		Ending Balance	8,000.00	
1500 Furniture & Fixtures				
		Beginning Balance	0.00	
1-1-00		Opening Entry	1,300.00	
		Ending Balance	1,300.00	
1550 Equipment				
		Beginning Balance	0.00	
1-1-00		Opening Entry	600.00	
		Ending Balance	600.00	

continues

continued

Date	Ref. No.	Description	Debit	Credit
2100 Loan Payable– First National Bank				
		Beginning Balance	0.00	
1-1-00		Opening Entry		5,000.00
		Ending Balance		5,000.00
3210 Capital				
		Beginning Balance	0.00	
1-1-00		Opening Entry		15,000.00
		Ending Balance		15,000.00
6300 Office Expense				
		Beginning Balance	0.00	
1-1-00		Opening Entry	200.00	
		Ending Balance	200.00	
6360 Rent Expense				
		Beginning Balance	0.00	
1-1-00		Opening Entry	500.00	
		Ending Balance	500.00	

GO TO ▶
Refer to Hour 18, "Reconciling the Bank Accounts and General Journal Entries," for a detailed explanation of General Journal Entries and how to post them to the General Ledger.

Entries posted directly to the General Ledger are called General Journal Entries and are usually assigned a number for reference. Because this is clearly marked as the opening entry, no reference number was assigned.

Posting each opening activity of the bookstore separately was not the only way to do it. The entry could have been calculated and written up as one entry.

Whenever a number of cash activities take place in the same time period, they can be posted as one entry. The way to do this with cash transactions such as the opening entry is to determine which accounts need to be debited and which need to be credited. The cash account is then posted with the difference between the debits and the credits.

Take another look at the original recap of the opening activities. This time they are listed showing how the amounts are to be posted to each individual account.

Account	Amount
Inventory	8,000.00 debit
Furniture & Fixtures	1,300.00 debit
Equipment	600.00 debit
Loan Payable–First National Bank	(5,000.00) credit
Capital	(15,000.00) credit
Office Expense	200.00 debit
Rent Expense	500.00 debit

Out of Balance	(9,400.00) credit

Without the cash account, the entry shows a remaining credit balance. This is the amount that should be posted to Cash in Checking as an offset or a debit.

Review the General Ledger as it looked after the individual postings. The balances in all the accounts would be exactly the same, but instead of having seven different entries to the cash account, there would only be one. The account would now look like this:

Date	Ref. No.	Description	Debit	Credit
1000 Cash in Checking				
		Beginning Balance	0.00	
		Opening Entry	9,400.00	
			------------	------------
		Ending Balance	9.400.00	

Whenever you have an entry that involves a number of different accounts, it is helpful to lay it out on paper before posting it to the General Ledger. Writing out the entry requires you to consider each account and what amount will be posted there. It also allows you to double-check for accuracy and make sure that the entry is in balance—for example, that debits equal credits.

HOUR'S UP!

You reviewed the charts, other information, and sample entries in this hour. Now try to answer the following questions to determine how much you have retained.

1. A fiscal year is one that begins in one calendar year and ends in the next calendar year.

   a. True

   b. False

2. Accounts that normally carry a debit balance include:

   a. Rent Expense, Land, and Sales Discounts

   b. Accounts Payable, Organization Costs, and Drawing

   c. Purchase Discounts, Inventory, and Cash in Savings

3. When income is received by a business, cash is debited.

   a. True

   b. False

4. The Chart of Accounts is transferred to the General Ledger in alphabetical order.

   a. True

   b. False

5. The receipt of loan proceeds would result in what entry?

   a. Debit Capital, Credit Accounts Payable

   b. Debit Cash, Credit Loan Payable

   c. Credit Cash, Debit Inventory

6. The General Ledger must always be in balance.

   a. True

   b. False

7. Accumulated Amortization normally carries a debit balance.

   a. True

   b. False

8. A credit balance in a General Ledger account indicates:

   a. A loss

   b. An error

   c. An offsetting debit

9. In the General Ledger, the ending balance will appear in either the debit or the credit column, depending on the balance of the account when it is reviewed.
    a. True
    b. False

10. Accounts that normally carry a credit balance include:
    a. Vehicles, Capital, and Telephone Expense
    b. Travel & Entertainment, Other Income, and Common Stock
    c. Accounts Payable, Interest Income, and Accrued Expenses

HOUR 4

Depreciable Assets, Prepaid Expenses, and Other Accounts

CHAPTER SUMMARY

LESSON PLAN:

In this hour you will learn about ...

- Depreciating assets
- Prepaid expenses
- Accounts specific to certain businesses
- Adding and eliminating accounts

An accounting system is structured around the needs of the business that uses it. Some businesses have depreciable assets, and some do not. Others add additional accounts to their General Ledger so that specific information can be obtained from the financial reports.

The Chart of Accounts and the General Ledger are designed to be flexible. It is this flexibility that enables the basic elements of accounting to work for any type of business enterprise.

DEPRECIATING ASSETS

You have already learned that separate accounts in the Asset section of the General Ledger are used to record the cost of major expenditures for property used for business purposes. You have also learned that depreciation accounts are set up for these assets to record the decrease in their value month to month and year to year.

Depreciation is an expense and a deduction for tax purposes. It is often recorded only at the end of the year after the company's tax return is filed. However, anyone who is managing an accounting system should know about depreciation and understand how it works.

Different types of depreciation are used for tax purposes. Accelerated depreciation, also known as declining balance depreciation, allows a larger portion of the asset to be written off in the first few years of its use. Tax law even allows a business to expense up to $18,500 in business property in one tax year.

PROCEED WITH CAUTION

A professional accountant who specializes in income tax and deductions should be consulted to determine what method would be most beneficial in reducing the company or individual's tax liability for the current year.

GO TO ▶
Refer to Hour 22, "End-of-the-Year Payroll Reports and Other Tax Reports," for instructions on personal and corporation tax returns, along with information on forms and requirements.

Keep in mind that these types of depreciation are mentioned only to make you aware of their existence. They are used for tax purposes only and cannot be used or recorded in an accounting system.

The only type of depreciation used on the books for accounting purposes is the straight-line method of depreciation. This method of depreciation is simple and easy to use on a monthly basis. In straight-line or book depreciation, the life of the asset is determined, and then the cost of the asset is written off over the course of that period of time.

In the Chart of Accounts, you set up various depreciable asset accounts. Each type of asset has a standard time period used for writing it off. The standard time periods are considered to be the normal, average, useful life for each type of business asset.

You may find that some businesses use different criteria based on heavy use of certain assets and the need for equipment that is out of the ordinary or that has a specified use for the particular business.

The following list gives the depreciable assets in your General Ledger and designates the standard time periods allowed for writing off their costs:

- Building: 40 years
- Vehicles: 5 years
- Furniture & Fixtures: 7 years
- Equipment: 3–5 years

A depreciation schedule should be set up to keep track of all the assets. This is necessary because while the company might have only one building, it may have more than one vehicle and various items that make up the categories of Furniture & Fixtures and Equipment. Each individual piece is listed separately on the depreciation schedule so that when and if an asset is sold or replaced, the information on its value and how much it has been depreciated is readily available.

The depreciation schedule is also kept for tax purposes. This is because when an asset is sold, the amount received for the sale could be taxable, depending on its original cost and how much it was depreciated during the time it was in service. Again, a tax accountant will make the final determination for the tax return. Your responsibility is in keeping the records accurate and up-to-date.

PROCEED WITH CAUTION

All bookkeepers and business owners should be aware of the tax laws governing the sale of property used in a business or profession. In some cases, depreciation used as a tax deduction must be reclaimed as income when an asset is sold. When in doubt, always seek the advice of a professional tax consultant.

Depreciation schedules are set up to meet the individual needs of a particular business. Because you are learning how to manage an accounting system on a monthly basis, the following example for a law firm is structured to write off the depreciation as a monthly expense.

Depreciation Schedule for John Jackson Law Firm

In-Service Date	Description	Cost	Term in Months	Monthly Depreciation
BUILDING				
3-1-99	One-Story Office	100,000	480	208.33
FURNITURE & FIXTURES				
3-1-99	Mahogany Desk	800	84	9.52
3-1-99	Secretary Desk	500	84	5.95
3-1-99	Conference Table	1,500	84	17.85
3-1-99	6 Chairs	600	84	7.14
				40.46
EQUIPMENT				
3-1-99	Tandy Computer	2,000	60	33.33
3-1-99	Telephone System	700	60	11.66
3-1-99	Gateway Computer	1,200	60	20.00
				64.99

continues

Depreciation Schedule for John Jackson Law Firm   (continued)

VEHICLES				
3-1-99	1999 Ford Taurus	20,000	60	333.33
	Total Monthly Depreciation			647.11

The date on the depreciation schedule is always the date the asset was first used as business property. The lawyer could have purchased the car in January 1999 but didn't open the law firm and begin using it as a business asset until March of that year. That means all of the assets placed into service in 1999 would only be depreciated from March on, or a total of 10 months for that year.

Based on this depreciation schedule, at the end of each month you would do an entry to record the depreciation. It would look like this:

Date	Reference No.	Account	Amount
3-31	3-1	1351 Accumulated Depreciation–Building	(208.33)
		1451 Accumulated Depreciation–Vehicles	(333.33)
		1501 Accumulated Depreciation–Furniture & Fixtures	(40.46)
		1551 Accumulated Depreciation–Equipment	(64.99)
		6160 Depreciation Expense	647.11

To record depreciation for March 1999

JUST A MINUTE

If the monthly depreciation expense is substantial, you may not want to write it off on a monthly basis because it will reduce the net profit shown on the financial statement. As stated earlier, the depreciation expense can be written off at the end of the year, as a means of reducing the tax liability.

Take note of the following items in the previous entry:

- Debits equal credits.
- A reference number was assigned.
- At the end of the entry, a brief explanation of the entry is written.

The reference number is usually the month that the entry is being recorded, with the number of the entry being made for that month.

In the previous sample, the reference number 3-1 means that this is the first entry recorded in the month of March. General Journal Entries should be written out as in the sample for the law firm and should be kept in a file folder.

GO TO ▶
Refer to Hour 10, "The Importance of Work Papers, Receipts, and Other Records," for more information on what files and papers to keep.

Regardless of whether the depreciation expense is written off monthly or yearly, a depreciation schedule listing the assets should be kept up-to-date. If an asset is sold, the date and price received should be entered on the schedule. If an asset is purchased, that item should be added to the schedule.

PREPAID EXPENSES

In the Chart of Accounts, you established an account called Deposits. As explained, this account holds the amounts of cash deposits paid in advance for rent or utilities. Although it is similar, it is not actually a Prepaid Expense because the dollar amount in that account is expected to be returned or carried over to the next year's lease.

A Prepaid Expense is an expense that would ordinarily be paid on a monthly basis but for one reason or another is paid in advance for a certain period of time. Paying an annual insurance premium would qualify as a Prepaid Expense. Rent paid on a quarterly basis would also be a Prepaid Expense.

In the asset portion of the Chart of Accounts, you add Prepaid Expense (Account 1260). This places the account right after Deposits (Account 1250) in the Chart of Accounts and the General Ledger.

Prepaid Expense is an asset because it is something of value owned by the business. In this case, assume it is one year's insurance coverage on the company vehicles.

GO TO ▶
Refer to Hour 1, "The Chart of Accounts/Balance Sheet Accounts," to review the information on setting up accounts and their proper placement in the accounting system.

Once the account is established, the dollar amount of the annual insurance premium is posted there. The insurance premium is for auto insurance on company-owned vehicles. Perhaps the company received a discount on the premium by paying it in advance rather than in monthly installments.

If the total amount of the premium is $2,400, the entry would look like this:

Date	Reference No.	Account	Amount
1-31	1-2	1000 Cash in Checking	(2,400.00)
		1260 Prepaid Expense	2,400.00

To record auto insurance paid for one year

Again, note that there is a reference number on the entry, telling you that this is the second General Journal Entry for the month of January. A brief explanation of the entry is also included.

When this entry is posted to the General Ledger, the new Prepaid Insurance account has a debit balance. If you reviewed this account in the General Ledger at this time, you would see the posting as follows:

Date	Reference No.	Description	Debit	Credit
1260 Prepaid Expense				
		Beginning Balance		0.00
1-31	1-2	Record Auto Insurance		2,400.00
		Ending Balance		2,400.00

The reference number is on the entry, along with the explanation of the entry, "Record Auto Insurance." These small details are always included in the General Ledger because they provide a point of reference for the entry and the reason that the account was debited for $2,400. Months later, you can look back at the General Ledger account and see when and why the debit was posted.

Because the financial statements should always reflect the most accurate monthly data, you would not want to post the entire year's auto insurance premium as an expense at the time it was paid. An annual premium of $2,400 means that the auto insurance expense is actually $200 per month. If you posted it all at once, you would have a $2,400 expense in January of the year and then nothing recorded for the remaining months of the year.

The annual premium is held or stored in the Prepaid Expense account in the Balance Sheet section, and each month the correct monthly premium is transferred to the proper account in the Profit & Loss section of the accounting system. With the expense spread across 12 months of the year instead of being lumped into one month, a more accurate monthly profit or loss is provided. Each month the following entry would be made:

Date	Reference No.	Account	Amount
2-28	2-1	1260 Prepaid Expense	(200.00)
		5150 Auto Expense	200.00

To expense monthly auto insurance premium

Remember that all expenses relating to the company vehicles are posted in the Auto Expense account.

After this entry is posted to the General Ledger, the Prepaid Expense account would look like this:

Date	Reference No.	Description	Debit	Credit
1260 Prepaid Expense				
		Beginning Balance	0.00	
1-31	1-2	Record Auto Insurance	2,400.00	
2-28	2-1	Monthly Auto Expense		200.00
		Ending Balance		2,200.00

You can see that the Prepaid Expense account has been reduced by a $200 credit. At the same time, the Auto Expense account has been debited or increased by the same amount.

JUST A MINUTE

If there are a number of prepaid expenses, a schedule like the one for depreciable assets could be made up. This would provide a quick, easy reference for anything that is prepaid that needs to be expensed each month.

ADDING OTHER ACCOUNTS TO THE GENERAL LEDGER

You have just seen how easy it is to add an account to the Chart of Accounts. You simply slip it into the proper section, placing it so that it will print out on the report in a logical place.

When you are setting up a Chart of Accounts, you include all the standard accounts the business will need. However, as time goes on, there will be changes that require modifications to the Chart of Accounts.

A manufacturing company provides the best example of the kinds of changes that can occur. A new company begins with one product but then begins to add others. All the products could be included in one Inventory account, but it may be more efficient to set up a new account for each one.

Another thing to consider with a manufacturing company is the way the products are put together. An inventory account for the raw materials required to produce the merchandise is often needed. Another inventory account for the finished goods is set up, and still another might be necessary for the merchandise that is still in the production stage.

These accounts would appear on the Chart of Accounts as follows:

- 1200 Inventory–Raw Materials
- 1210 Inventory–Finished Goods
- 1220 Inventory–W.I.P. (Work in Progress)

You should also have some knowledge of a few different companies and their individual requirements.

A construction firm would have an account set up for Inventory–Land, for any parcels of property where future housing developments were to be built. The same company would have an asset account for Construction in Progress and expense accounts for Masonry, Carpentry, Plumbing, Electrical, and all the other things that it might hire subcontractors to do.

Nonprofit organizations have accounts set up in all sections of the Chart of Accounts to monitor funds, grants, pledges, and donations.

 FYI For more information on the basic accounting structures used by different types of companies, you can read Introduction to Management Accounting by Charles T. Horngren, et al.

Keep in mind that although a particular company or business may have its own customized Chart of Accounts, its accounting procedures will not vary from what you are learning in this text.

If you are a new bookkeeper coming into an existing company, studying the Chart of Accounts will give you a good idea of how the business is operated. Appendix B, "Sample Forms," gives sample Charts of Accounts for various types of businesses.

ELIMINATING ACCOUNTS FROM THE GENERAL LEDGER

Eliminating an account from the General Ledger is not as simple as adding one. First of all, any account that has had posting activity should not be eliminated in the current year, even if it is no longer needed. It is best to wait until the current year is closed out, and then eliminate the account at the beginning of the new year before any transactions are posted.

In a computerized system, some accounts are considered control accounts. This means that the function of other accounts is related to them; the computer will not allow you to eliminate a control account. For example, Accounts Receivable and Accounts Payable are control accounts because they hold the totals for credit sales and credit purchases. Even if you don't have credit sales or credit purchases, a computerized accounting system would not allow you to delete either of these accounts.

Although you may have extraneous accounts in your General Ledger, they are not a problem. If an account has a zero balance, it is not printed in a computerized system unless it is specifically requested. If you are running a manual system, you are transferring the balances from the General Ledger to the financial statements. Again, an account with a zero balance does not need to be listed.

GO TO ▶
Refer to Hour 24, "Accounting Software Programs," for a discussion of a variety of computerized accounting systems and their use.

Sometimes you might want to reclassify an income or expense. You accomplish that by taking the balance from the old account and transferring it in full to the new account. If the old account has a debit balance, your General Journal Entry would credit that amount and then debit the same amount to the new account. For example, if you have very little activity in the Postage account, you might want to transfer it to the Office Expense account.

After a transferring entry, the two General Ledger accounts would look like this:

Date	Reference No.	Description	Debit	Credit
6290 Postage				
		Beginning Balance	0.00	
4-30	4-10	Cash Disbursements	33.00	
7-30	7-11	Transfer to 6300		33.00
			-----------	-----------
		Ending Balance	0.00	

continues

Date	Reference No.	Description	Debit	Credit
6300 Office Expense				
		Beginning Expense	0.00	
		Opening Entry	200.00	
4-30	4-20	Cash Disbursements	57.00	
5-31	5-10	Cash Disbursements	110.00	
6-30	6-12	Cash Disbursements	60.00	
7-30	7-11	Transfer from 6290	33.00	
			-----------	-----------
		Ending Balance	460.00	

Remember that the Chart of Accounts and the General Ledger are both functional and flexible. You can add accounts and eliminate accounts as needed. Just take care when transferring balances from one account to another that the entries offset each other.

Hour's Up!

This hour covered Depreciation, Prepaid Expenses, and additions and eliminations to the Chart of Accounts and the General Ledger. The following questions are based on what you have learned.

1. Vehicles are usually depreciation over what period of time?

    a. 5 years

    b. 7 years

    c. 3 years

2. When an asset is sold, depreciation taken as a tax deduction may have to be reclaimed as income.

    a. True

    b. False

3. You can always eliminate any account in the General Ledger.

    a. True

    b. False

4. A manufacturing company may have a separate inventory account for which of the following?

    a. Raw Materials

    b. Finished Goods

    c. Work in Progress

    d. All of the Above

5. Using a Prepaid Expense account provides a more accurate monthly profit or loss figure.

    a. True

    b. False

6. Depreciation is an expense used for tax purposes.

    a. True

    b. False

7. The Prepaid Expense account is found in what section of the Chart of Accounts?

    a. Liabilities

    b. Assets

    c. Expenses

8. The Prepaid Expense account usually has a credit balance.

    a. True

    b. False

9. What kind of depreciation is used on the books in an accounting system?

    a. Declining balance

    b. None

    c. Straight-line

10. The entry for depreciation on equipment for one month is:

    a. Debit Depreciation Expense, Credit Cash in Checking

    b. Credit Accumulated Depreciation–Equipment, Debit Depreciation Expense

    c. Credit Depreciation Expense, Debit Office Expense

QUIZ

HOUR 5

Organization and Proper Accounting Procedures

Of all the skills needed to manage an accounting system, organization and attention to detail may be the most important. Common sense dictates that if you approach any task with a plan and a purpose, it will go more smoothly.

Basic accounting procedures provide a firm structure on which to build your system. Organization and following those procedures on a daily basis will ensure the most efficient use of your time and avoid a multitude of problems.

ESTABLISHING AND MANAGING AN OPERATING ACCOUNT

Cash in Checking (Account 1000) is the account that you set up in the Chart of Accounts and the General Ledger as your operating account. This is the bank account that will receive deposits for incoming revenue and disburse all the expenses for your business.

The operating account should be opened at a bank that meets all of your business requirements. These would include but not be limited to the following:

- Convenient location
- Convenient banking hours
- Personal attention to your questions and business needs
- Reasonable fees

CHAPTER SUMMARY

LESSON PLAN:

In this hour you will learn about ...

- Establishing and managing an operating account
- Supplies
- Organizing accounting files
- Managing files and documents

You will spend a fair amount of time going to and from the bank, so choose a bank that is close to your business location. You don't want to spend precious time driving across town to do your banking.

The same holds true for the business hours of your bank. If you are operating a business for long hours Monday through Friday, perhaps you need a bank with branches that are open on Saturdays. Although electronic banking makes this less of a consideration today, extra fees are associated with this convenience.

FYI If you have access to the Internet, you may find that banks in your area offer online services.

A number of banks want you to do everything over the phone. When you need help, you are expected to choose your options from an electronically recorded menu. Be sure that the bank you deal with gives you the phone number of the banking office that you use. When you have a problem or a question about your operating account, you should be able to talk to a person who is familiar with you and your business.

Some banks charge you for every check and deposit. Others have set monthly fees. Still others may offer free or reduced-fee checking accounts if you sign up for additional banking services, such as credit lines and savings accounts.

Before you open the operating account for your business, shop around and find the bank that best suits all your needs. Your relationship with the bank and your personal banker is an important part of controlling the bank accounts. As an accountant who may be coming into an existing business, you may not have a choice of banks. In that case, make a personal visit to the bank and acquaint yourself with its procedures and services.

Once you've found the right bank for your business, you will be asked to choose checks for your account. Always order business voucher checks. These are the checks that come in a three-ring binder with a check stub that stays in the book after you've written the check and removed it. There are usually three checks to a page. This type of checkbook will make it easier to monitor and organize your accounting information. The checkbook for your operating account is a vital component of your accounting system because all cash transactions go through this account. Thus, it must be handled smartly and efficiently.

The voucher or check stub portion in the checkbook provides spaces to record deposits. Always note the date and amount of the deposit as soon as it is completed.

In certain types of businesses, such as law firms and property management companies, it is important to keep records of each check received for deposit. Any business that accepts client funds for future use or disbursement is considered to hold the client's funds in trust and must keep documentation of said funds. The easiest way to do this is to make a photocopy of the client's check before taking the deposit to the bank. This provides the best record of the receipt.

When you take the deposit to the bank, always check the receipt that the teller gives you. Make sure that the amount and your account number are accurately noted on the receipt. Then keep the deposit receipt in your files. Although it doesn't happen often, it is possible for a bank to make an error. Deposits can be lost or posted to the wrong account. The receipt proves that the deposit belongs to your business.

When you write a check, use the spaces provided for noting all the information that you will need later to post that disbursement to the General Ledger.

On the check stub, you should record the name of the payee, the amount, and a brief explanation of what invoice or service you are paying for. On the check itself, always include your account number or invoice number so that the vendor who is receiving the payment can record the payment to the correct account.

The few extra minutes that it takes to record checks and deposits properly in the checkbook will save you lots of extra minutes later if there is a question about a payment or receipt.

The other reason you should take care to record things carefully in the checkbook is that the information will help you keep a running total of the balance in the account. You will receive a bank statement only once a month, and in the interim you will need to know the status of your bank account. This is especially important for a new business that has not yet established a predictable cash flow.

Most banks have electronic or online systems that you can access to check your bank balance. The systems will also supply information on deposits and tell you whether a particular check has cleared your account. You can use

GO TO ▶ Refer to Hour 16, "Cash Disbursements Journal," to learn how disbursements should be recorded and posted to the General Ledger.

GO TO ▶ Refer to Hour 18, "Reconciling the Bank Accounts and General Journal Entries," to learn how to check the balance of your accounts with the monthly bank statements.

these automated banking features any time you have questions about your account that don't require a conversation with a bank employee.

Using this system to check the balance in your account is fine as long as you realize how it really works. The system does not know what checks you have written that have not yet cleared your account. Only you know how many checks are outstanding, so when you get the balance from the automated systems, you must then deduct the checks in your checkbook that are outstanding or that have not yet cleared the bank.

You also need to be aware that the speed of electronics means that checks clear your account quickly. Don't make the mistake of thinking that you can write checks today and deposit the money to cover them in a few days. Bank fees for returned checks are hefty—never write a check and mail it unless you have the funds in the bank to cover it.

Keeping your operating account in balance and in good order is imperative. Each time you complete a page in your check register, you should add the deposits and subtract the checks written; then note the balance on the bottom of the page in the space provided for it. That balance should be carried forward to the top of the next page in the check register.

Even if you are using a computerized system, this procedure should be done manually in the check register. At the end of the month, you will be cross-checking the balance in the checkbook against the balance in the General Ledger. In Appendix B, "Sample Forms," you will find a sample of a voucher check register.

Supplies

The bank will provide you with all the supplies you need for the operating account. This includes the checkbook, deposit slips, and a stamp for endorsing customers' checks for deposit into your account. If you don't have an endorser stamp, you can endorse the check by writing your business name on the back of the customer's check with the number of the bank account that you are depositing it into.

Additional supplies that you will need to organize your accounting system should be purchased and put into use as soon as possible. You will need some or all of the following items:

- Ledger paper
- File folders, regular or legal size

- Three-ring notebook or binder
- File cabinets/boxes
- Alphabetical expanding files

All of these supplies can be purchased at an office supply outlet or a variety store that carries stationery products.

Four-column ledger paper can be used for most accounting tasks. This paper has four columns for recording numbers, as well as a date column and a description column. It can also be used to list your Chart of Accounts. A separate page should be set up for each account to make up the General Ledger pages for balances and postings. This same paper can be used to write up depreciation schedules and General Journal Entries. Samples of these records written on four-column ledger paper can be found in Appendix B.

Other kinds of ledger paper with more or fewer columns can be purchased in pads of 50 sheets or more. If you prefer longer sheets or wider sheets, you can use them instead. The important thing is that you establish some type of tangible, written record of your accounting transactions.

Depending on the type of business you are working in, you can use regular file folders, standard 8.5 × 11 folders, or longer legal-size folders, at 8.5 × 14 inches. Whatever size accommodates your ledger paper or other files is fine.

You may or may not want to use labels to put on the files—that is up to you. Regardless, a file folder should be set up and designated to hold your Chart of Accounts, your General Ledger pages, Depreciation schedules or other schedules, General Journal Entries, and Financial Statements.

In place of file folders, you might want to use three-ring notebooks or binders. The ledger pads are already punched with three holes, so they can easily be inserted into a notebook or binder, if desired. Using a notebook or binder is actually the best choice to hold your Chart of Accounts and General Ledger sheets. You can use notebook dividers to separate Balance Sheet Accounts from Profit and Loss Statement accounts.

TIME SAVER

Even if you are using a computerized software program that stores all the data, you should set up a notebook to hold the Financial Statements that you print each month. Accountants are often asked to provide six months or a year of statements, and having them stored and ready to be copied saves time.

File folders or alphabetical expanding files should be used to keep track of customers or vendors. This puts the information and copies of sales slips and invoices at your fingertips whenever you need them.

You may also need file cabinets or boxes to store the various files. Office supply stores also carry plastic crates in a variety of sizes with hanging file folders. These are lightweight and can be stored on top of a desk or a table for easy access.

ORGANIZING ACCOUNTING FILES

In general, files should be set up for all the paperwork you produce each month. A computerized accounting system will keep records on customers and vendors, but there will still be paper documents to handle.

For example, a property management company may have hundreds of owners who receive monthly statements and copies of invoices for work done on their individual properties. A file for each owner should be set up to file the invoice copies. At the end of the month, when a statement is issued, the copies are ready and can be easily included with the property cash flow statement.

Many companies issue checks and invoices on the computer. However, there are still file copies to be sorted and stored. Whether you write manual checks or issue them from a computer, you will want to keep the canceled checks in order and easily accessible. When a vendor comes back to your business and claims that you didn't pay a particular invoice, you will be required to make a copy of the canceled check to prove that you did pay the bill.

GO TO ▶
Refer to Hour 10, "The Importance of Work Papers, Receipts, and Other Records," to learn how to cross-reference bills and checks so that you can retrieve information quickly and easily.

Some banks no longer return canceled checks with the monthly statements, but they do keep them on file. You can request a copy of the canceled check from the bank, if necessary.

Two files should be set up for both customers and vendors. One file for each should contain open or unpaid invoices. The other files should store paid invoices. You can do this in a couple of different ways, depending on the size of the business and the volume of the paperwork.

If the business does not have a lot of customers who buy on credit and need to be billed each month, you can simply file sales slips in an alphabetical expanding file during the current month, or keep them in date order in a file folder. You also can keep them in numerical order if your sales slips are numbered.

If you have credit sales to keep track of and bill, you will need to set up a file for each individual customer with name, address, and phone number information. You can use a ledger sheet to list the sales slips numbers, or you can just file a copy of the slip in the individual folders. A credit customer who buys goods on a regular basis should have his or her own ledger sheet to itemize the sales, payments, and current balance on the charge account.

You can set up customer files on ledger sheets and bind them in a notebook. You can also purchase blank ledger cards at an office supply store. The store will have files for storing the cards as well.

GO TO ▶
Refer to Hour 6, "Daily Sales Transactions," to take a more extensive look at credit sales and how to handle them.

The main consideration when setting up accounting files for a business is to devise a procedure and system that is accurate and provides quick and easy access to the information. At the end of the day, week, or month, the information must be in a clear, logical order so that it can be posted to the General Ledger.

Here is a sample of how a customer's ledger sheet could be set up:

John Madison
1234 Hickory Lane, New Apple, NJ
555-555-1000

Date	Invoice No.	Amount	Received on Acct.	Balance
1-1-00	321	$300.00		300.00

When additional sales or payments are made, the ledger sheet would be updated as follows:

John Madison
1234 Hickory Lane, New Apple, NJ
555-555-1000

Date	Invoice No.	Amount	Received on Acct.	Balance
1-1-00	321	$300.00		300.00
2-1-00	545	200.00		500.00
2-10-00			500.00	-0-

For all the bills that a business must pay each month, it is a good idea to keep the unpaid bills in alphabetical order in some sort of a file. If there are numerous bills, use an expanding file; if not, a single file folder will do. Again, the important thing is to keep them in good order.

GO TO ▶
Refer to Hour 9, "Cash Disbursements," to see how all the different types of disbursements should be handled and controlled.

As the bills are paid, you can file them in the file that you set up for paid bills. The paid bills file is usually kept in alphabetical order for the current year.

If the business buys goods from vendors, you should set up a ledger sheet for each one. The vendor cards will be much like the ledgers used for customers—they will keep track of all the purchases and payments to each individual vendor.

Of course, you will still have invoice copies to deal with: You can keep those with the individual ledgers until they're paid, and then file and store them in the paid bills file.

Organizing your records is a necessary part of managing an accounting system. Don't trust all your record keeping to a computerized system—if the computer fails or the system crashes, you'll spend hours, weeks, or maybe months trying to re-create your business transactions.

Of course, you should have a backup disk for all computerized systems, but you should have hard copies as well. At the end of each month, you should print out reports for Accounts Receivable, Accounts Payable, General Journal Entries, and Financial Statements, and store the reports in a safe place.

Proper accounting procedures rely on good information, set up conveniently and kept in an orderly manner.

A major advantage of keeping a good set of books is the ability to look back on prior months' reports when questions arise. If the files and the postings are not organized and current, the potential for problems is greatly increased.

MANAGING FILES AND DOCUMENTS

The best filing systems and the most effective organizational skills are born out of necessity. This depends on the individual and on the type of business that is being managed.

A medical practice requires one kind of record keeping for its accounting system, while a manufacturing company requires something entirely different. You may have to experiment a little to find out what works best for you and the accounting system you are managing. The important thing is to keep the records in an order that works well for you and the business you are in. The key word is *order*, which means keeping things in a regular and efficient arrangement so that the accounting system can run smoothly.

FYI Local business organizations and community colleges offer a lot of information on setting up and maintaining your records. There are also a number of good books on this subject, for example, **Taming the Paper Tiger at Work** by Barbara Hemphill.

Sorting through paperwork every day will help you keep your files organized and current. It only takes a few minutes to put things in their proper place. Some companies require that employees clear their desks at the end of each day—it's a good habit to cultivate.

If you run out of time, bundle up the day's transactions and put them in a file folder to keep them separate and ready to sort the first thing the next morning.

Buy a bulletin board and hang it next to your desk. You can quickly pin an important invoice or receipt to it so that it won't get swallowed up and lost in the clutter of the day's other transactions.

Post-It notes provide another quick and convenient way to label papers for handling later, but don't let those notes and papers pile up too long.

Another way to keep things organized and in perspective is to do the tasks that you dislike the most first. In other words, if you hate to file, then get it over with as soon as possible. If you've just paid bills, put the invoices in the paid file immediately. Letting them stack up will only cause you to be at the task that much longer when you need to find something.

Keep a file folder for transactions that require special handling, such as General Journal Entries. Keep the invoices, receipts, checks stubs, and whatever is needed in the file until the entry has been made.

Keep a close watch on the office supplies that you need as well. Running out of supplies such as file folders or ledger sheets can result in misplaced paperwork, which can result in a multitude of other problems.

Also make sure that you keep a copy of everything that leaves your accounting office. Checks should be recorded in your check register, or if they are computerized, an extra copy should be printed with the original. If someone in the company wants to borrow a customer's ledger, make a copy and give that out. Never give out an original to anyone, even your own mother, without having a backup copy of it for your records.

If you have a business deduction that is being questioned by the IRS, your excuse that you lent out the receipt and didn't get it back won't be acceptable. If you don't have a copy of the receipt or a canceled check to back up the deduction, it will be disallowed.

A good way to keep your files in order is to color-code them. This method is used by many businesses because it is simple to implement and because it helps you to instantly recognize needed files. Color-coded files are an excellent way of tracking special orders, special customers, or contracts that may otherwise get buried in your accounting files.

Office supply stores have aisle after aisle of folders, clips, and labels in wonderful eye-catching colors. Experiment with your files and set them up in living color. It will brighten your office and make your records easier to handle.

Just as the General Ledger must be kept in order, with debits equaling credits, so must the information that makes up the accounting transactions and financial activities of the business.

PROCEED WITH CAUTION

This hour emphasizes keeping accounting files in good order to save you time and, more importantly, to save you money at the end of the year. Professional tax preparers charge by the hour. If they have to spend time sorting through a jumble of accounting information, you will end up paying a much larger fee.

HOUR'S UP!

Without looking back on the preceding lesson, see if you can answer the following questions.

1. Financial Statements should be printed, reviewed, and filed.

   a. True

   b. False

2. Four-column ledger paper can be used to record which of the following?

   a. A Chart of Accounts

   b. Depreciation Schedules

   c. Customer accounts

   d. All of the above

QUIZ

3. With electronic banking, checks take a long time to clear your bank account.

    a. True

    b. False

4. Your operating account should be opened at a bank that provides which of the following?

    a. Free gifts

    b. Convenient location and banking hours

    c. Coffee and donuts

5. Deposit receipts safeguard your account against errors.

    a. True

    b. False

6. An outstanding check is

    a. One written for a large amount.

    b. A donation to charity.

    c. One that hasn't cleared your bank account.

7. A computerized accounting system eliminates the need for files.

    a. True

    b. False

8. When the IRS questions a deduction, you must provide

    a. A receipt or a canceled check.

    b. A sworn statement.

    c. A witness.

9. Unpaid and paid bills should be filed alphabetically for easy reference.

    a. True

    b. False

10. To prove that a vendor has been paid, you must provide

    a. A copy of the invoice.

    b. A canceled check.

    c. A notarized statement.

QUIZ

PART II

Daily Business Transactions

HOUR 6

Daily Sales Transactions

CHAPTER SUMMARY

LESSON PLAN:

In this hour you will learn about ...

- Processing daily business transactions
- Sales tax
- Posting sales and sales tax
- Accounts Receivable

The volume of daily business transactions will vary from day to day, week to week, and month to month. Establishing a new business enterprise takes time, so initially there may not be much information to put into the accounting system. However, whether there is one transaction or a hundred transactions to record, the process is the same. Establish good habits, orderly files, and proper procedures during those first few days and weeks, and you will be able to carry them through the busiest of times.

CASH SALES

A common transaction is the cash sale. Whether you are doing accounting for a sales or a service business, you will most likely have this type of transaction.

If you are involved in a retail business, you will have what is known as the point of sale. This is usually a cash register, a service counter, or any place where a customer can pay for and pick up merchandise.

Some stores have sales slips that are completed at the time of the sale. Some sales are simply rung up on a cash register. Either way, the customer receives a slip or a register receipt that gives a description of the merchandise purchased, the price of the merchandise, and, in most cases, the amount of sales tax charged.

GO TO ▷
Refer to Hour 10, "The Importance of Work Papers, Receipts, and Other Records," for details on the required reports and instructions for paying sales tax.

Both the customer and the merchant now have a record of the sale. For the merchant, this record will be used to enter information into the accounting system.

Whether the sales slip is handwritten or produced by an electronic cash register, it should contain the same standard information. Here is a sample of a standard sales ticket for a hardware store:

ACME HARDWARE

2-10-00

Item	No.	Price	Total
325 Hammer	1@	15.00	15.00
426 Nails	2@	3.00	6.00

			21.00
Sales Tax	@7%		1.47

			22.47
		Cash Tendered	23.00

		Change	.53

GO TO ▷
Refer to Hour 7, "Cost of Sales or Services," for information on inventory additions and subtractions, including a complete explanation of how the entries are done.

Although this sales slip is short, it contains a lot of information.

The items sold are listed with inventory identifying numbers next to them. This makes it possible to deduct the sold items from the current inventory total.

For now, you will concentrate on how the sale is recorded in the accounting system. Based on this particular sale, your entry would be as follows:

Date	Reference No.	Account	Debit	Credit
2-10-00	2-10	1000 Cash in Checking	22.47	
		2100 Sales Tax Collected		1.47
		4000 Sales of Goods		21.00
			--------	--------
			22.47	22.47

To record cash receipts for 2-10-00

Three different accounts from three different sections of the General Ledger are involved in this entry:

- **Cash in Checking** is an asset account. The amount of the sale is debited there to record the increase in the cash realized from this sale. A bank deposit for the amount of this sale would be prepared and taken to the bank.

- **Sales Tax Collected** is a liability account. The amount of the sales tax is credited into this section of the General Ledger because eventually this sales tax will have to be paid out to the state or city where the business is located. This liability account is simply holding the total amount of the taxes collected during the month. Although this cash went into the owner's checking account, it does not really belong to the business. It is therefore recorded as a liability because the business has the responsibility to pay it to the proper government agency.

- Finally, you have credited the net amount of the sale, without the sales tax, to the Income account **Sales of Goods or Services**.

You should also note that the date of the entry is the date of the transaction. In a business in which many sales are made each day, the sales should be totaled and recorded on a daily basis.

The cashier begins each day with a change fund. Assume that the change fund is $100. Whatever the amount of the change fund is, it should be recorded in the General Ledger account Cash on Hand.

At the end of the day, the cashier totals the sales and counts the money in the cash drawer. The amount of the change fund is then deducted from the total cash. The balance of the cash should then agree with the total amount of cash sales rung up that day.

TIME SAVER

Balance the cash sales and the change fund at the end of each business day. If there are discrepancies it is easier to find and correct them before the passage of time dulls the memory.

A retail business usually has a form that the cashier or store manager must complete at the end of the day. The form should have a simple format to recap the day's activities.

ACME HARDWARE

Date: 2-1-00

Beginning Change Fund	100.00
Cash Sales	2,572.00
Sales Tax	180.04

Total Cash	2,852.04
Bank Deposit	–2,752.04
Ending Change Fund	– 100.00

Cash Over/Short	-0-

Once the register is cleared, the change fund remains for the next day's business. Often the bank deposit is made immediately by the store manager/owner. Sometimes it is secured and left for the accounting department to handle the next day. Either way, the sales slips with all the information that each contains are transferred to the accounting department for processing.

The following is daily sales data for the hardware store for one week:

Date	Cash Sales	Sales Tax	Bank Deposit
2-1-00	2,572.00	180.04	2,752.04
2-2-00	3,100.00	217.00	3,317.00
2-3-00	1,856.00	129.92	1,985.92
2-4-00	2,817.00	197.19	3,014.19
2-5-00	984.00	68.88	1,052.88
2-6-00	3,841.00	268.87	4,109.87
	15,170.00	1,061.90	16,231.90

If these daily sales figures were posted every day, at the end of the week, the General Ledger accounts would look like this:

Date	Reference No.	Description	Debit	Credit
1000 Cash in Checking				
		Beginning Balance	0.00	
2-1-00		Sales	2,752.04	
2-2-00		Sales	3,317.00	
2-3-00		Sales	1,985.92	
2-4-00		Sales	3,014.19	
2-5-00		Sales	1,052.88	
2-6-00		Sales	4,109.87	
			------------	------------
		Ending Balance	16,231.90	
2100 Sales Tax Collected				
		Beginning Balance		0.00
2-1-00		Sales Tax		180.04
2-2-00		Sales Tax		217.00
2-3-00		Sales Tax		129.92
2-4-00		Sales Tax		197.19
2-5-00		Sales Tax		68.88
2-6-00		Sales Tax		268.87
			------------	------------
		Ending Balance		1,061.90
4000 Sales of Goods or Service				
		Beginning Balance	0.00	
2-1-00		Sales		2,572.00
2-2-00		Sales		3,100.00
2-3-00		Sales		1,856.00
2-4-00		Sales		2,817.00
2-5-00		Sales		984.00
2-6-00		Sales		3,841.00
			------------	------------
		Ending Balance		15,170.00

As you can see, the General Ledger accurately reflects the daily transactions of this business. Also note that the credits posted to the Sales and Sales Tax accounts total the amount of the debit posted to the Cash in Checking account.

CREDIT SALES

Many retail outlets offer charge accounts to their customers. A look at a credit sale in the shoe department in a department store will acquaint you with how these credit sales are handled in the accounting system.

As in the prior example, there is a point of sale and a sales receipt.

A.B. MARX

3-2-00

Invoice #67534

Item	No.	Price	Total
57 Big Foot	2@	56.00	112.00
Sales Tax		@7%	7.84

			119.84

Charge to Account 3232, George Foster.

Mr. Foster has just purchased two pairs of shoes and left the store with them. Instead of paying for the shoes at the time of the sale, the amount of his purchase will be collected from him at a later date.

Here is how the entry for this sale will be recorded in the General Ledger:

Date	Reference No.	Account	Debit	Credit
3-2-00	3-2	4000 Sales of Goods	112.00	
		2100 Sales Tax Collected		7.84
		100 Accounts Receivable	119.84	
			------------	------------
			119.84	119.84

To record sales for 3-2-00

You can see that this entry is basically the same as the cash sale entry, except that instead of debiting Cash in Checking, the total amount of the sale is debited to Accounts Receivable.

GO TO ▶
Refer to Hour 3, "Chart of Accounts Becomes the General Ledger," for information on debit accounts and credit accounts, and the importance of keeping entries in balance.

Take note of the fact that Sales Tax Collected is being credited for the sales tax. Even though it is not actually being collected at this time, it is still posted to the liability account and will have to be paid out to the state or city just as if it had actually been received in cash by the store.

Whenever Accounts Receivable is debited, an entry must also be made to the ledger card for the customer. George Foster's ledger card would be updated as follows:

3232 George Foster
   77 Burns Ave.
   Apple Tree, NJ 55555

Date	Invoice No.	Amount	Received on Acct.	Balance
3-2-00	67534	119.84		119.84

Eventually, Mr. Foster will receive a statement from A.B. Marx requesting $119.84 for the shoes he purchased.

Assume that Mr. Foster pays his bill on April 10. When the payment is received, it will be recorded on his ledger card. Because the payment will constitute a cash receipt, it will also be recorded as such in the General Ledger account.

3232 George Foster
   77 Burns Ave.
   Apple Tree, NJ 55555

Date	Invoice No.	Amount	Received on Acct.	Balance
3-2-00	67534	119.84		119.84
4-10-00		119.84		-0-

Mr. Foster's account balance is now zero because he has paid it in full. However, that is only the first part of the accounting process. The General Ledger will now receive the following entry to record the payment from Mr. Foster:

Date	Reference No.	Account	Debit	Credit
4-10-00	4-1	1100 Accounts Receivable		119.84
		1000 Cash in Checking	119.84	
			119.84	119.84

To record payments 4-10-00

TIME SAVER

A computerized accounting system automatically updates the customer's ledger at the same time that the General Ledger entry for the sale or the payment is made.

When the General Ledger entry is posted, the Accounts Receivable account will look like this:

Date	Reference No.	Description	Debit	Credit
1100 Accounts Receivable				
		Beginning Balance	0.00	
3-2-00	3-2	Record Sales	119.84	
4-1-00	4-1	Record Payments		119.84
		Ending Balance	0.00	

Combining Cash and Credit Sales

The shoe department of A.B. Marx also makes cash sales. On a typical business day, a number of both kinds of transactions will take place.

If an electronic cash register is used, a report will be generated to recap the sales activities of the day. It would look something like this:

A.B. MARX   SALES REPORT   4-10-00

Transaction

Number & Type Account #	Merchandise	Sales Tax	Total Sale
1-410 Cash	63.00	4.41	67.41
2-410 Cash	12.00	.84	12.84
3-410 Chg 3232	70.00	4.90	74.90

4-410 Cash	15.00	1.05	16.05
5-410 Chg 3251	140.00	9.80	149.80
6-410 Chg 3207	20.00	1.40	21.40
	320.00	22.40	342.40

This recap, along with copies of the sales slips, would be given to the accountant to process. The account numbers of the customers who purchased merchandise on credit are alongside the credit (chg) sale.

Before writing up the entry for this day's sales activity, you would go through the sales slips and make sure that the totals agreed with the recap. Then the cash sales would be separated from the credit sales, and each would be totaled.

Finally, the entry would be written up as follows:

Date	Reference No.	Account	Debit	Credit
4-10-00	4-10	1000 Cash in Checking	96.30	
		4000 Sales		320.00
		2100 Sales Tax Collected		22.40
		1100 Accounts Receivable	246.10	
			322.40	322.40

In reviewing this entry, you can see what accounts you will be posting the amounts to in the General Ledger. You can also see that the debits equal the credits, so you know that the entry is in balance.

Once you have posted this entry to the General Ledger, you will post the charge sales to the individual customer's ledger cards.

Three customer ledgers have to be updated:

Customer Account 3232	74.90
Customer Account 3251	149.80
Customer Account 3207	21.40
Total	246.10

GO TO ▶
Refer to Hour 15, "Cash Receipts Journal," to learn how to balance the customer ledgers with the General Ledger, to ensure accuracy.

Always double-check to make sure that the total posted to the customer ledger cards agrees with the total posted to the Accounts Receivable account in the General Ledger.

COMBINING CASH AND CREDIT SALES IN ACCOUNTS RECEIVABLE

In the next example of sales, you will review the daily transactions of a law firm. The law firm has initial consultations with clients and tries to determine the extent of the work that has to be done. Because this can be difficult to estimate, the law firm has a new client pay a *retainer.*

A retainer is a deposit that is collected against future fees. The retainer is a cash transaction; it is not the final settlement of the lawyer's fees or the client's bill. At the time the retainer is received, the final charges are not known, so a ledger or a charge account is set up for the client.

This procedure is used by other businesses, too. A retail store, for example, might require a customer to pay a deposit against the final cost of a special order.

JUST A MINUTE

In a business that takes retainers or deposits, an extra copy of the client's check or the cash receipt should be made and kept in the client's file. It will save calls to the accountant to verify that a retainer was paid.

Assume that Judy Jones contacts an attorney to obtain a patent on an invention. The attorney collects a retainer of $5,000.

When the retainer or deposit is received, it is posted to the General Ledger. The entry would be written up as follows:

Date	Reference No.	Account	Debit	Credit
4-15-00	4-15	1000 Cash in Checking	5,000.00	
		1100 Accounts Receivable		5,000.00
To record retainer received				

Once this entry is posted to the General Ledger, a customer account is set up for Judy Jones; the amount of the retainer is posted there also.

Two weeks later, the law firm completes the work on the patent application; the final bill for Jones is $5,802. Now that amount is posted to her customer or client account, and it is also posted to Accounts Receivable in the General Ledger.

The General Ledger account will now show the following postings and balance:

Date	Reference No.	Description	Debit	Credit
1100 Accounts Receivable				
		Beginning Balance	0.00	
4-15-00	4-15	Record Retainer		5,000.00
4-30-00	4-30	Fees Billed	5,802.00	
		Ending Balance	802.00	

The ledger for Judy Jones now looks as follows:

Judy Jones
1625 Marvel Ave.
East Apple, NJ

Date	Invoice No.	Amount	Received on Acct.	Balance
4-15-00			5,000.00	(5,000.00)
4-30-00	003	5,802.00		802.00

Again, notice that the ending balance of the customer's account agrees with the balance in the General Ledger for Accounts Receivable. If you have one customer ledger or a thousand, the open or outstanding balances on all of the customer accounts added together should agree with the total of the Accounts Receivable in the General Ledger.

The point-of-sale procedures used to handle daily business transactions are many and varied, depending on the type of enterprise that is operating.

If cash is changing hands and is being handled by employees, certain safeguards and security measures must be implemented. A process of checks and balances should be performed at the end of each business day. A form, similar to the sample shown previously, detailing all the cash and totaling all sales and refunds should be completed and verified.

This may or may not directly involve the accountant. However, if it does not, when the information is transferred to the accounting office, it should

GO TO ▶
Refer to Hour 19, "The Trial Balance," for information on accounting procedures that ensure accuracy.

be closely scrutinized for accuracy. The bank deposit should also be reviewed and verified by the accounting office and recorded in the check register.

Taking a little extra time to check and confirm the accuracy of daily business transactions before they are recapped and entered into the accounting system will prevent errors and keep the system and the information that it generates flowing the way it should.

HOUR'S UP!

Daily business transactions and related entries were explained in this hour. Try to answer the following questions that relate to the information you were given.

1. Sales Tax Collected is a liability because it has to be paid out to the state or city in a short time.

   a. True

   b. False

2. The point of sale in a retail business is a cash register or a service counter where the customer can pick up and pay for merchandise.

   a. True

   b. False

3. A credit sale is posted as follows:

   a. Debit Cash in Checking, credit Sales

   b. Debit Accounts Receivable, credit Sales and Sales Tax

   c. Credit Inventory, debit Cash in Checking

4. A retainer is not posted until the final bill is issued.

   a. True

   b. False

5. A customer ledger is updated with each sale or payment.

   a. True

   b. False

6. The total of all customer ledger balances should agree with:

   a. Accounts Payable balance

   b. Inventory balance

   c. Accounts Receivable balance

7. Items listed on electronic register receipts often include an inventory number.

    a. True

    b. False

8. The change fund of a retail store is included in the bank deposit with the sales revenue.

    a. True

    b. False

9. A cash sale is posted as follows:

    a. Debit Cash in Checking, credit Sales and Sales Tax

    b. Credit Inventory, debit Cash in Checking

    c. Debit Sales, credit Cash in Checking

10. A retainer is an advance payment for services posted to Accounts Receivable as a credit.

    a. True

    b. False

Quiz

HOUR 7

Cost of Sales or Services

LESSON PLAN:

In this hour you will learn about ...

- Purchases
- Inventory additions and subtractions
- Accounts Payable
- Posting to the General Ledger

Determining the sales price of goods or services is a crucial part of managing a business. If the sales price is too high, customers will go elsewhere. If the sales price is too low, the business will be operating at a loss. In order to strike the right balance, management relies on information generated by the accounting system.

The accounting system keeps track of the cost of merchandise and services so that sales prices can be adjusted up or down as needed. Recording and reporting these costs are one of the most important functions of an accounting system.

PURCHASES

Purchasing goods for resale or as materials for manufacturing or services is a big responsibility. Keeping track of those purchases and paying the vendors that supply the goods is just as challenging.

This is an area that must be monitored closely. Therefore, accounting procedures must be put into place that allow management to easily obtain the financial information needed to stay abreast of changes in the costs of goods.

The cost of goods and materials is one of the primary factors used to determine the sale price of merchandise and services.

This is especially true in manufacturing, and learning the procedures employed in that type of business will give you a good basic understanding of how purchases should be recorded.

To keep it simple, assume that your company manufactures and sells tote bags. Each tote bag requires one yard of cloth and one spool of matching thread. The cost to manufacture one bag is $1, and the company currently has an inventory of 2,500 tote bags. That means that the Inventory account currently has a balance of $2,500.

During the current month, your tote bag company purchased 750 yards of fabric and 750 spools of thread from Fabrics & Notions at a cost of $750. When the invoice comes in, the entry would be written up as follows:

Date	Reference No.	Account	Debit	Credit
2-10	562	4300 Purchases	750.00	
		2000 Accounts Payable		750.00

At the same time, the ledger card for the vendor, Fabrics & Notions, is updated. The ledger card for a vendor is posted differently than a ledger card for a customer. This sample will illustrate that difference.

Fabrics & Notions

225 Westchester

Apple Green, NJ

Date	Invoice No.	Amount	Paid/Ck#	Balance Due
2-10	562	−750.00		−750.00

GO TO ▶
Refer to Hour 16, "Cash Disbursements Journal," for detailed instructions for balancing the vendor cards to the General Ledger.

Note that the invoice amount has a minus sign in front of it, indicating that it is a credit. It is a credit to the tote bag company because this is a liability that must be paid out. The total of all the vendor ledgers should also agree with the total in Accounts Payable, which also carries a credit balance.

INVENTORY ADDITIONS/SUBTRACTIONS

With the materials purchased, your tote bag company manufactures an additional 750 tote bags.

At the end of the month, the sales recorded show that the company has sold 1,250 tote bags and deposited $3,750 in the bank account as revenue from these sales.

The company takes a physical inventory and verifies that there are now 2,000 tote bags.

Here's how the company's inventory worksheet would look:

February 2000

Beginning Inventory Balance	2500
Additional	750
Sales	−1250

Ending Inventory Balance	2000 (verified 2-28-00)

When this information is transferred to the accounting department, a General Journal Entry is made to adjust the Inventory account to the actual inventory on hand at the end of that month.

The entry to accomplish this is written up as follows:

Date	Reference No.	Account	Debit	Credit
2-28	2-28	1200 Inventory		500.00
		4300 Purchases	500.00	
To adjust inventory to actual				

If this inventory adjustment were not made, the Gross Profit on the Profit and Loss Statement would be distorted. To understand how this works, look at the company's Gross Profit without the Inventory adjustment entry.

JUST A MINUTE

The following financial statements show a minus sign in front of the Income amounts. This is to remind you that the Income accounts in the General Ledger usually carry credit balances. On an actual Profit and Loss Statement, these minus signs would not be shown.

February 28, 2000

Income:

Sales of Goods	$–3,750.00

Total Income	–3,750.00

Cost of Sales:

Purchases	750.00 (amount of invoice)
Total Cost of Sales	750.00 (.60 per tote bag)
Gross Profit	$–3,000.00

You already know that it costs the company $1 to manufacture one tote bag. Yet, without the adjustment to Inventory and Cost of Sales, the Gross Profit indicates that each tote bag costs only 60¢ to manufacture.

Now look at the Gross Profit after the entry has been posted to the proper accounts.

February 28, 2000

Income:

Sales of Goods	$–3,750.00
Total Income	–3,750.00
Cost of Sales:	
Purchases	1,250.00
Total Cost of Sales	1,250.00 ($1.00 per tote bag)
Gross Profit	$–2,500.00

With the Inventory adjustment made, the Cost of Sales—namely, the Purchases account—has been adjusted to reflect the true cost of $1 per bag.

GO TO ▶
Refer to Hour 18, "Reconciling the Bank Accounts and General Journal Entries," to learn more about making adjustments that affect the final outcome of the financial statements.

In addition to the financial statement reflecting an accurate Gross Profit for the tote bag company, the total dollar amount in the Inventory account now shows the actual number of tote bags available for sale at the end of the month, which is 2,000 @ $1 each, or a dollar amount of $2,000.

Based on this example, you can see how important it is to do a physical inventory and adjust the books to the actual amount of inventory on hand.

Now you will see how this same procedure helps management make informed decisions about the company and its financial future.

Having a standing order with Fabrics & Notions, the following month, the tote bag company receives another shipment containing 750 yards of fabric and 750 spools of thread.

Very often when a shipment comes into a warehouse, the shipping invoice lists only the total amount of goods that were ordered and shipped. Later, the accounting office receives the billing invoice for the total cost of the goods shipped.

This month's invoice from Fabrics & Notions totals $1,125 instead of $750, an increase of $375.

However, the company still can only make 750 tote bags from the materials. Again, it sells 1,250 tote bags totaling $3,750 in revenue.

At the end of the month, the physical inventory is taken, and it is determined that there are now 1,500 tote bags in stock for resale.

GO TO ▶
Refer to Hour 21, "The Monthly Profit and Loss Statement," to find information on tailoring the financial statements to the specific needs of the business.

The inventory worksheet is as follows:

March 2000

Beginning Inventory	2000
Additional	750
Sales	−1250
Ending Inventory	1,500 (verified 3-31-00)

The inventory adjustment would now be as follows:

Date	Reference No.	Account	Debit	Credit
3-31	3-31	1200 Inventory		500.00
		4300 Purchases	500.00	
To adjust inventory to actual				

Now see what the Gross Profit is without this entry being posted to the General Ledger.

March 31, 2000

Income:

Sale of Goods	$−3,750.00
Total Income	−3,750.00

Cost of Sales:

Purchases	1,250.00 (amount of invoice)

Total Cost of Sales	1,250.00 ($1.00 per tote bag)
Gross Profit	$-2,500.00

If the company's owner were to see this information, he or she would think that the tote bags were still costing the company $1 each. However, when the proper adjustment is made, the statement that the owner will see is this:

March 31, 2000

Income:

Sales of Goods	$-3,750.00

Total Income	-3,750.00

Cost of Sales:

Purchases	1,750.00 ($1.40 per tote bag)

Total Cost of Sales	1,750.00
Gross Profit	$-2,000.00

The owner now realizes that the cost to manufacture the tote bags has increased by 40¢ per bag. With this information, the owner can now make an informed decision about the future of the company. Either the owner can find another vendor who will supply the materials at a lower cost, or can raise the sales price of the tote bags.

As you can see, the proper accounting procedures provide valuable information and may keep the tote bag company from losing money on the following month's sales.

There are many different methods to control inventory and to figure the cost of goods and materials that make up the inventory. You have just learned the simplest method, called *specific identification*. If the tote bag company continues to purchase materials from the same vendor, the inventory value will be increased, and the sales price of the tote bags would most likely increase also.

Some companies only take inventory once a year; others use what is called the *perpetual inventory system,* in which the inventory is updated on a daily basis. Normally this is done through the use of electronic cash registers, which automatically deduct the inventory items as they are sold.

STRICTLY DEFINED

Specific identification is a method of inventory control in which the actual cost of each inventory item is determined and reported. The **perpetual inventory method** requires that each purchase be added to the inventory when it is received and that any item sold be deducted from the inventory at the time of the sale. This keeps the inventory balance updated on a daily basis. This method would be very difficult to maintain without a computerized system.

You may have heard the terms FIFO and LIFO with regard to inventory—they are mentioned here just to give you an idea of the different methods employed by some businesses. A brief explanation of what they are and how they work follows:

- **FIFO** stands for first in, first out. In this method, the oldest merchandise in stock is the first to be sold.

- **LIFO** stands for last in, first out. The most recently acquired merchandise is sold first.

With both of these methods, the inventory is evaluated by using the cost of each item left in stock. The result has a definite impact on the company's profit picture.

Another method of inventory evaluation is the average cost method. Rather than trying to identify the cost of each specific item remaining in stock at the end of the month, an average cost of all the inventory is calculated and then divided by the number of unsold units.

If you used this method for the tote bag company, based on the most recent information, your worksheet would be as follows:

Tote Bag Inventory Worksheet, March 2000

Beginning Inventory	2,000 × 1.00 each =	$2,000.00
Additional	750 × 1.40 each =	1,050.00
	2,750	3,050.00
Total Cost:	$3,050.00 ÷ 2,750 items =	$1.11 per bag
Inventory Sold	−1,250	
Ending Inventory	1,500 × 1.11 each =	1,665.00 dollar value

The determination of which inventory method should be used usually does not originate in the accounting department, but it is a management decision. The accountant's job is to use that method, whatever it is, to figure the value of the inventory for the accounting reports.

FYI
If you are going to work in a retail or manufacturing company with a substantial amount of inventory, or one that deals with a variety of different products, you can learn more by reading other books written on the subject of inventory and its valuation methods, such as *Basics of Inventory Management: From Warehouse to Distribution,* by J. David Viale.

ACCOUNTS PAYABLE

Accounts Payable, in the liability section of the General Ledger, is a control account. That means that its balance is a combination or a total of a number of individual accounts.

In large companies, Accounts Payable makes up a sizeable portion of the accounting system and is sometimes relegated to a special department that does nothing but process and pay the bills. Although there may be a variety of vendors and Expenses to be handled, Accounts Payable is not difficult to manage in any size company.

You have had a brief look at a vendor ledger, and you will now review some of the transactions that are common to the Accounts Payable section of the accounting system.

Companies that supply materials for manufacturing companies and merchandise for retail stores are just one type of vendor in the Accounts Payable liability section.

To give an accurate view of the financial condition of the business, all the Expenses that affect the bottom line or the net profit are included in Accounts Payable at the end of each month.

JUST A MINUTE

Remember that in an accrual-basis accounting system, Expenses that have not yet been paid can be included on the financial statements to provide a more accurate report for management and tax purposes.

Some companies pay all their bills at the beginning of the month, while others pay on the 10th of the following month. Still others pay bills once a week or so.

Whatever bills are paid during the current month are recorded in the liability or expense sections of the financial statements. Any bills that are unpaid at the end of the month that were incurred in the current month or that apply to the Income recognized in the current month should also be recorded in that month's financial statement, even if they are not actually scheduled for payment until the following month.

For example, the tote bag company pays its bills only once a month, on the 1st. Other than the rent on the business property, which is for the month of March, everything else that is paid on March 1st is an expense or a liability that was incurred during the month of February and that therefore was set up in Accounts Payable at the end of February.

The following is the Accounts Payable entry that was made for the tote bag company on February 28th.

Date	Reference No.	Account	Debit	Credit
2-28	AP2-28	6200 Equipment Rental	72.00	
		6220 Utilities	143.00	
		6300 Office Expense	25.00	
		6380 Repairs & Mtn.	47.00	
		6520 Supplies	22.00	
		6530 Telephone	64.23	
		2000 Accounts Payable		373.23
			373.23	373.23

To record Accounts Payable as of 2-28-00

Each one of these expense accounts will be debited for the amount listed, and Accounts Payable will credited as an offset. Once this is done, the information will flow through the General Ledger into the Balance Sheet and the Profit and Loss Statement for the month of February.

You have already reviewed the Gross Profit section of the Profit and Loss section, and now you can see how the rest of the statement will appear after this entry has been posted.

GO TO ▶
Refer to Hour 16, to learn how to pay the bills set up in Accounts Payable and how to post the disbursements to the General Ledger.

As you review the revised statement note that in the Cost of Sales section, the invoice from Fabrics & Notions that was posted to Accounts Payable when it was received is included in the total.

February 28, 2000

Income:

Sales of Goods	$3,750.00	
Total Income	3,750.00	
Cost of Sales:		
Purchases	1,250.00	(amount of invoice plus inventory adjustment)
Total Cost of Sales	1,250.00	($1.00 per tote bag)
Gross Profit	$2,500.00	
Expenses:		
Rent Expense	500.00	
Equipment Rental	72.00	
Utilities	143.00	
Office Expense	25.00	
Repairs & Mtn.	47.00	
Supplies	22.00	
Telephone	64.23	
Total Expenses	873.23	
Net Profit	1,626.77	

The minus signs have now been removed from the sample financial statements because you should be getting to the point where you know that Income accounts are credits, Cost of Sales and Expenses accounts are debits, and the difference between them is Net Profit.

Also note that the rent expense of $500 is part of the current month Expenses but not a part of Accounts Payable because it was paid before the month of February ended; all the other purchases and Expenses are not scheduled to be paid until the next month.

In a computerized accounting system, every bill that is set up in Accounts Payable has a ledger card. However, if you are working on a manual system, you can save time by doing ledger cards only for the vendors who supply materials and merchandise.

For other Expenses, such as phone bills and utilities, you can simply keep a copy of the unpaid invoice in an Accounts Payable bill file. This can be an expanding alphabetical file or just a file folder.

At the end of each month, you will review all the unpaid bills and recap them by the expense account where they will be posted. For example, you might have three bills that qualify as telephone Expenses: the regular service, the long-distance service, and the cellular phones or pagers. Although paying these bills would require three separate checks to be written, they can be added and combined into one entry for the expense account.

For the other vendors that supply materials for manufacturing and merchandise for resale, you cannot skip the ledger card because each one may have special payment terms or purchase discounts that must be tracked. The information on the purchases from these vendors also must be readily accessible for management questions.

Based on the information included in this hour for the tote bag company, here is how the Accounts Payable account would now appear in the General Ledger for this company at the end of February.

Date	Reference No.	Description	Debit	Credit
2000 Accounts Payable				
1-1-00		Beginning Balance		762.43
1-1-00	1-1	Cash Disbursements	762.43	
2-10-00	2-10	Purchases		750.00
2-28	2-28	A/P as of 2-28		373.23
		Ending Balance		1,123.23

GO TO ▶ Refer to Hour 8, "Discounts, Allowances, and Other Adjustments," for an overview of all the different adjustments that are made to customer and vendor ledgers and the related accounts in the General Ledger.

Note that the balance carried over from December was paid on January 1. It was originally posted as a credit to the account, offset by debits to the Cost of Sales and expense accounts. When these bills were paid on January 1, Accounts Payable was debited to clear it for January.

The next two postings are for the February purchase invoice from Fabrics & Notions that appears in the Cost of Sales section of the Profit and Loss Statement, and for the Expenses entered at the end of the month that are also listed on the Profit and Loss Statement.

The balance of Accounts Payable, which is a credit of $1,123.23 will appear in the Liabilities section of the Balance Sheet for February.

You may view a complete sample of a Balance Sheet and a Profit and Loss Statement in Appendix B, "Sample Forms."

HOUR'S UP!

Try to answer these questions on purchases, inventory, and Accounts Payable without referring back to this hour's text.

1. An inventory adjustment is made to obtain a more accurate Gross Profit.
   a. True
   b. False

2. At the end of the month, unpaid bills are recapped and posted to what account?
   a. Assets and Liabilities
   b. Accounts Payable, Purchases, and Expenses
   c. Income, Purchases, and Expenses

3. Income on a Profit and Loss Statement is assumed to have a credit balance.
   a. True
   b. False

4. The total of all vendor ledgers should agree with the balance in Accounts Payable.
   a. True
   b. False

5. The entry to post a reduction in Inventory is:

   a. Credit Inventory, debit Purchases

   b. Debit Sales, credit Accounts Payable

   c. Credit Purchases, debit Inventory

6. Accountants usually determine how inventory is evaluated.

   a. True

   b. False

7. The perpetual inventory system updates the inventory at the end of every month.

   a. True

   b. False

8. Accounts Payable can be found in what section of the General Ledger?

   a. Assets

   b. Liabilities

   c. Expenses

9. When posting Accounts Payable, the expense accounts are credited.

   a. True

   b. False

10. The entry to post an invoice for materials or merchandise to be paid at a later date is:

   a. Debit Inventory, credit Sales

   b. Debit Purchases, credit Accounts Payable

   c. Credit Accounts Payable, debit Sales

QUIZ

HOUR 8

Discounts, Allowances, and Other Adjustments

CHAPTER SUMMARY

LESSON PLAN:

In this hour you will learn about ...

- Sales discounts
- Sales refunds and allowances
- Purchase discounts
- Purchase refunds and allowances
- Interest calculations and adjustments
- Other miscellaneous adjustments
- Posting to the General Ledger

Each business day, situations arise that require special handling. Whether the revenue is derived from sales or services, there will always be adjustments that affect the final accounting figures.

You will find that many of these adjustments are simple, routine occurrences. Often procedures can be established that allow the adjustment to be made at the point of sale or service. As the manager of an accounting system, you should determine what kinds of adjustments can be done without your supervision and which ones require your personal attention.

As you review the various types of adjustments in this hour, you will find standard methods for making the adjusting entries in the accounting system.

SALES DISCOUNTS

Retailers often offer their customers special incentives to buy products. The newspapers are full of ads telling consumers how they can save money by buying merchandise on sale. The decision to lower prices may be due to an abundance of merchandise, a special purchase that the retailer has obtained, or just a ploy to entice customers into the store.

Whatever the reasons behind the discounts, they will necessitate adjustments for the accounting system.

GO TO ▶

Refer to Hour 2, "Profit and Loss Statement Accounts," for an explanation of why sales discounts are created and an illustration of their purpose in the General Ledger and on the financial statements.

In the last hour, you learned how to value inventory and adjust the total and cost at the end of the month. That will not change, regardless of how much the retail prices are lowered. Sales discounts and allowances affect only the Income or Sales account.

If the management of a computer store decides that it must make room for the new models that will be arriving soon, it offers the old models at a reduced price in order to sell them faster.

For example, a computer that ordinarily has a retail price of $2,500 is sold for 25 percent less than the original price.

The customer realizes a savings of $625 (2500 × .25 = 625), paying only $1,875 plus sales tax of 7 percent for the computer.

The entry to record this cash sale in the accounting system is as follows:

Date	Reference No.	Account	Debit	Credit
3-10-00	3-10	1000 Cash in Checking	2,006.25	
		4000 Sales		2,500.00
		2100 Sales Tax Collected		131.25
		4010 Sales Discounts	625.00	
			-----------	-----------
			2,631.25	2,631.25

To record sale of discounted item

This entry has been totaled to show that the debits equal the credits. Note that the actual cash received goes to Cash in Checking, and then the other particulars of the sale are distributed to the proper accounts.

Based on this entry, the financial statement would look like this:

Income:	
Sales	2,500.00 credit
Sales Discount	(625.00) debit

Total Income	1,875.00 credit

A number of other discounts could be offered on merchandise. The thing to remember is that the Sales account is credited for the price that was originally set on the item. The discount, regardless of how much or how little it is, is recorded as a debit in the Sales Discount account. When the two accounts are combined, the difference is the actual amount realized from the sale of the discounted merchandise.

SALES RETURNS AND ALLOWANCES

When a customer returns merchandise to a retail store typically a refund is issued. This transaction is handled a little differently because cash is being paid out rather than received by the business.

Various scenarios can apply to a refund or the attempts of a business to soothe a dissatisfied customer. The first and most common situation is that the customer returns the product, and the original price of the product is refunded to the customer.

Let's say that a woman buys a dress for $100 plus 7 percent tax. The entry to record this sale is as follows:

Date	Reference No.	Account	Debit	Credit
3-10	3-10	1000 Cash in Checking	107.00	
		4000 Sales		100.00
		2100 Sales Tax Collected		7.00
To record sale				

After the woman takes the dress home, she decides that she doesn't like it after all and brings it back to the store. The store takes the dress back and issues a refund. The entry in the accounting system would be written up as follows:

Date	Reference No.	Account	Debit	Credit
3-11	3-11	1000 Cash in Checking		107.00
		4020 Sales Returns and Allowances	100.00	
		2100 Sales Tax Collected	7.00	

To record refund on sale

As you can see, the debit to Cash in Checking recorded in the first entry has been canceled out by crediting the same amount to Cash in Checking in the second entry. The same is true for the sales tax collected.

Just to clarify this, look at the General Ledger after both of these entries have been posted.

Date	Reference No.	Description	Debit	Credit
1000 Cash in Checking				
		Beginning Balance	0.00	
3-10	3-10	Record Sale	107.00	
3-11	3-11	Record Refund		107.00
			---------	---------
		Ending Balance	0.00	

2100 Sales Tax Collected				
		Beginning Balance		0.00
3-10	3-10	Record Sale		7.00
3-11	3-11	Record Refund	7.00	
			---------	---------
		Ending Balance		0.00

4000 Sales of Goods or Services				
		Beginning Balance		0.00
3-10	3-10	Record Sale		100.00
			---------	---------
		Ending Balance		100.00

4020 Sales Returns and Allowances

		Beginning Balance	0.00	
3-11	3-11	Record Refund	100.00	
			---------	---------
		Ending Balance	100.00	

In this case, the refund eliminated the sale because the credit in Sales of Goods or Services is totally offset by the debit posted to Sales Returns and Allowances.

But what if the woman had actually purchased three dresses at $100 each plus 7 percent sales tax and then returned only one. The sale and the refund would be recorded in the same way, but if a financial statement were printed, the Income section would be as follows:

Income:	
Sales	$300.00 credit
Sales Returns and Allowances	(100.00) debit

Total Income	$200.00 credit

Of course, this is very similar to the way the Income statement appeared after the sale for the discounted computer was recorded. In both cases, there is an adjustment that reduces the amount of Income on the financial statement.

An allowance, such as a partial refund on a damaged item, would be entered and recorded in the accounting system the same as the total refund. The sales tax returned to the customer would be calculated on the exact amount of the refund.

If the original sale is made on credit, the posting to the General Ledger accounts is the same except that Accounts Receivable is substituted for Cash in Checking. The customer's ledger card must also be updated.

Paperwork should always be completed to support refunds and allowances. For example, the customer is usually required to sign a sales slip to verify that the money was returned.

Purchase Discounts

Just as a retail outlet offers discounts to its customers, vendors give discounts to their customers. Sometimes the discounts are given for purchasing a larger quantity of materials or goods for resale. Often a vendor will discount a purchase invoice if it is paid early.

When you set up the vendor cards in Accounts Payable, one of the things to be noted on the card is the payment terms that the vendor is extending to the company.

GO TO ▶
Refer to Hour 7, "Cost of Sales or Services," for samples of vendor ledger cards in the "Accounts Payable" section.

One of the most common discounts on purchases is a 2 percent cash discount provided if the invoice is paid by the tenth of the month following receipt of the goods. You may have seen the notation "2/10" on a purchase invoice.

If the computer store receives a shipment of 10 computers that cost $1,000 each, the total amount of the invoice would be $10,000. Under the terms 2/10, the computer store receives a discount of 2 percent, or $200, by paying the invoice early. Here's how the entry to set up that invoice for payment would be written up:

Date	Reference No.	Account	Debit	Credit
3-10	3-10	2000 Accounts Payable		9,800.00
		4300 Purchases	10,000.00	
		4310 Purchase Discount		200.00
			10,000.00	10,000.00

To record discount on purchase

Most vendor invoices are recorded in Accounts Payable for future payment. However, care must be taken to pay the invoice on time, so as not to lose the discount.

Just as the sales discount adjusted the Sales account in the Income section of the Profit and Loss Statement, this entry would adjust the Purchases account in the Cost of Sales section.

Cost of Sales:

Purchases	$10,000.00 debit
Purchase Discounts	(200.00) credit
Total Cost of Sales	9,800.00 debit

PURCHASE REFUNDS AND ALLOWANCES

If it is necessary to return goods or merchandise to a vendor, your company most likely will receive a credit memo rather than a cash refund. This is because your company processes the purchase invoices through Accounts Payable, while the vendors process the same invoices through their Accounts Receivable.

When the credit memo is received, the entry would be written up as follows:

Date	Reference No.	Account	Debit	Credit
3-15	3-15	2000 Accounts Payable	500.00	
		4330 Purchase Returns		500.00
To record credit memo				

Note that no entry is made to Purchases. The credit posted to Purchase Returns and Allowances simply reduces the debit amount originally posted there when the invoice was received.

INTEREST CALCULATIONS AND ADJUSTMENTS

Interest is the amount charged by an individual or a lending institution for borrowing funds. The terms of any loan should be negotiated and established in writing before a loan is accepted.

Simple interest is determined by the interest rate or percentage multiplied by the repayment period.

Think back to the bookstore in Hour 3, "Chart of Accounts Becomes the General Ledger," that borrowed $15,000 from the bank to get the business started. That was the amount posted to the liability account Loan Payable–First National Bank.

However, that is only the principal amount of the loan, not the amount that will actually be paid back to the bank. The total that the bank will receive is the principal of $15,000 plus the interest charged on the loan. If the loan has an interest rate of 8 percent per annum and is scheduled to be paid back over a five-year period, the interest would be figured as follows:

Principal times interest times term of the loan:

$$15,000 \times .08 = 1,200 \times 5 \text{ years} = \$6,000$$

The interest charged on the loan is \$1,200 per year, for a total of \$6,000 over the life of the loan. So, the bookstore will actually pay the bank \$21,000 for the use of the initial \$15,000.

If you divide that by the number of installment payments to be made (21,000 ÷ by 60 months), the bookstore will be making payments of \$350 per month on the loan.

GO TO ▶
Refer to Hour 9, "Cash Disbursements," for information on issuing checks and posting them to the General Ledger.

Each payment will be recorded in the accounting system. However, to do that accurately, you must first figure out how much of the payment should be posted to the principal amount in the Liabilities section of the General Ledger, and how much should be posted to the Interest Expense account.

To do that, you divide each part of the loan separately by the number of payments. Your worksheet will look like this:

Principal: 15,000

          60   equals \$250 per month

Interest: 6,000

          60   equals \$100 per month

Each month when the payment is made to First National Bank, the entry will be posted as follows:

Date	Reference No.	Account	Debit	Credit
2-1	2-1	1000 Cash in Checking		350.00
		2400 Loan Payable–First National Bank	250.00	
		6260 Interest Expense	100.00	

To record loan payment

Cash in Checking is credited as money is going out of the account. Loan Payable–First National Bank, which has a credit balance, is debited to reduce the amount of the liability.

Interest Expense is debited to record the amount of interest that has been included in the payment.

Look at the liability account in the General Ledger as the loan payments are made over a period of three months to understand how each payment posted reduces the liability amount.

Date	Reference No.	Description	Debit	Credit
2400 Loan Payable–First National Bank				
		Beginning Balance	0.00	
1-1		Opening Entry		15,000.00
2-1	2-1	Record Loan Payment	250.00	
3-1	3-1	Record Loan Payment	250.00	
4-1	4-1	Record Loan Payment	250.00	
		Ending Balance		14,250.00

The principal amount of the loan is not a deductible expense to the book-store, but it is important to update the account so that the Balance Sheet will show that the liability is being reduced each month.

There may be other types of business indebtedness recorded as Liabilities in the Balance Sheet accounts. Most of them will be simple interest loans as in the previous sample. Only the principal amount will be recorded in the liability account. You will figure the interest separately and make that entry to the expense account as you make each payment.

TIME SAVER

Most installment loans come with a payment coupon book. As soon as you figure the interest and principal amounts of the payment, note the breakdown in the payment book. That way you will have the information on hand and can note it on the check stub so that it can be posted accurately.

If the business owns a building, it may also have a mortgage loan. A mortgage is a long-term loan used to finance a particular piece of real estate. Some mortgages have fixed interest rates that stay in effect for the entire repayment period. Other mortgages have adjustable interest rates. These are commonly referred to as adjustable rate mortgages (ARMs).

This means that the interest rate can be adjusted either up or down during the life of the loan. Usually the adjustment is based on some type of standard, such as the prime interest rate set by the Federal Reserve Board.

Interest on both types of mortgages is compounded—that is, the interest charged for one period is added to the principal before the interest for the next period is calculated. The result is that the allocation of principal and interest changes with every payment.

Some lenders send out monthly statements that show the breakdown of principal and interest for the prior month, so your entry could be based on that statement. If the mortgage lender does not send out a monthly statement, ask for an amortization chart that will allow you to estimate the amount of the interest month by month. You can review a sample of an amortization schedule in Appendix B, "Sample Forms."

At the end of the year, the lender is required to send a statement that itemizes the principal, interest, taxes, and insurance paid during the year. When that is received, the mortgage interest for the year can be adjusted to the actual amount.

OTHER MISCELLANEOUS ADJUSTMENTS

If the business does have a building, you will also have taxes and insurance to post to the expense accounts. Ordinarily, if there is a mortgage, there is an *escrow account*. A portion of the monthly payment is allocated to the escrow account, from which the lender then pays out the taxes and insurance.

STRICTLY DEFINED

With respect to a mortgage loan, an **escrow account** is a cash account maintained by the lender. A portion of each mortgage payment is deposited into the escrow account and kept on hand to pay Expenses such as taxes and insurance on the mortgaged property.

The portion of the monthly payment that goes toward taxes and insurance is calculated by the lender. The amount is based on the amount paid out for taxes and insurance in the prior year. Like the interest amount, you can estimate the monthly taxes and insurance and then, if necessary, adjust them at the end of the year.

The monthly tax amount is posted to the Other Taxes account in the expense section. The monthly insurance is posted to the Insurance–General account. These postings are done at the time the mortgage payment is made each month.

If the business sells merchandise or goods on credit, you will most likely have many customer ledgers in Accounts Receivable. With a number of accounts to collect, there will be a few that will default and not pay their bill.

GO TO ▶
Refer to Hour 16, "Cash Disbursements Journal," for detailed information and instructions for posting all the checks and payments that are made during the month.

Because the Income that will be reported on the tax return is based in part on the sales recorded in Accounts Receivable, you will have to adjust them to reflect only the accounts that are collectable. You don't want to pay Income tax on amounts that will never be collected.

To write off these uncollectable accounts, you will need to add an account titled Bad Debts (Account 6560) to the General Expense section of your Chart of Accounts and General Ledger.

Bad debts can be written off at any time during the year, but most companies review the customer ledgers that make up Accounts Receivable at the end of each year and determine which ones need to be eliminated.

If a department store reviews its accounts at the end of the year and determines the combined balance of bad debts to be $2,000, for example, the entry to write them off the books would be as follows:

Date	Reference No.	Account	Debit	Credit
12-31	12-31	1100 Accounts Receivable		2,000.00
		6560 Bad Debts	2,000.00	
To write off bad debts				

Accounts Receivable, which has a debit balance, would be credited to reduce that balance. Bad Debts would be debited to record the expense that offsets the original sales taken as Income and credited to the sales account.

At the same time, the customer ledgers that make up the bad debts would be pulled from Accounts Receivable, marked as bad debts written off, and filed with the accounting records.

These are the most common miscellaneous adjustments that need to be calculated and recorded in the accounting system. These adjustments will not apply to every business.

GO TO ▶
Refer to Hour 24, "Accounting Software Programs," to examine and explain a variety of accounting software programs.

In previous hours you learned about other adjustments. In a computerized accounting system, it is possible to set up a general journal entry to automatically post reoccurring monthly adjustments such as depreciation and prepaid Expenses.

As you continue to move forward in this book, you will encounter more samples of entries and review more detailed General Ledger postings, which will include some of the adjustments you learned about in this hour and in previous hours.

HOUR'S UP!

Answering the following questions will help you review and retain some of the information that you studied in this hour.

1. Simple interest on a loan is calculated as follows:
   a. Principal × rate
   b. Principal × rate × term
   c. Rate × term

2. A refund is posted as a debit to Sales Returns and Allowances.
   a. True
   b. False

3. Interest on a business loan is not recorded as an expense.
   a. True
   b. False

4. The insurance premium paid on business property is recorded as a debit to:
   a. Miscellaneous Expense
   b. Building
   c. Insurance–General

5. An entry to Bad Debts offsets the Income recorded for the original sale.
   a. True
   b. False

6. The principal amount of a business loan is recorded as a debit to the liability account.

    a. True

    b. False

7. When merchandise is sold at a reduced price, the amount of the discount is recorded as:

    a. A credit to Sales

    b. A debit to Sales Discounts

    c. A credit to Cash in Checking

8. Vendor terms 2/10 allows a discount for paying the invoice early.

    a. True

    b. False

9. A purchase discount is recorded as:

    a. A debit to Sales

    b. A credit to Accounts Payable

    c. A credit to Purchase Discounts

10. An expense account for Bad Debts is used to record unpaid Accounts Payable.

    a. True

    b. False

HOUR 9

Cash Disbursements

CHAPTER SUMMARY

LESSON PLAN:

In this hour you will learn about ...

- Accounts payable
- General Expenses
- Writing checks
- Posting the disbursements

When you are managing an accounting system, you are usually responsible for processing and paying all the monthly bills. This includes the vendors set up in Accounts Payable and all the general Expenses.

You will have control of the business checking account, and you will have to keep it updated and in balance.

BUSINESS CHECKING ACCOUNT

The following is a sample of a voucher stub from a business checking account:

Check No. 001

Balance _____

Date_____

To_____   Deposits _____

For_____

Balance _____

This check stub already has spaces allocated for all the information that you will need to post the check or cash disbursement to the General Ledger.

Before you begin reviewing the checks written for the month, you will need to study the financial statements for a sample company, a profitable catering service run by a mother and a daughter. You will be reviewing year-to-date financial statements.

The ladies started the business, located in rented space in an industrial complex, in January 1999. The following is their Balance Sheet report:

GO TO ▶
Refer to Hour 5, "Organization and Proper Accounting Procedures," for an explanation of how to set up and manage the operating account.

GO TO ▶
Refer to Hour 21, "The Monthly Profit and Loss Statement," to learn how to produce monthly and year-to-date statements, as well as how to tailor the statements to the needs of an individual business.

S & S CATERING SERVICE
BALANCE SHEET
April 30, 2000

ASSETS:

Cash in Checking	23,522.83
Cash in Savings	5,132.00
Cash on Hand	200.00
Accounts Receivable	1,234.00
Inventory	781.00
Leasehold Improvements	2,800.00
Accumulated Depreciation–LH	(746.56)
Vehicles	22,100.00
Accumulated Depreciation–Vehicles	(5,893.28)
Equipment	17,500.00
Accumulated Depreciation–Equipment	(7,777.76)
Furniture & Fixtures	1,200.00
Accumulated Depreciation–F & F	(533.28)
Organization Costs	1,500.00
Accumulated Amortization–Org.	(666.56)
Deposits	750.00

TOTAL ASSETS	61,102.39

LIABILITIES AND EQUITY
LIABILITIES:

Accounts Payable	2,225.24
Loan Payable–Merchants Bank	11,000.00

TOTAL LIABILITIES	13,225.24

EQUITY:

Retained Earnings	34,400.00
Net Profit (Loss)	13,477.15

Capital #1	15,000.00
Capital #2	15,000.00
Drawing #1	(15,000.00)
Drawing #2	(15,000.00)

TOTAL EQUITY	47,877.15

TOTAL LIABILITIES AND EQUITY	61,102.39

You should notice a few things when reviewing this Balance Sheet. First of all, it is obvious that the owners have a profitable, solvent business enterprise. In their first year, the net profits averaged $2,800 per month.

Each of the women invested $15,000 in the business, and they were able to withdraw their initial investments before the end of the second year. Now four months into the second year, the profits are averaging $3,300 per month, a gain of $500 per month over the previous year.

The other thing to take note of is that the depreciation and amortization appear to be written off on a monthly basis. Remember that these Expenses are not cash expenditures, but a reduction in the value of the Assets.

Now you will review the current year's Profit and Loss Statement for the catering company:

S & S CATERING SERVICE
PROFIT AND LOSS STATEMENT
April 30, 2000

INCOME:	
Sales of Goods or Services	28,400.00
Other Income	52.00
Interest Income	120.00

TOTAL INCOME	28,552.00
COST OF SALES:	
Purchases–Food	4,013.00
Purchases–Paper Products	579.87

TOTAL COST OF SALES	4,592.87

GROSS PROFIT	23,979.13
GENERAL EXPENSES:	
Advertising	800.00
Auto Expenses	896.00
Bank Charges	40.00
Depreciation Expense	3,737.72
Amortization Expense	166.64
Dues & Subscriptions	72.00
Equipment Rental	184.30
Utilities	425.32
Insurance–General	400.00
Interest Expense	400.00
Legal & Accounting	450.00
Miscellaneous Expense	128.00
Postage	132.00
Office Expense	216.00
Rent Expense	1,600.00
Repairs & Maintenance	21.00
Other Taxes	53.00
Supplies	428.00
Telephone Expense	352.00
TOTAL EXPENSES	10,501.98
NET PROFIT (LOSS)	13,477.15

GO TO ▶ Refer to Hour 22, "End-of-the-Year Payroll Reports and Other Tax Reports," to learn how the accounting information is transferred to business and personal tax returns.

One piece of information that you should take note of in the Profit and Loss Statement is that the owners are not paying wages. This is one reason that the profits are so good.

The profits from the business will be transferred to the owners at the end of the year and will be reported on their personal tax returns.

ACCOUNTS PAYABLE

The first bills to be paid in the month of May for the S & S Catering Service are the ones that were set up in Accounts Payable at the end of April.

The unpaid bills at the end of April were as follows:

Wholesales Grocers	842.35
Paper Products Plus	579.87
Business Promotions	150.00
Accounting Associates	450.00
Mar's Auto Repairs	203.02

Total Accounts Payable	2,225.24

GO TO ▶
Refer to Hour 23, "Closing the Books at the End of the Year," to learn how the end-of-the-year closing zeroes out all the accounts in the profit and loss section of the General Ledger.

The total of these unpaid bills was posted into Accounts Payable, and although these expenditures had not yet been paid out, they were included in the financial statements as of April 30, 2000.

Look back on the Balance Sheet, and you will see the total amount of $2,225.24 listed in the Accounts Payable account. These bills were also included in the Profit and Loss Statement. The paper products invoice and the bill for doing the prior year's tax returns (Legal & Accounting) are the same amounts as listed here because these are the first Expenses recorded in those specific accounts for the current year.

Look at the following checks written for two of these bills in Accounts Payable:

Check No. 185

	Balance>	23,522.83

Date 5-1-00

To: <u>Wholesale Grocers</u>

	<Deposits

For: Accounts Payable

	This Check>	842.35
	Balance>	22,680.48

Check No. 186

Date: 5-1-00

To: Accounting Associates

continues

continued

		<u>Deposits</u>
For: Accounts Payable		
	This Check>	<u>450.00</u>
	Balance>	<u>22,230.48</u>

You can see that these checks were written for the amounts listed in the Accounts Payable schedule. You should also note that in the description portion of the check, the words "Accounts Payable" are written.

GO TO ▶

Refer to Hour 7, "Cost of Sales or Services," for a demonstration and explanation of the process of posting unpaid bills to the expense accounts and the offsetting entry to Accounts Payable.

That area of the check stub is to note the General Ledger account that the check amount will be recorded in. Because these bills were already posted to the individual expense accounts, the check will now be posted to Accounts Payable, the account used to record the offsetting entry for each bill that remained unpaid at the end of the month.

By posting these checks to Accounts Payable, you are clearing the balance in that account and getting it ready to accept the new total of the current month's unpaid bills.

The entry to record the previous two checks is as follows:

Date	Reference Number	Account	Debit	Credit
5-1	Ck 185	1000 Cash in Checking		842.35
		2000 Accounts Payable	842.35	
5-1	Ck 186	1000 Cash in Checking		450.00
		2000 Accounts Payable	450.00	

The Cash account is credited because money is being taken out of the checking account. Accounts Payable is debited because that is where these bills were posted at the end of the month.

Once all the bills on the Accounts Payable list are paid and posted, this is how the Accounts Payable account in the General Ledger will look for S & S Catering Service for the current month:

Date	Reference Number	Description	Debit	Credit
2000 Accounts Payable				
5-1-00		Beginning Balance		2,225.24
5-1-00	Check	Record # 185	842.35	
5-1-00	Check	Record # 186	450.00	
5-1-00	Check	Record # 187	150.00	

5-1-00	Check	Record # 188	579.87	
5-1-00	Check	Record # 189	203.02	
		Ending Balance	0.00	0.00

At the end of every month, the balance in the Accounts Payable account should reflect the total of the unpaid bills for the current month only.

Vendor ledgers will also have to be updated to include the payments that were made. When this is done, the total of all the vendor accounts should be the same as the Accounts Payable balance in the General Ledger.

GENERAL EXPENSES

Usually a number of other bills need to be paid during any given month. Here is a list of bills for the catering company that are due on or before May 15th:

Acme Industrial Plaza	$400.00
Edison Electric Co.	49.00
Exxon Gasoline Co.	101.00
Handy Man Inc.	27.32
Computers for Rent	32.00
Paper Products Plus	17.00

When the checks for these bills are issued, the check stubs will be completed as follows:

Check No. 190

Balance>   21,297.59

Date: 5-13-00
To: Acme Industrial Plaza

<Deposits

For: Rent Expense

This Check>   400.00
Balance>   20,897.59

Check No. 191
Date: 5-13-00
To: Edison Electric Co.

<Deposits

For: Utilities

This Check> 49.00
Balance> 20,848.59

Check No. 192
Date: 5-13-00

<Deposits

To: Exxon Gasoline Co.
For: Auto Expense

This Check> 101.00
Balance> 20,747.59

Check No. 193
Date: 5-13-00

<Deposits

To: Handy Man, Inc.
For: Repairs & Mtn.

This Check> 27.32
Balance> 20,720.27

Check No. 194
Date: 5-13-00
To: Computers for Rent

<Deposits

For: Equipment Rental

This Check> 32.00
Balance> 20,688.27

Check No. 195

Date: 5-13-00

To: Paper Products Plus

	<Deposits
For: Supplies	
This Check>	17.00
Balance>	20,671.27

Each check is written to the vendor for the specified amount. In the description section of the check stub, the account that the check should be posted to is designated.

TIME SAVER

When you are using a manual accounting system, you don't need to post each check to the Cash in Checking account individually. You can recap the checks and post one total to the cash account.

The entry to post these six checks to the General Ledger can be recapped and written up as follows:

Date	Reference No.	Account	Debit	Credit
5-13	Ck # 190	6360 Rent Expense	400.00	
	Ck # 191	6220 Utilities	49.00	
	Ck # 192	5150 Auto Expense	101.00	
	Ck # 193	6380 Repairs & Mtn.	27.32	
	Ck # 194	6200 Equipment Rental	32.00	
	Ck # 195	6520 Supplies	17.00	
		1000 Cash in Checking		626.32
			----------	----------
			626.32	626.32

POSTING DISBURSEMENTS TO THE GENERAL LEDGER

It is very important that you understand how these entries, when posted to the General Ledger, affect the financial reports of the company.

A financial statement can be produced at any time during the month. The report will reflect whatever has been posted to the General Ledger accounts up to that point.

The following chart shows the balances in the General Ledger accounts as they were reported on April 30, 2000, and as they are now, after the cash disbursements were posted:

General Ledger Accounts	Balance 4-30-00	Balance 5-13-00
Cash in Checking	23,522.83	20,671.27*
Cash in Savings	5,132.00	5,132.00
Cash on Hand	200.00	200.00
Accounts Receivable	1,234.00	1,234.00
Inventory	781.00	781.00
Leasehold Improvements	2,800.00	2,800.00
Acc. Depreciation–LH	(746.56)	(746.56)
Vehicles	22,100.00	22,100.00
Acc. Depreciation–Vehicles	(5,893.28)	(5,893.28)
Equipment	17,500.00	17,500.00
Acc. Depreciation–Equipment	(7,777.76)	(7,777.76)
Furniture & Fixtures	1,200.00	1,200.00
Acc. Depreciation–F & F	(533.28)	(533.28)
Organization Costs	1,500.00	1,500.00
Acc. Amortization–Org.	(666.56)	(666.56)
Deposits	750.00	750.00
Accounts Payable	(2,225.24)	0.00*
Loan Payable–Merchants Bank	(11,000.00)	(11,000.00)
Retained Earnings	(34,400.00)	(34,400.00)
Capital #1	(15,000.00)	(15,000.00)
Capital #2	(15,000.00)	(15,000.00)
Drawing #1	15,000.00	15,000.00
Drawing #2	15,000.00	15,000.00
Sales of Goods/Services	(28,400.00)	(28,400.00)
Other Income	(52.00)	(52.00)

General Ledger Accounts	Balance 4-30-00	Balance 5-13-00
Interest Income	(120.00)	(120.00)
Purchases–Food	4,013.00	4,013.00
Purchases–Paper Products	579.87	579.87
Advertising	800.00	800.00
Auto Expenses	896.00	997.00*
Bank Charges	40.00	40.00
Depreciation Expense	3,737.72	3,737.72
Amortization Expense	166.64	166.64
Dues & Subscriptions	72.00	72.00
Equipment Rental	184.30	216.30*
Utilities	425.32	474.32*
Insurance–General	400.00	400.00
Interest Expense	400.00	400.00
Legal & Accounting	450.00	450.00
Miscellaneous Expense	128.00	128.00
Postage	132.00	132.00
Office Expense	216.00	216.00
Rent Expense	1,600.00	2,000.00*
Repairs & Maintenance	21.00	48.32*
Other Taxes	53.00	53.00
Supplies	428.00	445.00*
Telephone Expense	352.00	352.00
Net Profit	(13,477.13)*	(12,850.81)*

The accounts with asterisks (*) are the only accounts affected by the activity posted in the beginning of May. All the other accounts stayed the same because nothing was posted to them.

The profit and loss section accounts that changed are these:

Account	4-30-00	5-13-00	Difference
Auto Expense	896.00	997.00	101.00 debit
Equipment Rental	184.30	216.30	32.00 debit
Utilities	425.32	474.32	49.00 debit

continues

continued

Rent Expense	1,600.00	2,000.00	400.00 debit
Account	*4-30-00*	*5-13-00*	*Difference*
Repairs & Mtn.	21.00	48.32	27.32 debit
Supplies	428.00	445.00	17.00 debit

The Balance Sheet accounts that changed are these:

Account	*4-30-00*	*5-13-00*	
Cash in Checking	23,522.83	20,671.27	(2,851.26) credit
Accounts Payable	(2,225.24)	0.00	2,225.24 debit
			0.00

In the postings, debits offset credits, as they should, but the postings have resulted in the net profit being reduced $626.32, even though the total amount that was posted was actually $2,851.26. Why is that?

Remember that the first checks written were for the bills in Accounts Payable. They were already posted to the expense accounts in April. Posting the checks for these bills simply moved the total from Accounts Payable to Cash in Checking and did not affect the net profit.

Cash disbursements are made all month long and can be posted as the checks are written or posted all together at the end of the month.

Just be sure to keep the checkbook balance updated. You should always know how much money is in the bank account.

HOUR'S UP!

These questions are a way to test what you have learned in this hour. Take a few minutes to answer them.

1. The vendor ledgers are updated only when a purchase is made.

    a. True

    b. False

2. The Balance Sheet shows the previous year's profit as Retained Earnings.

    a. True

    b. False

QUIZ

3. The check written to pay the electric bill is debited to what account?

   a. Rent

   b. Supplies

   c. Utilities

4. S & S Catering Service's profits are transferred to the owners' personal tax returns at the end of the year.

   a. True

   b. False

5. To save time, the checkbook balance doesn't have to be updated every time a check is written.

   a. True

   b. False

6. The check written for a monthly lease payment is posted as follows:

   a. Credit Cash in Checking, debit Equipment Rental

   b. Credit Accounts Payable, debit Cash in Checking

   c. Credit Cash in Checking, credit Rent Expense

7. Proper completion of the check stub makes posting disbursements easier.

   a. True

   b. False

8. When paying bills recorded in Accounts Payable, the check is posted as follows:

   a. Credit Cash in Checking, debit Purchases

   b. Debit Accounts Payable, credit Cash in Checking

   c. Credit Accounts Payable, debit Cash in Checking

9. Cash disbursements can be posted as the checks are written or all together at the end of the month.

   a. True

   b. False

10. A cash disbursement to auto repairs is debited to what account?

    a. Vehicles

    b. Repairs & Maintenance

    c. Auto Expense

QUIZ

Hour 10

The Importance of Work Papers, Receipts, and Other Records

- The records to keep
- How to store records and for how long
- Reconciling and paying vendor accounts
- Completing sales tax reports and paying the taxes

Documents that support the data in your accounting system are extremely important. If you have ever been through an audit, you know that those documents are always requested and carefully reviewed by the auditor. This holds true whether the audit is conducted by an independent, outside accounting firm or a government agency.

Many nonprofit organizations are subject to annual audits, as are companies such as property management companies that keep funds in trust for their clients. In addition, state audits are conducted in connection with sales tax and workers' compensation insurance.

As you learned earlier, the IRS will not accept your word for a tax deduction. If you cannot produce a canceled check, a receipt, or other documentation, the deduction is disallowed, and interest and penalties are promptly assessed.

Not only do the proper records have to be retained, but they also have to be kept in good order so that, when requested, they can be easily accessed.

The Records to Keep

Work papers that support general Journal Entries should always be filed and kept in date order. For example, if you opt to post cash disbursements at the end of the month instead of as the checks are written, you will have a work paper that recaps and distributes the check amounts to the proper accounts.

GO TO ▶
Refer to Hour 5, "Organization and Proper Accounting Procedures," for valuable information on organizing and filing accounting records.

Any time you have a refund or an entry that needs calculations, such as a tax report or a workman's compensation report, you will have a work paper to support the report. That work paper should be stapled to the report and filed with the report.

Bank reconciliations usually require a work paper. Once the bank account balance has been verified, the work paper should be attached to the bank statement, so it can be filed with the bank statement.

Always write the date and the check number directly on your copy of any invoice you pay. The invoices should then be filed alphabetically in a file reserved for paid bills.

GO TO ▶
Refer to Hour 18, "Reconciling the Bank Accounts and General Journal Entries," to find detailed instructions and samples to follow when reconciling bank accounts and other statements.

When the canceled checks are returned with the bank statement, put them in numerical order and keep them in a file. Putting them in numerical order will also put them in date order.

If a question arises on an invoice, it is easier to find an invoice filed in alphabetical order than to go through stacks of canceled checks. Once the invoice is located, you will have the number of the check that was used to pay it, and you will be able to determine whether that check cleared the bank account.

Whenever cash is paid out, some sort of documentation is required. Whether it's a petty cash expenditure, a cash refund, or a cash purchase, you need to get a receipt; if appropriate, have the person who is receiving the cash sign the receipt.

Obviously, you should handle a cash receipt the same way. A sales slip, a photocopy of a check, or some other documentation should be available to verify the cash received.

All sales records need to be kept and filed in good order. Besides the obvious reasons, such as refund requests or complaints about merchandise or services, the sales records are needed for audit purposes. State, city, and county officials often audit sales records to determine whether sales tax was properly reported and remitted.

Payroll records should also be kept in order and filed in a place where they can be retrieved. Time cards, personnel records, and canceled payroll checks should all be carefully filed. Each year, as payroll tax reports and any work papers that relate to them are completed, copies of them must be retained and filed.

Government agencies often request additional information on payroll tax reports. You must be able to produce a copy of anything that you sent, along with documents to support the reports, if necessary.

In this age of computers, you may be tempted to skip some of the steps necessary to keep and maintain good written records, but remember that anyone can enter information into a computer. Proving that the information is true and accurate takes more than your word for it.

GO TO ▶
Refer to Hour 13, "Posting Payroll, Computing Taxes, and Conforming to Federal and State Rules and Regulations," for instructions on filing federal and state tax returns.

Having the proper documentation on hand to support the revenue, disbursements, payroll, and any other miscellaneous transactions that go through the accounting system is vital. These records protect you and your company.

Audits, tax disputes, legal claims, and any and all questions that arise from the information entered in an accounting program require written, tangible proof in order to be satisfied.

STORING RECORDS

Various methods of storing records can be used. The manner chosen depends on the company, the number of files, and how accessible they must be.

Current-year files should be kept readily available in file cabinets, drawers, or boxes. Fireproof vaults or file cabinets with locks can be used to protect sensitive records, such as personnel files.

Office supply stores sell a variety of boxes for storing files. These provide an inexpensive alternative to more costly metal files, and as long as records are properly placed in the boxes, in a neat, logical order, they work very well.

Backup disks for computerized files should be stored somewhere away from the computer, where they will be safe from fire or unauthorized hackers.

HOW LONG SHOULD RECORDS BE RETAINED?

Again, the length of time that records should be kept depends on the company and its needs.

In general, records should be available for the current year and three years before that. A few years ago, the Internal Revenue Service agreed not to go back farther than three years to audit an individual or a business. Other agencies and auditors adopted the same policy.

Of course, some records should be kept longer. Personnel records, for instance, should be retained for as long as the person is in the company's employment, and then for three years after termination.

Any accounting records that relate to long-term contracts or warranties must also be kept for the life of the contract or the guarantee.

JUST A MINUTE

Banks, newspapers, and libraries keep many of their records on microfilm. This is a good way to retain records when storage space is limited.

All the paperwork that flows through your accounting office is your responsibility. It is usually up to you to determine how it should be filed and stored. When someone needs documentation, you are the person who will receive the request.

With that in mind, keep your files in a way that makes it easy for you to access whatever is needed.

RECONCILING AND PAYING VENDOR ACCOUNTS

Most vendors send out monthly statements detailing the invoices that were issued for purchases.

If you are working for a large company, you may have a number of statements to reconcile each month. This is another reason to keep the vendor ledgers updated and the unpaid invoices filed in good order.

The statements should be reviewed and checked for accuracy. Make sure that there are no outstanding balances from the previous month on the statement.

The unpaid invoices should be compared to the invoices listed on the statement. The vendor's statement should also agree with the balance on the vendor ledger that you have for that company. If there are discrepancies, call or write the vendor to get them resolved. Keeping your ledger in balance with the vendor's records will keep your company's credit rating good and avoid any problems with future orders to be shipped on credit.

Some companies issue purchase orders for all goods and supplies ordered. A purchase order is a memo to the vendor authorizing the shipment of goods.

If that is the case, your company's purchase order number should have been noted on the vendor's original invoice.

While it is important to check all the vendor statements to make sure that the vendor has updated the ledger kept on your company with the proper purchases and payments, you should not pay bills based on statements.

Get in the habit of paying by invoice only. This will avoid a lot of problems. If you don't have a copy of an invoice listed on a vendor's statement, call the company and request a copy of it. Once you receive the copy, you can verify that the merchandise on that invoice was actually received in good order by your company.

This procedure should be followed for two reasons:

1. Statements usually list only the invoice number and the amount. A description of the purchases is detailed on the invoices and is not included on the statement.

2. If there is an invoice listed on the statement that you don't have a copy of, it could mean that your company did not order the merchandise. It could also mean that the order was placed but never received by your company.

Paying by invoice only also eliminates the possibility of paying the same invoice twice. It is possible to have paid an invoice, but for some reason the payment does not appear on the current vendor statement. This can happen for a variety of reasons, including postal delays or the vendor's failure to process the payment in a timely or accurate manner.

If you are paying only invoices that are in your unpaid bill file, the chances of paying one twice or overlooking one that did not get posted on the vendor's statement are unlikely. Of course, all the invoices for purchases of goods and merchandise that are in your unpaid bill file should be recorded on the vendor ledger for that particular company.

GO TO ▶
Refer to Hour 19, "The Trial Balance," to find out how to implement a series of checks and balances that will help you avoid errors.

Following this process establishes a chain of checks and balances.

Mistakes cost time and sometimes money. While paying the same invoice twice or neglecting to pay one at all is probably not going to put your company in real jeopardy, it can be costly. Also, if you don't pay an invoice when it's due, you may lose a discount or have to pay late fees.

The following is a sample of a vendor ledger that has been properly updated with purchases and payments:

Fabrics & Notions
225 Westchester
Apple Green, NJ   Terms: 30 days

Date	Invoice No.	Amount	Paid/Ck#	Balance Due
2-10-00	562	−750.00	−750.00	
3-10-00			750.00 (201)	0.00
3-15-00	617	−925.00		−925.00
3-25-00	674	−272.00		−1,197.00
4-1-00			1,197.00 (256)	0.00
4-10-00	728	−875.00		−875.00

If Fabrics & Notions sends out monthly statements, this statement should be checked against the open invoices in the unpaid bill file and this vendor ledger.

If the amounts don't agree or reconcile, try to pinpoint the source of the error and correct it. Sometimes a phone call can iron out a problem in a few minutes.

TIME SAVER

Whenever you discover an error or problem in the accounting system or the records, try to find the source and correct it immediately. Putting it off for another day may just serve to compound the error and cause you to lose more time because it has become more complicated to fix.

Managing an accounting system requires that you pay attention to details. If you keep the small tasks organized and under control, you will find that the bigger tasks go more smoothly.

Reconciling vendor statements and keeping vendor ledgers updated and in balance are just some of those small details that cannot be overlooked.

COMPLETING SALES TAX REPORTS AND PAYING THE TAXES

Although reporting and paying sales tax does not apply to every business venture, an accountant should at least have a working knowledge of the procedures.

The state, county, or city in which the business is being conducted regulates the tax rates, rules, and reporting requirements. In most cases, sales tax is collected when tangible goods or products are sold. Those products can be anything from clothing to computer software programs.

A retail business is usually required to get a sales tax license before it begins to operate. Each taxing entity issues its own license and assigns a license number to the business applicants.

Wholesalers, those who sell products to retailers, do not charge sales tax to their customers because it is assumed that the tax will be collected and paid when the retailer sells the products to the public. However, the retailer must provide the wholesaler with a valid resale tax number issued by the state, city, or county.

You may be located in an area where only state sales tax is required to be collected and paid. Or, you could be in an area where both state and city sales taxes are in effect.

The burden of responsibility is on the taxpayer—that is, the person who is selling the retail merchandise. If you are not sure of sales tax requirements in your area, you must contact the state, city, or county offices to get the necessary information and apply for whatever licenses are needed.

In your Chart of Accounts, in the liability section of the General Ledger, you set up the account Sales Tax Collected. In Hour 6, you learned that the tax was charged as a percentage on retail sales, and you learned how to post it as part of cash and credit transactions.

Again, depending on the area where the retail business is operating, the sales tax is scheduled to be reported and paid on a specified date. Generally, the tax is payable every month. For instance, the reports and the taxes may be due on or before the 15th of the month following the reporting period. The reporting period is the month in which the sales were made and the tax was collected.

GO TO ▶ Refer to Hour 7, "Cost of Sales or Services," for an explanation on how to collect and post the sales tax to the liability account.

Very often the tax rate is split between state and city. For example, in Phoenix, Arizona, the sales tax rate is 7 percent. The state of Arizona gets 5 percent of the tax, and the city of Phoenix is entitled to the other 2 percent.

Both the city and the state send out tax reports that must be completed and returned with the tax remittances.

A retailer that uses an electronic cash register can program the tax rate into the register, and the tax will be automatically calculated on each sale. If there is no electronic device at the point of sale, the tax can be figured by multiplying the sales price by the tax rate.

In lieu of either of these methods, sales tax charts can be used that show the amount of sales tax that should be collected on any sales' total.

At the end of each month, after all the sales have been posted to the General Ledger, the Sales Tax Collected account will have a credit balance, as in the sample that follows:

Date	Description	Debit	Credit
2100 Sales Tax Collected			
	Beginning Balance		0.00
2-5-00	Sales Tax		180.04
2-10-00	Sales Tax		217.00
2-15-00	Sales Tax		129.92
2-20-00	Sales Tax		197.19
2-25-00	Sales Tax		68.88
2-29-00	Sales Tax		268.87
	Ending Balance		1,061.90

For most sales tax reports, you will also have to know the gross amount of sales for the month you are reporting. Here is the Sales account that goes with the previous Sales Tax sample:

Date	Description	Debit	Credit
4000 Sales of Goods or Service			
	Beginning Balance		0.00
2-5-00	Sales		2,572.00
2-10-00	Sales		3,100.00
2-15-00	Sales		1,856.00
2-20-00	Sales		2,817.00
2-25-00	Sales		984.00
2-28-00	Sales		3,841.00
	Ending Balance		15,170.00

If all the tax collected goes to one entity, the following information would be filled in on the report:

Acme Hardware	Reporting Period: 2-1/2-28-00	
4275 E. Maple Ave.		
Harbor Light, MN	State Sales Tax # 55-5555	
Gross Sales	Tax Rate	Tax Collected
$15,170.00	7%	1,061.90

Total Tax Remitted		1,061.90

The report would then be signed and dated, and mailed with a check for $1,061.90.

If the taxing authorities in your area divide the tax between city and state, you would have two reports to complete and two checks to write, as in the following samples:

Acme Hardware	Reporting Period: 2-1/2-28-00	
4275 E. Maple Ave.		
Harbor Light, MN	State Sales Tax # 55-5555	
Gross Sales	Tax Rate	Tax Collected
$15,170.00	5%	758.50

Total Tax Remitted		758.50

Acme Hardware	Reporting Period: 2-1/2-28-00	
4275 E. Maple Ave.		
Harbor Light, MN	City Sales Tax # 66-6666	
Gross Sales	Tax Rate	Tax Collected
$15,170.00	2%	303.40

Total Tax Remitted		303.40

Based on the second example, in which two taxing authorities are being paid, the Sales Tax Collected account in the General Ledger would be posted as follows:

Date	Description	Debit	Credit
2100 Sales Tax Collected			
	Beginning Balance		0.00
2-5-00	Sales Tax		180.04
2-10-00	Sales Tax		217.00
2-15-00	Sales Tax		129.92
2-20-00	Sales Tax		197.19
2-25-00	Sales Tax		68.88
2-29-00	Sales Tax		268.87
3-10-00	State Tax Paid	758.50	
3-10-00	City Tax Paid	303.40	
		------------	------------
	Ending Balance		0.00

The debits posted to the Sales Tax Collected account clear the balance, showing that the tax has been remitted. The other side of these entries is a credit to Cash in Checking to record the two checks that were written from that account.

Although these entries have been made and the General Ledger shows that the tax has been paid, if there is ever a question, the accountant would have to produce copies of the sales tax reports filed, along with copies of the canceled checks that paid the tax.

Also bear in mind that the examples given here are generic. They are meant only to give you a basic idea of how the sales tax is reported and paid. The taxing authorities in your own area will have their own versions of the reporting forms that may require more information or a variation on the procedure.

GO TO ▶

Refer to Hour 14, "Payroll Tax Reports," to understand the importance of timely reporting and payment of taxes.

The most important thing to remember when reporting and paying any type of tax is that it must be done in a timely manner. Taxes should always be reported and paid on or before the due date to avoid interest and penalties.

This brings us to a final word on work papers and other documents. It is a good idea to date and write your initials on papers to establish a point of reference. If the document is a copy of a tax report, initial it and write the date that the form was mailed to the taxing authority.

Above all, keep all the documentation in a neat, orderly fashion. Sales tax reports should all be filed together, as should bank statements and the reconciliations that go with them.

In any office or accounting situation, sometimes you'll need to put your hands on a particular document in a hurry. The person you will help most by organizing them properly is yourself.

HOUR'S UP!

The information that you have reviewed in this hour should have prepared you to answer the following questions.

1. The work papers for the bank reconciliation should be filed with:

    a. Canceled checks

    b. Bank statements

    c. Paid bills

2. The date and check number should be noted on a paid invoice before it is filed.

    a. True

    b. False

3. Canceled checks should be filed in alphabetical order.

    a. True

    b. False

4. Most accounting records should be kept for:

    a. Seven years

    b. One year

    c. The current year plus three prior years

5. One of the most important things to remember about sales tax is that it must be reported and paid on time.

    a. True

    b. False

6. After sales tax is paid, the entry to record the payment should be:

    a. Credit Cash in Checking, debit Sales Tax Collected

    b. Credit Sales Tax Collected, debit Accounts Payable

    c. Credit Cash in Checking, debit Other Taxes

QUIZ

7. The retailer is responsible for collecting sales tax.

    a. True

    b. False

8. Work papers should be kept for which of the following:

    a. Bank reconciliations

    b. General Journal Entries

    c. Calculations for tax reports

    d. All of the above

9. Vendors should be paid based on the monthly statement that you receive.

    a. True

    b. False

10. What is required to satisfy audit questions, tax disputes, and legal claims?

    a. Computer entries

    b. Written documentation

    c. Witnesses

PART III

Employees and Payroll

HOUR 11
Salary and Wages

In an accounting system, payroll and the taxes associated with it are in their own special category.

Becoming proficient in this area requires more than one hour of instruction because the requirements, tax rates, and tax credits are as varied as the employers and wage earners that are governed by them.

To manage payroll and payroll taxes, you must first become familiar with the required procedures that should be put in place before that first employee is hired.

Some companies have personnel departments or employ services that handle all the aspects of payroll, but this is another area where the accountant should have at least a working knowledge of the procedures and requirements. In most small businesses, processing the payroll and the necessary reports falls to the accountant.

If your company is not incorporated, you will need to obtain an Employer Identification Number. This number is used by the IRS to track your employees, the wages they receive, the payroll taxes, and tax credits associated with those wages.

In other words, the Employer Identification Number, often shortened to EIN, is your account number with the federal government. If your company is already incorporated, you will already have this number—it is the same tax identification number that is assigned when you apply for corporation status with the IRS.

GO TO ▶
Refer to Hour 14, "Payroll Tax Reports," for an explanation about all the taxes associated with payroll.

If you do business in a state that has an Income tax, that state will assign its own number but will also reference all reports with your federal Employer Identification Number.

In addition to Income taxes, most states also require employers to pay into a fund for unemployment benefits. This is a percentage of the gross amount of your employees' wages. A separate account number is assigned for reporting and paying this tax.

Unemployment taxes are deposited in a fund that is used to pay benefits to people who have lost their jobs. For instance, if you decide to reduce your work force and lay off some of your employees, they are eligible to collect unemployment while they look for another job. The benefits that your former employees collect are charged against the funds that you have contributed to this program.

The federal government has its own unemployment tax that is imposed on employers. However, the federal program allows you to claim credit for the taxes you are paying to fund your state unemployment benefits. The account number for federal unemployment taxes is the same Employer Identification Number used for the other federal taxes.

It is a good idea to contact the appropriate federal and state tax agencies and apply for your account numbers so that you will have it in place before you actually hire employees. These agencies will send you the forms and all the paperwork needed to obtain your account numbers.

TIME SAVER

The state agencies use your Federal Employer Identification number as a reference, so you should obtain that number first. Once that number has been assigned, you can use it to apply to the other tax authorities.

A copy of the form used to apply for the federal Employer Identification Number appears in Appendix B, "Sample Forms."

HIRING EMPLOYEES

When you receive your tax numbers, you will also receive the official publications outlining your duties as an employer and stating what qualifies a person as your employee.

Anyone who performs services for you, providing that you can control what will be done and how it will be done, may be considered your employee.

In general, self-employed professionals such as doctors, lawyers, contractors, and others tradesmen who offer their services to the public are not considered employees. However, if their companies are incorporated, corporate officers who work in the business can be employees as well as employers.

GO TO ▶
Refer to Hour 14 to learn how the owner reports and pays his personal wages and taxes.

REQUIRED GOVERNMENT FORMS

When you hire an employee, that person must provide you with a valid Social Security number. In addition, recent legislation requires that you also verify that the employee is a citizen of the United States.

To protect yourself, have the prospective employee show you his or her Social Security card and another valid piece of identification. This can be a driver's license or a birth certificate. Make a photocopy of these documents, and keep them in the employee file along with a copy of the employee's application and copies of the other government forms that are required.

The official employer publications from the IRS contain information on ordering the following forms that must also be kept on file.

FORM W-4

This is the form that a new employee fills out for tax withholding. It tells you if the employee is married or single and also how many dependents he or she has.

The information on this form determines the amount of federal withholding tax that you will deduct from the employee's pay. This amount is based on marital status and withholding allowances. Withholding allowances are the number of dependents the employee is claiming.

Employees may claim fewer withholding allowances than they are entitled to claim. However, you are required to send certain copies of the W-4 to the IRS. Send a W-4 to IRS when the following circumstances arise:

- An employee claims more than 10 withholding allowances.
- An employee, who is expected to earn more than $200 per week, claims to be exempt from withholding tax.

To be exempt from withholding taxes, the employee is certifying that he or she will have no tax liability on a personal tax return and therefore would receive a total refund of any tax withheld from wages. This exemption might apply to students and retired persons working part-time.

FORM I-9

This is a form for the Immigration and Naturalization Service (INS), to verify that the employee is legally eligible to work in the United States. The copy of the Social Security card and other identification supports this document.

FORM W-5

The Earned Income Credit Advance Payment Certificate is used for an employee with a qualifying child who is eligible to receive an Earned Income Credit. When properly completed, this form requires the employer to make advance payments on the Earned Income Credit that the employee is entitled to receive on his or her federal tax return.

For complete information on the Earned Income Credit and advance payment program, read Circular E, "Employer's Tax Guide," a publication of the Department of the Treasury and the IRS.

There is no difference between full-time and part-time workers with regard to the required government forms and payroll tax deductions. Copies of these required forms can be found in Appendix B.

VARIOUS TYPES OF WAGES AND PAY PERIODS

It is up to you and your employees to determine the type of wages that will be paid for services. However, bear in mind that you must follow federal and state labor laws.

Many employers pay an hourly wage. If the employee is working full-time, the hourly wage must be at least the hourly minimum wage set by the federal government. Part-time workers do not fall under the minimum wage requirements, but other regulations apply to them, especially if the employees are underage. It is prudent to become familiar with the federal laws and the laws of your state before hiring employees.

Time clocks and time cards are widely used to keep track of the hours that an employee works. When the employee reports for work, the time card is inserted into the clock, and the time is recorded on the card. At quitting time, the time card is inserted into the clock again, and the time the employee left for the day is recorded. Some companies also have their employees use the time clock to record the times that they start and end their lunch breaks.

Some smaller companies have employees complete a time slip on which they manually record the hour that they began work and the hour that they ended work each day.

Either way, at the end of the pay period, the time cards or time slips are turned over to the accounting office so that the employees' hours can be totaled. Even if the company uses an outside payroll service to issue the paychecks, the job of calculating the number of hours that each employee worked in that pay period usually falls to the accountant. The hours are then recorded on the payroll service's form and are sent in for processing.

A number of accepted pay periods are used today:

- Weekly: 52 pay periods per year
- Biweekly: 26 pay periods per year
- Semimonthly: 24 pay periods per year
- Monthly: 12 pay periods per year

The frequency with which a company issues paychecks is determined by several factors. The size of the company, the number of employees, and whether the payroll is done in-house or is sent out to a payroll service may affect the decision of how and when to pay employees.

Regardless of how often the paychecks are issued, the number of hours worked in the pay period is multiplied by the hourly rate, and the result is the employee's gross wages. All payroll taxes are based on the gross wages.

For an employee who earns $8 per hour and normally works 40 hours per week, the calculation to figure the paycheck for a biweekly period is as follows:

$8 hourly rate

× 80 hours worked in a two-week or biweekly period

$640 gross wages

GO TO ▶

Refer to Hour 12, "Payroll Taxes: Employee/Employer," to learn how to calculate the taxes on gross wages.

Gross wages for salaried employees are usually a set amount each week or pay period. These employees may or may not be exempt from overtime.

Overtime wages go into effect when an employee works more than 8 hours in a day or more than 40 hours in a week. To be exempt from overtime, the employer cannot exert certain controls over the employee. For example, if the employer sets the hours that the employee works, the worker cannot be considered exempt from overtime.

Overtime wages are paid at time-and-a-half or 1.5 percent of the hourly rate. To calculate overtime wages, you must first know the regular hourly rate for the employee. Using the previous example, if you increase the hours worked to 90 hours, or 5 hours of overtime each week, in the pay period, the calculation would be done as follows:

$8.00 × 80 hours = 640.00 (regular hours)

8.00 × 10 hours × 1.50 = 120.00 (overtime hours)

$760.00 gross wages

To calculate overtime for a salaried employee, you must first determine the hourly rate. To obtain the hourly rate of a salaried employee, you divide the yearly salary by 2,080. This is the number of hours that an employee is considered to work per year, based on 40 hours a week for 52 weeks (40 × 52 = 2,080).

For an employee who earns a gross salary of $2,500.00 per month, you would calculate the hourly rate as follows:

$2,500 × 12 months = 30,000 ÷ 2,080 = 14.42 per hour

GO TO ▶

Refer to Hour 17, "Payroll Journal and Employee Expense Accounts," to learn how to keep payroll records accurately and efficiently.

Assume that the employee is paid twice a month, or semimonthly. The gross salary for one payroll period is $1,250. If the employee worked three hours of overtime for that same period, you would figure the wages for that payroll period as follows:

Regular wages $1,250.00

Overtime wages   3 × 14.42 × 1.50 = 64.89

Total wages $1,314.89

Some businesses pay their employees on a commission basis. A salesperson, for instance, might be paid a commission on the total product sold each pay period. If the commission rate is 10 percent and the salesperson sold $20,000 in products, the salary would be computed as follows:

20,000 × .10 = $2,000 gross wages

Some salespeople are paid a salary against commissions. This is a little more involved. In this case, think of the salary as an advance or a draw against commissions. This is how it works.

On a monthly basis, a car salesman receives a salary or a draw of $1,500. This is paid on the 1st of each month. He also receives a commission of 10 percent for every automobile that he sells. If by the end of the month he has sold two cars for a total of $44,000, this is how his paycheck would be calculated:

$44,000 × 10% = 4,400

Minus draw −1,500

$2,900 gross wages

The taxes on the salesman's salary may be figured on the commission amount of $4,400 (if no taxes were deducted from the draw). If taxes were deducted from the draw amount, at the end of the month, taxes would be calculated on the net amount of $2,900, the difference between the commission amount and the draw.

Some companies offer a commission structure designed to encourage the sales staff to work harder. This method may be referred to as a graduated commission scale or sliding commission scale. For instance, the employees may earn 5 percent commission on the first $10,000 in sales and then 7 percent on all sales over that amount.

GO TO ▶
Refer to Hour 12 to learn how to calculate the taxes on a variety of wage classifications.

Based on this method, if a salesperson sells $12,000 in merchandise in one pay period, the gross wages would be computed as follows:

$10,000 × .05 = $500

$2,000 × .07 =   40

$540

Keep in mind that whenever employees are being paid on a commission basis, the commission is figured on the employee's sales minus any refunds, returns, or allowances.

GO TO ▶
Refer to Hour 8, "Discounts, Allowances, and Other Adjustments," for instructions on handling refunds and other adjustments to sales.

Employees of businesses such as restaurants are in their own special class. Although they usually earn a small hourly wage, they also receive tips paid to them directly from the customers.

The idea is that the combination of the hourly wage and the tips received will constitute a fair wage. The employee must report tips to the owner so that they can be added to the hourly wages and taxed. Tips are reported on Form 4070, "Employee's Report of Tips to Employer." A sample of this form is included in the appendix with the other employment forms.

In lieu of using the government Form 4070, the employer can make up their own statement for the employee to report tips. The statement must be signed by the employee and include the following information:

- The employee's name, address, and Social Security number
- The employer's name and address
- The month or period that the report covers

The tips are added in, taxed, and then deducted again because the employee has already received the tips in cash.

For example, if a restaurant employee earns a base wage of $2.50 per hour, has worked 30 hours in the weekly pay period, and reported $200 in tips, the paycheck would be calculated as follows:

Base wages $2.50 × 30 = $ 75.00

Tips reported 200.00

Gross taxable wages $275.00

Once the taxes are calculated, the taxes and the amount of the tips are deducted, and the result is the employee's *net pay*.

STRICTLY DEFINED

Net pay is the amount left after the taxes and other deductions are subtracted from the employee's gross wages. The actual paycheck is written for this amount.

There are a number of variations on the methods used to pay employees. Those outlined in this hour were chosen to give you an overview of the many ways gross wages can be calculated. These are standard procedures that can be modified and applied to most businesses.

The addition of employees automatically expands the accounting system. Payroll checks, taxes, and reports become integral functions of the system and must be managed and maintained.

Using a payroll service may lesson the workload for the accountant, but it does not relieve the entire burden. The information supplied by the payroll service still needs to be included in the company's financial data.

Timely payments of the taxes associated with payroll also remain the responsibility of the employer. Therefore, all reports generated by the payroll service should be reviewed and checked for accuracy.

A good basic knowledge and understanding of payroll and taxes is definitely an asset to an accountant and a business owner.

HOUR'S UP!

Information on employees, employment forms, and wages was presented in this hour. See how much you have retained by trying to answer the following questions.

1. An employee is someone whom a business owner pays to perform a service.
   a. True
   b. False

2. A salaried employee's hourly rate is calculated as follows:
   a. Divide salary by hours worked
   b. Divide annual salary by 2,080
   c. Divide annual salary by 365

3. Employers may be required to pay both state and federal unemployment taxes
   a. True
   b. False

4. Tips are not taxable.
   a. True
   b. False

5. In a biweekly payroll system, paychecks are issued how many times a year?

    a. 29

    b. 24

    c. 26

6. Government Form I-9 is used to report employee tips.

    a. True

    b. False

7. A copy of employees' W-4 forms should always be sent to the IRS.

    a. True

    b. False

8. A new employee must provide an employer with:

    a. A Social Security number

    b. A driver's license

    c. A birth certificate

9. An Employer Identification Number (EIN) is assigned by:

    a. The state

    b. The IRS

    c. The city magistrate

10. A commission structure that increases after sales exceed a designated amount is called a graduated commission scale.

    a. True

    b. False

QUIZ

HOUR 12

Payroll Taxes: Employee/Employer

CHAPTER SUMMARY

LESSON PLAN:

In this hour you will learn about ...

- Social Security tax
- Medicare tax
- Federal withholding tax
- State withholding tax
- Calculating payroll checks
- Unemployment taxes

Once an employee is hired, the employer assumes the responsibility of collecting and paying the taxes the government imposes on the employee's wages. In addition, the employer's Expenses increase because the employer is required to contribute matching amounts for some of the taxes deducted from the employees' paychecks.

Anyone who has held a job is familiar with the taxes that are deducted from an employee's wages. Now you will look at the taxes from the employer's perspective and see how they are calculated, remitted to the government, and processed into the accounting system.

SOCIAL SECURITY TAX

The Federal Insurance Contributions Act (FICA) provides for a federal system of benefits. The one commonly associated with this program is the retirement program. There are also benefit plans for the survivors of people who have paid into the system, such as spouses and minor children. Still another facet of FICA oversees a federal disability program.

To fund these programs, the federal government imposes and collects a tax on the wages of workers. In addition, a matching amount of tax is imposed and collected from the employers of those workers. The employer portion is also based on the gross wages of the employee.

The current tax rate for Social Security is 6.2 percent, making the total combined contributions for employer and employee 12.4 percent. There is a ceiling or a maximum dollar amount of wages subject to the Social Security tax. This maximum dollar amount may increase from year to year.

In the year 2000, the wage base limit was $76,200. That means that wages exceeding that amount were no longer subject to Social Security tax.

As with all payroll taxes, the burden and responsibility of collecting and paying Social Security tax lies with the employer. Self-employed individuals are not exempt from this tax; it is just reported and paid a little differently.

GO TO ▶
Refer to Hour 14, "Payroll Tax Reports," to learn how taxes are imposed and collected from self-employed individuals.

In the Chart of Accounts that you created, a Balance Sheet account was established for Accrued Payroll Taxes. This account is much like Sales Tax Collected, in that the taxes collected from employees are posted to that account with the understanding that they will be paid out within a short period of time.

In the profit and loss section of the Chart of Accounts, an expense account was created called Payroll Taxes. As you may have surmised, the employer's portion of the Social Security tax is posted to this account because it is a business expense.

GO TO ▶
Refer to Hour 17, "Payroll Journal and Employee Expense Accounts," to learn how to post the various payroll taxes to the General Ledger.

Social Security tax is initially computed only on the gross wages of the employee. If an employee earns $1,000 in a single pay period, the Social Security tax would be calculated as follows:

Gross wages	$1,000.00
	$\times .062$

	$62.00 employee's Social Security tax

The employee's portion of the Social Security tax is deducted from the amount of the gross wages.

MEDICARE TAX

The Federal Insurance Contributions Act (FICA) also has a provision for medical benefits that go along with the retirement benefits. When a taxpayer reaches retirement age, in addition to collecting a monthly retirement check from Social Security, that person receives medical benefits, or Medicare. Medicare is designed to replace the health insurance benefits that the worker is no longer entitled to once employment has ended.

Like the Social Security tax, Medicare tax is imposed and collected from the wage earner and the employer. Unlike Social Security tax, there is no limit on the wages subject to this tax. Medicare tax is collected on all wages.

The current tax rate for Medicare tax is 1.45 percent. Using the same example of a worker who has earned $1,000 in gross wages in one pay period, the employee's portion of the Medicare tax would be computed as follows:

Gross wages	$1,000.00
	× .0145

	$14.50 employee's Medicare tax

Remember that both Social Security tax and Medicare tax are deductions that are calculated and then subtracted from the gross wages.

FEDERAL WITHHOLDING TAX

The federal withholding tax can be a percentage of gross wages or a set amount taken from a tax table supplied by the IRS.

Each year, employers should receive a copy of Circular E, "Employer's Tax Guide." In addition to general information about all the taxes and forms, the guide contains the withholding tax tables for the current year.

FYI Circular E, "Employer's Tax Guide," is automatically sent to employers on or about January 1st each year. In addition to information and tax tables, it gives the current rates for Social Security and Medicare taxes, and the current base wage limit for Social Security tax.

The guide includes a variety of tax tables for computing the withholding tax by the percentage method and tables that present a set amount of tax to be withheld, depending on the employee's marital status and the number of exemptions that the employee has claimed on the W-4 in your payroll files.

The tables are also based on whether the payroll periods are weekly, biweekly, semimonthly, or monthly. The following is a sample of a tax table using the percentage method for withholding tax:

Biweekly Payroll Period

[a] SINGLE person (including head of household)

[b] MARRIED person

If the amount of wages is:

Over	But not over	The amount of Income tax to withhold is:	Of excess over:
$102	$1,050	15%	$ 102
$1,050	$2,250	$142.20 plus 28%	$ 1,050
$2,250	$5,069	$478.20 plus 31%	$ 2,250
$5,069	$10,950	$1,352.09 plus 36%	$ 5,069
$10,950		$3,469.25 plus 39.6%	$10,950

PROCEED WITH CAUTION

The tax tables in this book are meant as samples only—do not use them to calculate actual payroll taxes. Current tax rates and tables should be requested from the IRS.

The sample table can be used for both married or single employees and the rates are based on a biweekly pay period. Using this table, you can calculate the payroll check of an employee whose gross wages in this pay period total $2,200. It should be computed as follows:

Gross Wages	Withholding Tax
$2,200.00	$142.20
– 1,050.00	
------------	------------
1,150 × .28 =	$322.00

	Total $464.20

The other type of tax tables that can be found in the IRS booklet are columnar charts listing the withholding tax according to the salary range and the number of exemptions claimed by the employee. The following is an abbreviated but reasonable facsimile of that type of table:

Married Persons—Weekly Payroll

If the wages are: And the number of withholding allowances claimed are:

At least	But less than	0	1	2	3	4
$740	750	93	85	77	69	61
750	760	95	87	79	71	63
760	770	96	88	80	72	64
770	780	98	90	82	74	66
780	790	99	91	83	75	67

Notice how close all the categories are for wages and the tax that should be withheld on those wages. Of course, the actual tables start with 0 wages and 0 tax, and increase in small increments up to approximately $1,400 in wages. After the employee's gross wages reach that level, you are advised to use the percentage tax table to figure the withholding tax. In an actual tax table, more columns are listed for withholding allowances to accommodate employees who have five, six, seven, and more dependents.

Circular E contains separate tax tables for the different types of pay periods, and each is designated for either single or married employees. Samples of these tables can be reviewed in Appendix B, "Sample Forms."

No calculations are needed if you are using this type of table. Simply find the salary range, go across to the number of allowances that the employee has claimed on the W-4 form, and you will find the amount of withholding tax that should be deducted from the gross wages.

TIME SAVER

Worksheets that list the names of the employees, their marital status, their withholding allowances and any other information pertinent to payroll can be made up and used to help you calculate the payroll checks each pay period.

STATE WITHHOLDING TAX

If you are working in a state that has its own Income tax, that state will supply you with the information and the forms needed to withhold the necessary taxes from your employees' paychecks.

In some states, such as Arizona, the state withholding tax is a percentage of the federal withholding amount. In these states, you may be required to withhold 10, 15, or 20 percent of the federal withholding tax and pay it to the state.

Other states have withholding tables similar to the federal tables that you just reviewed. The state tax is determined by those tables and is deducted from the employee's gross wages.

In a state in which the withholding tax is a percentage of the federal tax, you may have an additional form for the employees to complete that designates the percentage that should be used to compute the state withholding tax. This is usually similar to the Federal W-4 form.

For the purpose of the following example, assume that you are working in a state that bases its withholding tax on 15 percent of the federal withholding amount.

The employee's gross wages for one week are $765. The employee is married and claims two withholding allowances. The state withholding tax will be computed as follows:

Gross Wages	Federal Withholding	State Withholding
$765.00	80.00 × 15 =	12.00
	(from tax table)	

If the state in which you are located provides tax tables, you determine the state tax the same way that you determine the federal tax.

JUST A MINUTE

Many computerized payroll systems have the tax rates for the federal and state programmed in. Once the employee's information and the gross wages are input, the computer automatically figures and deducts all applicable taxes.

CALCULATING PAYROLL CHECKS

Regardless of the number of employees on the payroll, you can compute the checks easily and accurately by using a spreadsheet.

Set up the spreadsheet so that it reflects the employees' names and includes abbreviations that tell you each one's marital status and withholding allowances. For example, a married person with two allowances would be designated as M-2, while a single person with no allowances would be S-0.

The spreadsheet needs to have enough columns across to accommodate all the taxes and other deductions that apply to payroll in your particular area. The percentages needed to calculate Social Security, Medicare, and, if applicable, state withholding can be penciled in for easy reference. Your spreadsheet may look something like the following example:

Name:	Gross Wages	SS (.062)	Med (.0145)	FWH	SWH (.15)	Net Ck.
J. Brown (M-1)	765.00	–47.43	–11.09	–88.00	–13.20	605.28
M. Smith (M-1)	780.00	–48.36	–11.31	–91.00	–13.65	615.68
V. Johnson (M-3)	785.00	–48.67	–11.38	–75.00	–11.25	638.70
Totals	2,330.00	–144.46	–33.78	–254.00	–38.10	1,859.66

Before issuing the actual payroll checks, total your worksheet as shown in the example. Cross-check it to be sure that it is in balance—that is, the total of gross wages minus the total of all tax deductions should equal the total of the net paychecks.

When the payroll checks are distributed, the employees also should be given a breakdown that lists the gross wages and the deductions. If there is room on the check itself, you can write this information on the check. Otherwise, you can include some other type of voucher or slip that provides this information.

Payroll checks can be ordered through your bank or stationery suppliers that have a detachable check stub to record the particulars of each check issued. This enables your employees to detach the stub and retain it for their records.

If the business has a large number of employees, you may want to establish a separate bank account just for payroll, funding it as needed from the regular operating account.

Also remember that the employer will have to match the amounts deducted from the employees' checks for both Social Security and Medicare. The total

GO TO ▶
Refer to Hour 13, "Posting Payroll, Computing Taxes, and Conforming to Federal and State Rules and Regulations," to learn how to post the payroll to the General Ledger.

GO TO ▶
Refer to Hour 14 to learn about honoring deadlines and conforming to federal and state regulations.

of the employer and the employee portions of these two taxes plus the federal withholding tax should be remitted to the IRS in accordance with its regulations and deposit schedules.

Unemployment Taxes

Each state operates its own unemployment program that is funded by contributions from employers. Only Alaska currently collects unemployment taxes from employees. In all the other states, unemployment taxes are strictly an employer's expense.

In most states, if you are subject to the federal unemployment tax, you must also pay state unemployment tax. To be subject to the federal tax, an employer must have had at least one employee for 20 calendar weeks during the current or preceding year, or paid at least $1,500 in wages during any calendar quarter. Broader rulings apply in some of the states, so an employer could be liable for state unemployment taxes even if that employer is not liable for federal unemployment taxes.

GO TO ▶
Refer to Hour 11, "Salary and Wages," to find information on applying for federal and state unemployment tax accounts.

State unemployment rates are assigned to employers based on their prior experience record. A new employer who has not paid into the system may pay a higher rate at first until an experience record has been established.

If the employer has claims against his or her account from previous employees, the employer's rate may be increased. An employee who has been fired or laid off due to lack of work or a reduction in the work force is eligible to file a claim for unemployment benefits. These claims become a part of the employer's experience record and affect his or her unemployment tax rate. The rates are reviewed every year, and the employer is notified of the rate that will be in effect for the current year.

In most states, the unemployment tax is reported and paid on a quarterly basis. Gross wages for that quarter are multiplied by the employer's assigned rate, and the result is the tax that must be remitted.

There is a ceiling on the amount of wages that an employer pays unemployment tax on for each employee in any given year. When the employee's wages exceed the limit in that state, for the current year, the employer no longer has to pay unemployment taxes on that employee's wages.

Federal unemployment taxes are remitted to the IRS. As you learned earlier, an employer receives credits that reduce the federal tax based on how much the employer has paid in state unemployment taxes.

The following chart shows a sampling of states and their unemployment rates and wage limits:

State	Rates	No Experience Rate	Wage Limit
Arizona	0.05%–5.4%	2.7%	$7,000.00
California	0.7%–5.4%	3.4%	7,000.00
Colorado	0 %–5.4%	3.1%	10,000.00
Florida	0.12%–5.4%	2.7%	7,000.00
Illinois	0.6%–6.8%	3.1%	9,000.00
New York	0.0%–7.3%	3.4%	7,000.00
North Dakota	0.2%–5.4%	2.2%	15,600.00
Texas	0.24%–6.24%	2.7%	9,000.00

As you can see, each state has its own rates and wage limit, so it is important that a new employer contact the unemployment department of the state where the business is located to get all the necessary forms and information.

Federal unemployment taxes are reported on an annual report, but the tax may have to be paid quarterly, depending on the size of the business and the number of employees.

The normal rate for federal unemployment tax for employers who are making contributions to their state is 0.8 percent, and the wage limit is $7,000.

In both state and federal unemployment tax calculations, you will need to know the amount of the exempt wages. Exempt wages are the wages of each employee that are over the wage limit.

GO TO ▶
Refer to Hour 14 for instructions on calculating tax and preparing unemployment tax reports.

For example, if a business has two employees and each earned $15,000 in one year, the federal unemployment tax would be computed as follows:

Total wages	$30,000.00
Exempt wages	– 16,000.00

Taxable wages	$14,000.00
	× .008

Tax due	$112.00

There is no doubt that employees, payroll, and payroll taxes generate extra work for an accountant. However, advance organization and scheduling will establish a routine that will make the process simple and less time-consuming.

QUIZ

Hour's Up!

Review and answer these questions on payroll taxes without looking back at this hour's lessons.

1. The employee's deduction for Social Security tax is calculated as follows:

   a. Net wages × Social Security tax rate

   b. Gross wages – allowances × Social Security tax rate

   c. Gross wages × Social Security tax rate

2. The burden and responsibility of collecting and paying payroll taxes falls to the employer.

   a. True

   b. False

3. State withholding tax is the employer's expense.

   a. True

   b. False

4. Employers are required to match the employees' deductions for:

   a. Federal withholding tax

   b. Medicare

   c. Unemployment tax

5. The designation on the payroll worksheet for a married employee with two allowances is:

   a. M-2

   b. M-0

   c. S-2

6. Employers pay federal unemployment tax on all wages.

   a. True

   b. False

7. Federal withholding tax is determined in part by an employee's martial status.
   a. True
   b. False

8. Circular E, "Employer's Tax Guide," contains:
   a. Tax forms
   b. Wage charts
   c. Withholding tax tables
   d. All of the above

9. Unemployment taxes are withheld from employees who work in:
   a. All states
   b. New York
   c. Alaska

10. State withholding tax is always a percentage of the federal withholding tax.
    a. True
    b. False

QUIZ

Hour 13

Posting Payroll, Computing Taxes, and Conforming to Federal and State Rules and Regulations

Whether the payroll is being done manually in-house or is sent out to a payroll tax service, payroll ledgers will have to be established and updated for the individual employees.

Updating the individual employee ledgers can be done any time before the end of the month, but posting the payroll to the General Ledger should be done as each pay period is completed.

All the taxes that will be paid to the federal and state tax entities can be posted to the Balance Sheet account Accrued Payroll Taxes (Account 2300). However, to make it easier to understand the various taxes, especially those that require the employer to pay a matching amount, you will be adding accounts to the Liabilities section of the Balance Sheet in the Chart of Accounts.

The additional accounts are as follows:

- Federal Withholding Tax Payable (Account 2200)
- Social Security Tax Payable (Account 2210)
- Medicare Tax Payable (Account 2212)
- State Withholding Tax Payable (Account 2220)
- Accrued FUTA (Account 2280)
- Accrued SUTA (Account 2290)

The last two accounts are to record unemployment taxes. FUTA is the accepted abbreviation for federal unemployment tax; SUTA stands for state unemployment tax.

CHAPTER SUMMARY

LESSON PLAN:

In this hour you will learn about ...

- Posting payroll and payroll taxes
- Computing tax liability
- Payroll tax deposits
- Avoiding penalties
- Conforming to federal and state requirements

GO TO ▶
Refer to Hour 4, "Depreciable Assets, Prepaid Expenses, and Other Accounts," for instructions on adding accounts to the Chart of Accounts and the General Ledger.

You will use a worksheet that you prepared for the payroll checks issued in the pay period, or you will receive one from the payroll tax service.

You will be posting from the sample worksheet that was displayed in the last hour. It is the payroll for a weekly pay period as follows:

Name:	Gross Wages	SS (.062)	Med (.0145)	FWH	SWH (.15)	Net Ck.
J. Brown (M-1)	765.00	−47.43	−11.09	−88.00	−13.20	605.28
M. Smith (M-1)	780.00	−48.36	−11.31	−91.00	−13.65	615.68
V. Johnson (M-3)	785.00	−48.67	−11.38	−75.00	−11.25	638.70
Totals	2,330.00	−144.46	−33.78	−254.00	−38.10	1,859.66

You will only be posting the totals for this pay period. Your entry will be written up as shown here:

Date	Ref. No.	Account	Debit	Credit
4-8	PR 4-8	6000 Salaries & Wages	2,330.00	
		2200 FWH Payable		254.00
		2210 SS Payable		144.46
		2212 Medicare Payable		33.78
		2220 SWH Payable		38.10
		1000 Cash in Checking		1,859.66
			2,330.00	2,330.00

All you are doing is transferring the totals from the spreadsheet to this entry. The figures for the individual payroll checks will be used to update the employee's ledgers at another time.

Now assume that the employees all earned the same amount for each week in the month of April, and each week the payroll entry was written up and posted to the General Ledger as in the previous sample entry. At the end of the month, the General Ledger payroll accounts would be as follows:

Date	Ref. No.	Description	Debit	Credit
2200 Federal Withholding Tax Payable				
4-1		Beginning Balance		0.00
4-7	PR 4-7	Record Payroll		254.00
4-14	PR 4-14	Record Payroll		254.00
4-21	PR 4-21	Record Payroll		254.00
4-28	PR 4-28	Record Payroll		254.00
		Ending Balance		1,016.00
2210 Social Security Tax Payable				
4-1		Beginning Balance		0.00
4-7	PR 4-7	Record Payroll		144.46
4-14	PR 4-14	Record Payroll		144.46
4-21	PR 4-21	Record Payroll		144.46
4-28	PR 4-28	Record Payroll		144.46
		Ending Balance		577.84
2212 Medicare Tax Payable				
4-1		Beginning Balance		0.00
4-7	PR 4-7	Record Payroll		33.78
4-14	PR 4-14	Record Payroll		33.78
4-21	PR 4-21	Record Payroll		33.78
4-28	PR 4-28	Record Payroll		33.78
		Ending Balance		135.12
2220 State Withholding Tax Payable				
4-1		Beginning Balance		0.00
4-7	PR 4-7	Record Payroll		38.10
4-14	PR 4-14	Record Payroll		38.10
4-21	PR 4-21	Record Payroll		38.10
4-28	PR 4-28	Record Payroll		38.10
		Ending Balance		152.40

continues

continued

Date	Ref. No.	Description	Debit	Credit
6000 Salaries & Wages				
4-1		Beginning Balance		0.00
4-7	PR 4-7	Record Payroll		2,330.00
4-14	PR 4-14	Record Payroll		2,330.00
4-21	PR 4-21	Record Payroll		2,330.00
4-28	PR 4-28	Record Payroll		2,330.00
		Ending Balance		9,320.00

The difference between the debit and credit balances in this example is a debit of $7,438.64 ($1,859.66 × 4), which is the net amount of the paychecks for the four pay periods in April. This amount has been offset by a credit for that amount posted to the Cash in Checking account.

With the four payrolls posted to the General Ledger, you have the total employee taxes recorded in the liability accounts that will have to be paid out to the federal and state tax authorities. However, you still must compute the employer's share of taxes that must be added in and paid.

GO TO ▶
Refer to Hour 16, "Cash Disbursements Journal," to learn how to issue the payments for tax Liabilities and post them to the General Ledger.

There is more than one way to compute the employer's portion of the taxes. You could simply double the employee's Social Security and Medicare tax deductions. However, the following formula is the accepted standard of figuring the employer's taxes because it the same formula used to compute the payroll tax report at the end of the quarter.

Gross wages for April:

$9,320 × .124 =   1,155.68 Social Security tax

9,320 × .029 =   270.28 Medicare tax
Total   1,425.96

        + 1,016.00 Federal withholding tax

Total   2,441.96 Tax liability for April payroll

Remember that the employer and employee each pay 6.2 percent of gross wages for Social Security tax. That equals a total of 12.4 percent that must be remitted. Each pays 1.45 percent of gross wages for Medicare tax, making that total 2.9 percent.

PROCEED WITH CAUTION

Keep in mind that the tax rates in this book are based on the rates in effect at the time it was written. By the time you put these procedures into practice, the rates may have changed. Always check the current Circular E for the prevailing rates for the year you are working in.

Since the employee's portion of these taxes has already been posted to the General Ledger, your general journal entry to record the employer's portion will be as follows:

Date	Ref. No.	Account	Debit	Credit
4-30	GJ4-30	2210 SS Tax Payable		577.84
		2212 Medicare Tax Payable		135.16
		6490 Payroll Taxes	713.00	
			------------	------------
			713.00	713.00

Look back at the amounts already posted for the four payroll periods to the two liability accounts, and you will see that adding this entry to the General Ledger brings the accounts up to the amounts calculated for the total taxes due from the employer and employee for Social Security and Medicare taxes for the month of April. There is no change in the federal or state withholding tax accounts because those taxes apply only to the employee.

Also take note that all these liability accounts have credit balances, so to increase the balances in any of these accounts, additional credits are posted.

The final item to consider is that the offsetting debit is posted to an expense account in the profit and loss section of the General Ledger. The employer's portion of these taxes is an expense to the business. Just as amounts posted to Accounts Payable can be recorded as Expenses before they are actually paid, so can amounts posted to other accrual accounts, such as payroll taxes payable.

GO TO ▶
Refer to Hour 1, "The Chart of Accounts/Balance Sheet Accounts," for an explanation of operating an accounting system on an accrual basis.

PAYROLL TAX DEPOSITS

With the exception of the federal unemployment report, which is filed annually, the payroll tax reports are filed quarterly. The quarters and due dates of reports and any unpaid taxes are as follows:

Reporting Period	Due Date of Reports
January 1 to March 31	On or before April 30
April 1 to June 30	On or before July 31
July 1 to September 30	On or before October 31
October 1 to December 31	On or before January 31 of the following year

Although the federal tax reports, *Form 941,* are filed quarterly, the taxes are not necessarily paid the same way. The IRS has specific guidelines for paying the taxes in a more timely manner.

STRICTLY DEFINED

Federal tax report **Form 941** is sent to employers every quarter. It must be completed and filed by the due dates outlined. This report is a recap of wages and taxes for that quarter, as well as all deposits made to cover the quarterly tax liability.

Income tax withheld and both the employer and employee Social Security and Medicare taxes are paid during the quarter by making tax deposits to authorized financial institutions or Federal Reserve banks. Most banks are authorized to accept tax deposits. The frequency of the deposits is determined by the schedule assigned to the employer by the IRS.

Currently, there are two types of deposit schedules: monthly or semiweekly. These schedules tell you when a deposit is due after a tax liability is incurred—that is, when an employer has a payday.

Before the beginning of each calendar year, you must determine which of the two schedules you are required to use. The deposit schedule that you must use is based on the total tax liability that you reported on Form 941 during a four-quarter lookback period. Your deposit is not determined by how often you pay your employees or make deposits.

For purposes of this determination, the lookback period begins July 1 and ends June 30. If you reported $50,000 or less of taxes for the lookback period, you are a monthly schedule depositor. If you reported more than $50,000, you are a semiweekly schedule depositor.

During the first calendar year, new employers with no reporting periods to look back on are generally determined to be monthly depositors.

Most small businesses are monthly depositors. Under that deposit schedule, the employer must deposit Form 941 taxes on payments made during a calendar month by the 15th day of the following month. For example, the tax liability that you calculated for the month of April of $2,441.96 must be deposited by May 15.

Semiweekly depositors should go by the following schedule:

If the Payday Falls on a:	Deposit Taxes by:
Wednesday, Thursday, or Friday	The following Wednesday
Saturday, Sunday, Monday, or Tuesday	The following Friday

JUST A MINUTE

In the unlikely possibility that a new employer or any employer accumulates a tax liability of $100,000.00 or more on any day during a deposit period, the employer must deposit the tax by the next banking day. Consult Circular E for more details.

Form 8109, "Federal Tax Deposit Coupon," must accompany your deposit to the bank. If you are a new employer, the IRS will send you a coupon book five to six weeks after you receive an Employer Identification Number (EIN).

Since these coupons can be used to deposit taxes other than the Form 941 taxes, it is very important to clearly mark the correct type of tax and tax period on each coupon. This information is used by the IRS to credit your account. Follow the instructions in the coupon book. A sample of Form 8109 can be found in Appendix B, "Sample Forms."

The check that is used to pay your tax deposit should be made out to the bank where the deposit is being made. As a rule, you must make the tax deposit at the bank where your checking account is located. This is because the bank must verify that the funds are in your account before it can accept the deposit.

In some instances, you may make a payment with your Form 941 instead of depositing it. For a complete explanation of these circumstances, consult Circular E or a tax advisor.

If you have accumulated less than a $1,000 tax liability during the quarter, you may pay the tax with the 941 report.

Although the federal unemployment tax (FUTA) reported on Form 940 is filed annually, the accumulated tax may have to be paid more often. Form 8109 Federal Tax Deposit Coupon, properly marked, should accompany the check made out to your financial institution.

GO TO ▶
Refer to Hour 14, "Payroll Tax Reports," to learn how to compute taxes and prepare the tax reports that must be filed quarterly or annually.

If your FUTA tax liability for a quarter is $100 or less, you do not have to make a deposit. In that case, you may carry the amount forward to the next quarter until the tax liability reaches $100 or more, and then make a deposit.

State withholding taxes are usually not deposited but are mailed directly to the state with a form that the state supplies. Unless the employer has a large number of employers and accumulates a substantial liability for state withholding tax, the tax is remitted with the quarterly report.

Avoiding Tax Penalties

Be cautious and accurate when calculating tax Liabilities. Whenever there is doubt about the amount of tax liability that will accumulate during the quarter, make monthly deposits in accordance with the scheduling requirements to avoid penalties.

It is better to make small deposits each month than to find at the end of a quarter that the liability has exceeded $1,000 and incur penalties.

Penalties for failure to make required deposits on time can be as high as 20 percent of the unpaid tax liability. If a deposit is required to be made on a day that is not a banking day, the IRS will considered the deposit made on time if it is made by the close of the next banking day. In addition to federal and state bank holidays, Saturdays and Sundays are treated as nonbanking days. If a deposit is due to be made on a Friday, and that Friday is a nonbanking day, the deposit will be considered timely if it is made on the following Monday.

You are required to deposit 100 percent of your tax liability on or before the deposit due date. However, there is some leeway for honest errors, provided that the shortage is not substantial and that it is paid in a responsible timely manner. Again, for specific information, refer to Circular E or a professional tax advisor.

Tax penalties can be forgiven and reversed if you supply the taxing authority with a valid, reasonable explanation. However, tax penalties cannot be ignored. To do so only causes more penalties and interest to be assessed.

TIME SAVER

 If you have access to the Internet, you can contact the IRS via its Web site at www.irs.gov. There you will find information and referrals for questions, as well as downloadable tax forms.

CONFORMING TO FEDERAL AND STATE REGULATIONS

Perhaps the most difficult thing about payroll and payroll taxes is mastering all the rules and regulations of the various taxing authorities.

For the most part, the state agencies conform to the same deadlines set up by the federal government. State unemployment tax reports and withholding reports are due quarterly at the same time the Federal 941 must be filed.

As you learned earlier, when a business applies for an employer account for federal or state payroll taxes, information packets are sent to answer many questions. If you are still in doubt, you can request a number of other free publications from those same agencies. You can also contact them through their Internet sites and phone numbers for taxpayer assistance.

Whenever you are in doubt about a tax matter, get your questions answered as soon as possible. Most of the time, you will receive a notice from IRS advising you of your deposit schedule. You will also automatically receive all the reports that must be filed--they all come with instructions. However, if your business does not receive a notice or a form that needs to be filed, it is your responsibility to rectify the situation. Make phone calls, obtain forms, or do whatever is needed to conform to the regulations.

Don't ever let a tax deadline pass without taking action. If you need a form, call and request it, or make up a reasonable facsimile and file it.

Again, samples of many federal tax forms are included in Appendix B. Review them and become familiar with the information needed to complete them.

HOUR'S UP!

These questions will help you determine how many tax facts you have mastered from this hour.

1. Tax deposits due on a Saturday can be deposited on the following Monday without incurring a penalty.

    a. True

    b. False

2. To increase the balance in a liability account, the account is debited.

    a. True

    b. False

3. To calculate the Medicare tax liability for both the employer and the employee, the formula is:

   a. Gross wages × .029

   b. Gross wages × .124

   c. Net wages × .029

4. The net amount of the employee's paychecks is posted to Salaries and Wages.

   a. True

   b. False

5. The entry to record the employer's portion of Medicare tax after a pay period is:

   a. Debit Payroll Tax Expense, credit Cash in Checking

   b. Credit Medicare Tax Payable, debit Payroll Tax Expense

   c. Credit FUTA, debit Payroll Tax Expense

6. An employer who is designated a monthly depositor is required to deposit taxes when?

   a. On the 1st of each month

   b. On the Wednesday following the pay period

   c. On the 15th of the month

7. To be a semiweekly depositor, tax liability in the lookback period must have exceeded $50,000.

   a. True

   b. False

8. Tax accrual accounts are used to record the liability for payroll taxes as they are paid.

   a. True

   b. False

9. The standard abbreviation for federal unemployment tax is:

   a. SUTA

   b. FUTA

   c. FICA

10. You are required to deposit at least 50 percent of your tax liability on or before the deposit due date.

    a. True

    b. False

QUIZ

HOUR 14
Payroll Tax Reports

CHAPTER SUMMARY

LESSON PLAN:

In this hour you will learn about …

- Employee ledgers
- Federal tax reports
- State tax reports
- Unemployment reports
- How the owner gets paid

Federal and state taxing authorities allow an employer thirty days from the time the quarterly payroll period ends to file the payroll tax reports. This is a task that should not be taken lightly. The deadline is not flexible and penalties and interest are imposed on employers who do not file reports in a timely manner.

If your company uses a payroll tax service, the reports will be issued by the service. If the payroll is done in-house, you will be responsible for the reports as well. The reports are preprinted forms with line-by-line instructions. Completing them is not difficult as long as you look ahead and make sure you have all the required information.

In this hour you will find simple methods of compiling data and calculating taxes that will make filing the payroll tax reports quick and easy.

EMPLOYEE LEDGERS

Before any payroll reports can be completed and filed, the employee ledgers should be updated and totaled. Each employee should have a separate sheet that details the total earnings for each quarter. The ledger sheet should have the employee's name, address, Social Security number, and withholding allowances noted on it.

If possible, update the ledgers on a monthly basis. However, as long as you've kept your payroll spreadsheets in order, the ledgers can be updated any time before the end of the quarter.

Using the sample payroll from Hour 13, "Posting Payroll, Computing Taxes, and Conforming to Federal and State Rules and Regulations," and assuming that the payroll was the same for each month of the quarter, the first employee's ledger would be as follows:

J. Brown
2233 N. Jackson St.
Big Bear, AZ 85755   SS# 555-55-5555   M-1

Date	Gross	SS	MED	FWH	SWH	Net Pay
4-00	3,060.00	189.72	44.36	352.00	52.80	2,421.12
5-00	3,060.00	189.72	44.36	352.00	52.80	2,421.12
6-00	3,060.00	189.72	44.36	352.00	52.80	2,421.12
Q-2	9,180.00	569.16	133.08	1,056.00	158.40	7,263.36

As you can see, the total payroll for each month is listed and then the quarterly earnings are totaled.

GO TO ▶
Refer to Hour 23, "Closing the Books at the End of the Year," to learn how the information entered on the employee's ledger is used to prepare W-2s.

Always cross-check the employee ledgers to be sure they are in balance before continuing. If there is an error on an employee's ledger, it will carry over into your reports.

After you have updated and balanced all the employee ledgers, you are ready to start on the payroll tax reports.

FEDERAL TAX REPORTS

Form 941, "Employer's Quarterly Federal Tax Return," must be prepared and filed on or before the due date each quarter. If you are a monthly depositor, you should already have calculated the tax Liabilities and deposited the taxes.

Usually, Form 941 sent by the IRS to an employer already has the employer's name, address, and Employer Identification Number filled in on the top of it. The form also has a place to notify the IRS of an address change.

The next step is to do a worksheet for the 941. On the worksheet, you lay out all the information that needs to be entered on the form. The worksheet is your opportunity to check all the figures and calculations for accuracy so that you can complete Form 941 correctly and neatly.

Still using the payroll sample from Hour 13, and assuming that the three employee ledgers have been updated and balanced, their quarterly earnings are transferred to the worksheet. Based on this payroll, the tax deposits were $2,441.96 each month, as calculated in Hour 13.

Although Form 941 does not ask for the individual quarterly earnings of each employee, some of the other payroll reports do require this information. The same worksheet is used to assemble the information and calculate the tax for all the quarterly reports.

The following example is one way that a worksheet for quarterly reports can be written up:

Employee & SS#	Gross	SS	MED	FWH	SWH
J. Brown					
555-55-5555	9,180.00	569.16	133.08	1,056.00	158.40
M. Smith					
111-11-1111	9,360.00	580.32	135.72	1,092.00	163.80
V. Johnson					
222-22-2222	9,420.00	584.04	136.56	900.00	135.00
Totals	27,960.00	1,733.52	405.36	3,048.00	457.20

Form 941 calculations:

$27,960.00 \times .124 =$	$3,467.04
$27,960.00 \times .029 =$	810.84
	4,277.88
Federal W/H	3,048.00
Total for Qtr.	7,325.88
FTD 5-15-00	−2,441.96
FTD 6-15-00	−2,441.96
FTD 7-15-00	−2,441.96
Tax Due	-0-

GO TO ▶

Refer to Hour 13, "Posting Payroll, Computing Tax Liabilities, Conforming to Federal and State Regulations," for instructions on calculating payroll taxes on monthly payroll totals.

The employees' quarterly earnings have been transferred to the worksheet. Each employee's name and Social Security number is listed because that information will be needed for another report.

The employees' net earnings are not included on the worksheet because those figures are not needed for any of the reports.

Note that the calculations for the quarterly 941 tax are the same as the calculations used for the monthly tax in Hour 13.

This provides a more accurate figure. You can see that at the end of the quarter, the federal tax deposits (FTD) made on the 15th of each month for the previous month's payroll balance with the quarterly tax figure. The tax due is zero, and all the information needed for Form 941 is on the worksheet.

The following copy of Form 941 is filled out with the information from this worksheet:

PROCEED WITH CAUTION

Although Form 941 could be completed without the use of the worksheet, it is a step that should not be skipped. By doing a worksheet, you verify the accuracy of your information and avoid filing erroneous reports. Making an error on a tax report can result in penalties. Also, correcting a report is a lot more difficult and time-consuming than doing a worksheet.

STATE TAX REPORTS

Currently, only the following states do not have a personal Income tax:

- Alaska
- Tennessee
- Florida
- Texas
- Nevada
- Washington
- New Hampshire
- Wyoming
- South Dakota

All the other states have a personal Income tax. If you are doing business in a state that has an individual Income tax, it is likely that there is also a requirement that employers withhold state tax from employees' wages and file a quarterly report.

*Form 941 completed
per worksheet.*

Form **941**			**Employer's Quarterly Federal Tax Return**	

Form **941**
(Rev. January 1996)
Department of the Treasury
Internal Revenue Service (O)

4141

► See separate instructions for information on completing this return.

Please type or print.

OMB No. 1545-0029

Enter state code for state in which deposits made ► [A-Z] (see page 3 of instructions).

Name (as distinguished from trade name)
TYA Sample Company

Trade name, if any

Address (number and street)
1234 Apple Avenue

Date quarter ended
6-30-00

Employer identification number
00-000000

City, state, and ZIP code
Big Bear, AZ 85755

T	
FF	
FD	
FP	
I	
T	

If address is different from prior return, check here ►

IRS Use

1 1 1 1 1 1 1 1 1 | 2 | 3 3 3 3 3 | 4 4 4
5 5 5 | 6 | 7 | 8 8 8 8 8 | 9 9 9 | 10 10 10 10 10 10 10 10 10 10

If you do not have to file returns in the future, check here ► ☐ and enter date final wages paid ►

If you are a seasonal employer, see **Seasonal employers** on page 1 of the instructions and check here ► ☐

1	Number of employees (except household) employed in the pay period that includes March 12th ►			
2	Total wages and tips, plus other compensation	2	27,960	00
3	Total income tax withheld from wages, tips, and sick pay	3	3,048	00
4	Adjustment of withheld income tax for preceding quarters of calendar year	4		
5	Adjusted total of income tax withheld (line 3 as adjusted by line 4—see instructions)	5	3,048	00
6a	Taxable social security wages . . . . $ 27960 00 × 12.4% (.124) =	6a	3,467	04
b	Taxable social security tips . . . . $ × 12.4% (.124) =	6b		
7	Taxable Medicare wages and tips . . . . . $ 2796000 × 2.9% (.029) =	7	810	84
8	Total social security and Medicare taxes (add lines 6a, 6b, and 7). Check here if wages are not subject to social security and/or Medicare tax . . . . ► ☐	8	4,277	88
9	Adjustment of social security and Medicare taxes (see instructions for required explanation) Sick Pay $ _____ ± Fractions of Cents $ _____ ± Other $ _____ =	9		
10	Adjusted total of social security and Medicare taxes (line 8 as adjusted by line 9—see instructions)	10	4,277	88
11	**Total taxes** (add lines 5 and 10)	11	7,325	88
12	Advance earned income credit (EIC) payments made to employees, if any	12		
13	Net taxes (subtract line 12 from line 11). **This should equal line 17, column (d) below** (or line D of Schedule B (Form 941))	13	7,325	88
14	Total deposits for quarter, including overpayment applied from a prior quarter	14	7,325	88
15	**Balance due** (subtract line 14 from line 13). See instructions	15	— 0 —	
16	Overpayment, if line 14 is more than line 13, enter excess here ► $ _____ and check if to be: ☐ Applied to next return **OR** ☐ Refunded.			

• All filers: If line 13 is less than $500, you need not complete line 17 or Schedule B.

• **Semiweekly schedule depositors:** Complete Schedule B and check here ► ☐

• **Monthly schedule depositors:** Complete line 17, columns (a) through (d), and check here . . . . ► ☒

17	Monthly Summary of Federal Tax Liability.			
	(a) First month liability	(b) Second month liability	(c) Third month liability	(d) Total liability for quarter
	2441.96	2441.96	2441.96	7325.88

Sign Here

Under penalties of perjury, I declare that I have examined this return, including accompanying schedules and statements, and to the best of my knowledge and belief, it is true, correct, and complete.

Signature ►

Print Your Name and Title ►

Date ►

For Paperwork Reduction Act Notice, see page 1 of separate instructions.   Cat. No. 17001Z   Form **941** (Rev. 1-96)

The look of these forms varies from state to state. However, most of them require the same information as the federal report, such as gross wages and taxes withheld. That information is already on the worksheet.

For example, the state of Arizona currently has an individual Income tax. The law of that state requires employers to withhold taxes. As in the sample payroll, the state Income tax in Arizona is a percentage of the federal withholding tax.

The following quarterly report for the state of Arizona is completed using the information from the sample worksheet:

Quarterly return for the state of Arizona withholding taxes.

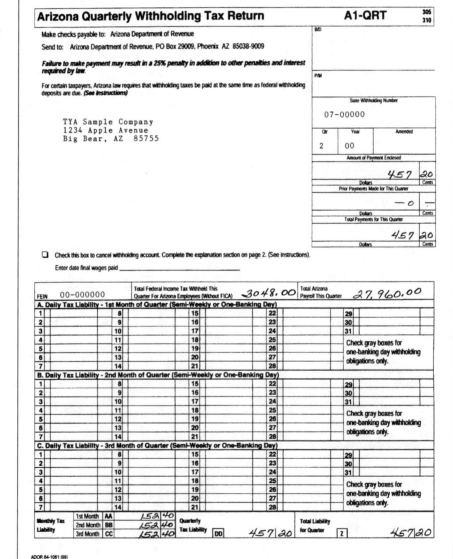

One difference between the state withholding report and the federal Form 941 is that the tax for the state is usually paid with the report. The top of the report has a voucher that is filled out for the payment.

JUST A MINUTE

Although it is not shown in the completed sample, federal Form 941 also comes with a payment voucher. Employers whose tax liability for the quarter is less than $1,000 can pay their tax when they file the form. In that case, the voucher would be completed and sent along also.

UNEMPLOYMENT REPORTS

In most states, the report that requires the most information is the unemployment tax report. That is because the earnings of each employee must be reported.

The state keeps a record of each employee's wage history. If and when one of them applies for unemployment, the state can access the employee's records in the computer system and quickly determine whether the employee is eligible for unemployment benefits.

GO TO ▶ Refer to Hour 12, "Payroll Taxes-Employee/Employer," to find information on unemployment tax rates and wage limits.

To calculate the state unemployment tax, continue to use the sample payroll from the state of Arizona. Assume that the company just began operations and has no experience record.

On the same worksheet, the additional information needed for the state unemployment tax report is added, and the tax is calculated:

Employee & SS#	Gross	SS	MED	FWH	SWH
J. Brown					
555-55-5555	9,180.00	569.16	133.08	1,056.00	158.40
M. Smith					
111-11-1111	9,360.00	580.32	135.72	1,092.00	163.80
V. Johnson					
222-22-2222	9,420.00	584.04	136.56	900.00	135.00
Totals	27,960.00	1,733.52	405.36	3,048.00	457.20

continues

continued

Employee & SS#	Gross	SS	MED	FWH	SWH
Form 941 calculations:					
27,960.00 × .124 =		$3,467.04			
27,960.00 × .029 =		810.84			
		4,277.88			
Federal W/H		3,048.00			
Total for Qtr.		7,325.88			
FTD 5-15-00		−2,441.96			
FTD 6-15-00		−2,441.96			
FTD 7-15-00		−2,441.96			
Tax due		-0-			
Unemployment Tax:					
Total wages		27,960.00			
Exempt wages		−6,960.00			
Taxable wages		21,000.00 × .027 = 567.00 state unemployment			
		21,000.00 × .008 = 168.00 federal unemployment			

Remember that the wage limit for the state of Arizona is $7,000 for each employee. Since each of the three employees in this example earned more than that in the quarter, the excess wages are exempt from tax. Also, because the federal wage limit is $7,000 as well, the federal computation can be done at the same time.

A completed unemployment tax report for the state of Arizona follows using the information from this worksheet.

Based on this report, unless this employer hires new employees, that employer will not have to pay any additional unemployment taxes for the remainder of the calendar year. However, the employer will still have to file reports on the employees' wages even though all the wages will be exempt from tax.

ARIZONA DEPARTMENT OF ECONOMIC SECURITY   FORM INCOMPLETE. DO NOT FILE.   REPORT UC-018 (PAGE)
PO BOX 52027
PHOENIX, AZ 85072-2027   ARIZONA ACCOUNT NUMBER   00000

                                          CALENDAR QUARTER ENDING   6-30-00

                                          TO AVOID PENALTY MAIL BY   7-31-00

TYA Sample Company   FEDERAL ID NO. 00-000000
1234 Apple Avenue
Big Bear, AZ 85755
                                          USE BLACK INK ONLY

UNEMPLOYMENT TAX AND WAGE REPORT   Telephone (602) 248-9354

A. NUMBER OF EMPLOYEES -   **C. WAGE SUMMARY** - Computation of payment due.
Report for each month, the number of full and part-time covered   (See instructions for assistance)
workers who worked during or received pay subject to UI Taxes
for the payroll period which includes the 12th of the month.   1. **TOTAL WAGES PAID IN QUARTER**   27,960.00
                                                     From Section B. Wage Listing

                                                 2. **SUBTRACT EXCESS WAGES**   6,960.00
                                                     Cannot exceed Line 1 - see instructions
                    3
                                                 3. **TAXABLE WAGES PAID**   21,000.00
                                                     Up to $7000 per Employee - Line 1 minus line 2

                    3   4. **TAX DUE**   567.00
                                                     Line 3 × Tax Rate of   2.7
                                                     The decimal equivalent =   .027
                    3
                                                 5. **ADD INTEREST DUE**
                                                     1% of Tax Due for each month payment is late

                                                 6. **ADD PENALTY FOR LATE REPORT**
                                                     0.10% of Line 1 ($35 min / $200 max)

B. WAGES -   7. **TOTAL PAYMENT DUE**   567.00
List all employees in Social Security Number order, or   Check Payable to DES-Unemployment Tax
alphabetically by last name. Please use white paper in the
same format for additional employees. If you have ten or more   8. **AMOUNT PAID**   567.00
employees, consider reporting via magnetic media. Ask for
"Arizona Magnetic Media Reporting" (PAU-430). We support
diskette, tape, and cartridge media.   LIEN MAY BE FILED WITHOUT FURTHER NOTICE ON DELINQUENT TAXES.

1. Employee Social Security Number	2. Employee Name *(Last, First)*	3. Total Wages Paid in Quarter
565-55-5555	BROWN, J.	9,180.00
222-22-2222	JOHNSON, V.	9,420.00
111-11-1111	SMITH, M.	9,360.00
	TOTAL WAGES THIS PAGE	27,960.00
Signature:	TOTAL WAGES ALL PAGES	27,960.00
Title:	Prepared by:	
Date:	Telephone:	

PHOTO COPY FOR YOUR RECORDS

Completed report for state of Arizona unemployment tax.

The same is true for federal unemployment because all the employees have exceeded $7,000 in gross wages. An annual unemployment tax report will have to be filed at the end of the year. However, the tax calculated on the worksheet exceeds $100, so a federal tax deposit should be made using a Form 8109 coupon.

GO TO ▶
Refer to Hour 13, "Posting Payroll, Computing Taxes, and Conforming to Federal and State Rules and Regulations," for information on federal unemployment tax and the required deposits.

The calculation on the worksheet for federal unemployment tax was easily done because the wage limit for the federal tax and the state tax are the same.

If you're working in a state with a wage limit different than the federal wage limit, such as New York state, the calculations would be done as follows:

Unemployment Tax:

Wage limit	$8,500.00 × 3 (employees) = $25,500.00 taxable wages
Gross wages	$27,960.00 – 25,500.00 = $2,460.00 exempt wages
Total wages	$27,960.00
Exempt wages	–2,460.00
	‑‑‑‑‑‑‑‑‑‑‑‑‑‑
Taxable wages	25,500.00 × .034 = $867.00 state unemployment

Federal Unemployment:

Total wages	$27,960.00
Exempt wages	–6,960.00
	‑‑‑‑‑‑‑‑‑‑‑‑‑‑
Taxable wages	21,000.00 × .008 = $168.00 federal unemployment

A copy of the worksheet should be retained and filed with the copies of the quarterly payroll tax reports.

How the Owner Pays Taxes

GO TO ▶
Refer to Hour 10, "The Importance of Work Papers, Receipts, and Other Records," to learn about the importance of retaining work papers.

A small business owner is referred to as a sole proprietor. You have already touched on the fact that at the end of the year, the profit or loss from the business is transferred to the owner and is reported on his or her personal Income tax return.

The form used to report this business Income is Schedule C, "Profit or Loss from a Business or Profession." The sole proprietor is not considered an employee of the business, however the sole proprietor can and often does have employees.

During the year, the sole proprietor can draw funds out of the business. Remember that the owner's initial investment is recorded in the Capital account and that the owner also has a Drawing account.

How much or how little the owner withdraws from the business during the year does not affect the net profit of the company. Whatever the net profit is at the end of the year, it is assumed for tax purposes to be the owner's Income. The information from the Profit and Loss Statement is transferred to Schedule C and becomes part of the owner's personal tax return (Form 1040).

The Schedule C Income is subject to personal Income tax and is also subject to Social Security and Medicare taxes. Of course, this means that there is another tax form to be completed. That form is Schedule SE, "Self-Employment Income."

Although the self-employed person is not required to file Form 941 payroll tax reports on his Income during the year, he or she is not exempt from these taxes. Actually, the rate for Social Security and Medicare tax is higher than the combined tax on employees' earnings.

In addition, the sole proprietor may be required to file another tax form to estimate his Income. Then the taxes based on the estimated Income are paid to the IRS in regular installments throughout the year.

Because the employment tax rates are higher on a self-employed individual, and because this person is paying both the employee and employer share of Social Security and Medicare taxes, many small businesses owners choose to incorporate their companies.

GO TO ▶
Refer to Hour 22, "End-of-the-Year Payroll Reports and Other Tax Reports," for information on transferring business Income to the owner's personal tax return.

When the business is incorporated, the owner can be considered an employee of the corporation and is subject to the same tax rates as the other employees.

In Appendix B, you will find copies of the federal tax forms, as well as Schedule C, Schedule SE, and Schedule ES used by sole proprietors.

Hour's Up!

Payroll tax reports are an important accounting function. These questions test the knowledge you have acquired in this hour.

1. The worksheet for quarterly payroll tax reports is used:
    a. To send to the IRS
    b. For the employees' records
    c. To verify accuracy

2. Form 941 requires a breakdown of each employee's individual earnings.

   a. True

   b. False

3. All states conform to the federal unemployment tax wage limit.

   a. True

   b. False

4. Employee payroll ledgers should include:

   a. Name and address

   b. Social Security number

   c. Year-to-date earnings

   d. All of the above

5. Some tax forms have vouchers to be completed and mailed with tax payments.

   a. True

   b. False

6. Which of the following states does not have a personal Income tax?

   a. California

   b. Texas

   c. Arizona

7. A sole proprietor is exempt from payroll taxes.

   a. True

   b. False

8. States keep records of the individual earnings of employed workers.

   a. True

   b. False

9. The wage limit for federal unemployment tax is:

   a. 8,500

   b. 7,000

   c. 5,000

10. Federal Form 941 must be filed on or before the due date each quarter.

   a. True

   b. False

QUIZ

PART IV

End-of-the-Month Accounting Tasks and Procedures

Hour 15

Cash Receipts Journal

Chapter Summary

LESSON PLAN:

In this hour you will learn about …

- Current month and year-to-date financial data
- Cash/credit transactions and sales
- Posting receipts and sales to the General Ledger
- Balancing Accounts Receivable
- Statements to customers

All revenue is recorded in the Cash Receipts Journal. It is this section of the accounting system that processes incoming cash and distributes it to various accounts in the General Ledger.

The distribution of revenue to the appropriate accounts enables a business owner to track the products or services that are most profitable and helps the owner identify potential problems such as a slow down in a particular sales area.

The Cash Receipts Journal also provides a record of bank deposits that can be used to monitor cash flow.

Current Month and Year-to-Date Financial Data

Every entry that goes into an accounting system during the month becomes a part of the financial statements issued at the end of the month. As each month ends, its financial data is added to the year-to-date accounting information.

The year-to-date information is an account-by-account total of all the months to that point in the calendar year. For example, at the end of November, the current month shown on the Profit and Loss Statement is the month ending November 30. The year-to-date information on the Profit and Loss Statement is a total of the accounting data entered from January 1 through November 30.

GO TO ▶

Refer to Hour 23, "Closing the Books at the End of the Year," to go through the year-end accounting procedures and learn the year-end closing procedures.

In the next hours, you will go through the last month of the year for two different types of businesses. You will learn how to close out the books for these companies for the month and then the year.

The first business you will study is a simple one-man operation, Caricatures by Ed. Edward Brown is an artist who rents space in a large shopping mall on weekends. Every Saturday and Sunday, he sells caricature drawings to the mall shoppers. Ed is a sole proprietor and he keeps a simple set of manual books.

The following is Ed's Chart of Accounts:

Chart of Accounts for Caricatures by Ed

1000	Cash in Checking	Balance Sheet/Asset
1050	Cash on Hand	Balance Sheet/Asset
2100	Sales Tax Collected	Balance Sheet/Liability
3040	Retained Earnings	Balance Sheet/Equity
3210	Capital	Balance Sheet/Equity
3220	Draw	Balance Sheet/Equity
4000	Sales	P & L Stmt./Income
5100	Advertising	P & L Stmt./Expense
5150	Auto Expense	P & L Stmt./Expense
6300	Office Expense	P & L Stmt./Expense
6360	Rent	P & L Stmt./Expense
6520	Supplies	P & L Stmt./Expense

Ed is mainly selling his artistic abilities. Since he draws the caricature as it is requested, he has no inventory. The only real liability Ed has is the sales tax he must collect and remit to the state. Ed began operating this business in January 2000.

The Balance Sheet for Caricatures by Ed as of November 30 is as follows:

Assets:
Cash in Checking $1,774.50
Cash on Hand   100.00

Total Assets   1,874.50
Liabilities:
Sales Tax Collected   91.50

Total Liabilities	91.50
Equity:	
Retained Earnings	9,252.00
Capital	500.00
Draw	(7,969.00)

Total Liabilities & Equity	1,874.50

From this Balance Sheet, you can see that the money Ed has been taking out of the business is recorded in his Draw account. However, remember that at the end of the year it is the profit or loss of this business enterprise that will be transferred to Ed's personal tax return, not the amount he has withdrawn from it.

The Balance Sheet also shows that Ed has no Assets other than his checking account and the change fund he uses. There is no equipment and therefore no depreciation to consider.

The Profit and Loss Statement for Ed's business as of November 30 is as follows:

GO TO ▶
Refer to Hour 22, "End-of-the-Year Payroll Reports and Other Tax Reports," to learn how to transfer the financial data of the business to the sole proprietor's personal tax return.

Caricatures by Ed

Income Statement as of November 30, 2000

	November 1 through November 30, 2000	January 1 through November 30, 2000
Income:		
Sales	$1,830.00	$18,300.00
	------------	------------
Total Income	$1,830.00	$18,300.00
Expenses:		
Advertising Expense	52.00	574.00
Auto Expense	40.00	526.00
Rent Expense	500.00	5,500.00
Supplies	300.00	2,448.00
	------------	------------
Total Expenses	$892.00	$9,048.00
	------------	------------
Net Profit (Loss)	$938.00	$9,252.00

Note that the Income and Expenses for the month are listed separately before they are added into the year-to-date financial information.

Keeping the books for a small, simple business enterprise does not require a lot of time and effort, yet all the financial data is recorded and presented properly because Ed is following standard accounting procedures.

The other business you will study in this hour and succeeding hours is more complex. John Carter, DDS, incorporated his dental practice and is an employee of the corporation. Carter also employs a dental assistant, and Carter's wife works there two days a week handling bookkeeping and billings. Mrs. Carter enters all the accounting data into a computerized accounting system that produces the financial statements.

GO TO ▷
Refer to Hour 24, "Accounting Software Programs," to learn how to set up and use a computerized accounting system.

This is the third year of business for Carter, and his practice has become more profitable each year. Carter's Chart of Accounts is going to look a little different than the ones you've reviewed earlier for other companies.

This Chart of Accounts comes from a computerized accounting system that automatically formats the financial statements according to the type of business the accountant has selected from the choices the computer allows.

In Appendix B, "Sample Forms," you will find other chart of account samples that were computer-generated and therefore formatted much like the one for John Carter, DDS.

As you have learned, the Chart of Accounts designates the way the accounts will appear in the General Ledger and how they will be presented on the financial statements. You will see the correlation between the Chart of Accounts and Carter's financial statements as follows:

John Carter, DDS

Chart of Accounts

Account Number	Name	Type	Balance Sheet/Income Statement Section
1000	Cash in Checking	Asset	Current Assets
1050	Cash in Savings	Asset	Current Assets
1080	Petty Cash	Asset	Current Assets
1100	Accounts Receivable		Assets
1400	Leasehold Improvements	Asset	Other Current Assets
1401	A.D. L.H. Improvements	Asset	Other Current Assets
1500	Furniture & Fixtures	Asset	Property & Equipment

Account Number	Name	Type	Balance Sheet/Income Statement Section
1501	A.D. F & F	Asset	Property & Equipment
1550	Equipment	Asset	Property & Equipment
1551	A. D. Equipment	Asset	Property & Equipment
2000	Accounts Payable	Liability	Current Liabilities
2200	Federal W/H Tax	Liability	P/R Taxes Payable
2210	Social Security Tax	Liability	P/R Taxes Payable
2212	Medicare Tax	Liability	P/R Taxes Payable
2220	State W/H Tax	Liability	P/R Taxes Payable
2280	Accrued FUTA	Liability	P/R Taxes Payable
2290	Accrued SUTA	Liability	P/R Taxes Payable
2300	Loan–Merchants Bank	Liability	Long-Term Debt
3040	Retained Earnings	Equity	Equity
3210	Capital	Equity	Equity
3220	Drawing	Equity	Equity
4000	Fees–Patients	Income	Income
4200	Interest–Savings	Income	Income
4300	Misc. Income	Income	Income
5100	Dental Supplies	Expense	Expense
5150	Brochures & Catalogs	Expense	Expense
5200	Auto Expense	Expense	Expense
5230	Laboratory Fees	Expense	Expense
5650	Rent	Expense	Expense
6000	Salaries & Wages	Expense	Expense
6030	Telephone	Expense	Expense
6050	Utilities–Gas & Electric	Expense	Expense
6140	Office Supplies/Postage	Expense	Expense
6160	Dues & Subscriptions	Expense	Expense
6180	Educational Expense	Expense	Expense
6220	Insurance–General	Expense	Expense
6230	Insurance–Empl. Group	Expense	Expense
6240	License Fees	Expense	Expense
6490	Payroll Taxes	Expense	Expense
6510	Interest Expense	Expense	Expense
6530	Depreciation Expense	Expense	Expense
6550	Income Taxes	Expense	Expense
6560	Bad Debts	Expense	Expense

The Chart of Accounts in Carter's computerized accounting system is reflected in the financial statements that follow:

Balance Sheet for John Carter, DDS.

John Carter DDS Inc.
BALANCE SHEET
November 30, 2000

ASSETS

CURRENT ASSETS

Cash in Checking	$	21,402.70
Savings Account		42,000.00
Petty Cash		50.00
Accounts Receivable		14,300.00

TOTAL CURRENT ASSETS		$	77,752.70

Leasehold Improvements	$	25,600.00
A.D. Leasehold Improvements		(7,466.55)

PROPERTY AND EQUIPMENT

Furniture & Fixtures		3,600.00
A.D. Furniture & Fixtures		(1,499.40)
Equipment		13,350.00
A.D. Equipment		(7,775.60)

TOTAL PROPERTY AND EQUIPMENT	$	7,675.00
TOTAL ASSETS	$	103,561.15

John Carter DDS Inc.
BALANCE SHEET
November 30, 2000

LIABILITIES AND EQUITY

CURRENT LIABILITIES

Accounts Payable	$	5,140.00
PAYROLL TAXES PAYABLE		4,901.74
CURRENT PORTION LONG-TERM DEBT		25,694.60

TOTAL CURRENT LIABILITIES	$	35,736.34

EQUITY

Retained Earnings	$	28,328.94
Capital		10,000.00
NET INCOME (LOSS)		29,495.87

TOTAL EQUITY	$	67,824.81
TOTAL LIABILITIES AND EQUITY	$	103,561.15

John Carter DDS Inc. INCOME STATEMENT For The Period			
	November 01, 2000 To November 30, 2000		January 01, 2000 To November 30, 2000
INCOME			
Fees - Patients	$ 28,600.00	$	328,600.00
Interest Income	0.00		1,200.00
Total INCOME	$ 28,600.00	$	329,800.00
EXPENSES			
Dental Supplies	$ 1,051.00	$	10,251.00
Brochures and Catalogues	400.00		4,400.00
Laboratory Fees	4,004.00		65,720.00
Rent	1,500.00		16,500.00
Salaries & Wages	15,500.00		170,500.00
Telephone	85.00		928.00
Utilities - Gas & Electric	232.00		2,210.00
Office Supplies & Postage	122.00		1,652.00
Dues & Subscriptions	20.00		560.00
Professional Fees	0.00		890.00
Insurance-General	316.00		3,476.00
Insurance - Employee Group	328.00		3,608.00
License Fees	0.00		250.00
Taxes - Payroll	460.36		10,430.87
Interest Expense	333.33		3,666.63
Depreciation Expense	478.33		5,261.63
Total EXPENSES	$ 24,830.02	$	300,304.13
Total NET OPERATING INCOME (LOSS)	$ 3,769.98	$	29,495.87
NET INCOME (LOSS) BEFORE TAX	$ 3,769.98	$	29,495.87
NET INCOME (LOSS)	$ 3,769.98	$	29,495.87

Income Statement as of November 30, 2000, for John Carter, DDS.

Take note of the fact that the computer-assigned designations allow it to combine accounts into one total on the financial statement. The payroll accrual accounts are the best example of this. All the accounts that bear this label in the Chart of Accounts are totaled into PAYROLL TAXES PAY-ABLE in the liability section of the Balance Sheet. However, in the General Ledger each account is listed separately as shown in the Chart of Accounts.

You can review the balances directly from the General Ledger as they appear on the *Trial Balance.*

GO TO ▶
Refer to Hour 19, "The Trial Balance," to learn more about the Trial Balance and how it is used to ensure accuracy.

The **Trial Balance** is a report that can be done manually or generated by a computerized system that lists all the accounts in the General Ledger with their year-to-date balances. It is used to review the accounts before the financial statements are issued. This report will also show if the debit balances equal the credit balances.

The Trial Balance for Carter shows the following credit balances in the payroll accrual accounts:

2200	Federal W/H Tax Payable	$3,317.52
2210	Social Security Tax Payable	471.20
2212	Medicare Tax Payable	449.50
2220	State W/H Tax Payable	663.52

Payroll Taxes Payable (Balance Sheet)		$4,901.74

Please take some extra time to review the Chart of Accounts and the year-to-date financial statements for the manual system used by Caricatures by Ed and the same reports issued by the computerized system used by John Carter, DDS.

Although these two businesses are very different and the accounting systems are also different, the accounting procedures and the resulting reports are very similar.

CASH/CREDIT TRANSACTIONS

Ed does not have an actual store. He runs his business from space in the walkway of a shopping mall; therefore, his sales are strictly cash and carry. The price list Ed displays includes the sales tax of 5 percent he must pay to the state.

At the end of each business day, Ed uses a simple form to balance his cash and total his sales. Then he separates the sales tax from the total sales so that it can be posted properly.

Here is a sample of Ed's cash receipts form completed for one business day:

12-2-00

Total Cash	$674.00
Less Change Fund	−100.00

Total Sales	574.00
Sales Tax Computation:	574.00 ÷ 1.05 = 546.67
	574.00 − 546.67 = 27.33 sales tax
Sales	$546.67
Sales Tax	27.33

	$574.00

The formula Ed uses to separate the sales from the sales tax is a basic math computation you can use to reduce a figure down to what it was before a percentage was added to it. To prove that this is correct, you can check it by multiplying the reduced figure by the percentage ($546.67 base sales × .05 = 27.33 sales tax).

Once Ed has the figures he needs, he enters the totals in his cash receipts journal. At the end of December, Ed's cash receipts journal is as follows:

Cash Receipts Journal

December 2000

Date	Sales	Sales Tax	Total Cash	Bank Deposit
12-2	546.67	27.33	574.00	
12-3	236.19	11.81	248.00	822.00 (12-4)
12-9	407.62	20.38	428.00	
12-10	500.95	25.05	526.00	954.00 (12-11)
12-16	264.76	13.24	278.00	
12-17	354.28	17.72	372.00	650.00 (12-18)
12-23	271.42	13.58	285.00	285.00 (12-26)
12-30	236.19	11.81	248.00	248.00 (1-2-01)
	2,818.08	140.92	2,959.00	2,959.00

POSTING CASH RECEIPTS AND SALES TO THE GENERAL LEDGER

From this cash receipts journal, Ed writes up the following entry to be posted to the General Ledger:

Date	Ref. No.	Account	Amount
12-31	CR12-1	4000 Sales	(2,818.08)
		2100 Sales Tax Collected	(140.92)
		1000 Cash in Checking	2,959.00

			-0-

GO TO ▶
Refer to Hour 6, "Daily Sales Transactions," for instructions and samples of posting cash receipts and sales to the General Ledger accounts.

In the preceding entry, the credits to be posted are shown in brackets rather than listing them in a separate column marked "Credit." Either way is acceptable, as long as the entry is in balance. Ed has proved that his entry balances by adding it up and seeing that the credits plus debits equals zero.

The bookkeeper at John Carter's office uses a computer to enter the cash and Credit Sales. In a computerized system, a ledger card is set up for every patient. The accountant designates the sale as either cash or credit. If it is a credit transaction, the computer automatically debits Accounts Receivable and the patient's ledger. The accountant must then enter the Income account that should be credited for the sale. In this case, all patient fees, both cash and charge sales, are recorded as Fees–Patients (Account 4000).

At the end of the month, reports like those shown in the following reports are generated.

As you can see, the customer sales journal report shows the sales posted in December. Each sale listed is designated as CS (cash) or CI (credit invoice). Also note that, to save time, the accountant has set up an account called Cash Payments. All cash sales for a given day can be added together and entered as one total.

Just as you would post these transactions in a manual system, the computer posts the sales as follows:

- **Cash sales.** Credit Income–Patient Fees, debit Cash in Checking
- **Credit sales.** Credit Income–Patient Fees, debit Accounts Receivable and patient ledger

John Carter DDS Inc.
CUSTOMER SALES JOURNAL
12/ 1/00 To 12/31/00

DATE	TT	ID	NAME	SLS	REF NO	AMOUNT
12/01/00	CS	900	Cash Payments			522.00
12/04/00	CI	123	Jack Hensley		00001201	440.00
12/04/00	CI	MARYSMITH	Mary Smith		00001202	276.00
12/04/00	CS	900	Cash Payments			675.00
12/04/00	CS	900	Cash Payments			935.00
12/05/00	CI	261	Kenneth Graun		00001203	2,360.00
12/06/00	CS	900	Cash Payments			2,762.00
12/07/00	CI	362	Robert Gonzales		00001209	572.00
12/07/00	CI	360	Kevin Flight		00001210	365.00
12/07/00	CI	328	Tammi Varin		00001211	1,689.00
12/08/00	CS	900	Cash Payments			485.00
12/11/00	CS	900	Cash Payments			422.00
12/14/00	CI	352	Fran Birkhead		00001204	592.00
12/15/00	CI	192	Elisa Maxwell		00001208	540.00
12/15/00	CS	900	Cash Payments			3,416.00
12/18/00	CI	171	Laura Gonzales		00001213	425.00
12/19/00	CS	900	Cash Payments			632.00
12/20/00	CI	154	Joyce Martin		00001205	290.00
12/20/00	CI	167	Marilyn Caponegri		00001206	62.00
12/20/00	CI	168	William Caponegri		00001207	62.00
12/20/00	CS	900	Cash Payments			975.00
12/22/00	CI	184	Sybil Tiedemann		00001212	386.00
12/23/00	CS	900	Cash Payments			2,545.00
12/23/00	CS	900	Cash Payments			1,875.00

Customer Sales Journal.

John Carter DDS Inc.
CUSTOMER SALES JOURNAL
12/ 1/00 To 12/31/00

DATE	TT	ID	NAME	SLS	REF NO	AMOUNT
			TOTAL SALES:			23,303.00
			CI - Invoices			8,059.00
			CS - Cash Sales			15,244.00
			CF - Finance Charge			0.00
			CX - Credit Memos			0.00

BALANCING ACCOUNTS RECEIVABLE

The next end-of-the-month report to be accessed is from the Accounts Receivable section. It is a report of all the open invoices in Accounts Receivable detailing the individual patients, their account numbers, and how much each was billed during the month.

In a manual accounting system, you get this information by adding up the balances on the ledger cards and comparing that total to the Accounts Receivable balance in the General Ledger.

Either way, if the figures do not agree, you will have to review the postings for that month and see where the error occurred.

The following is a copy of the Accounts Receivable report from John Carter, DDS, which would be generated by the computer:

Once the report of open invoices is reviewed, you can generate a copy of the General Ledger report for Accounts Receivable (Account 1100).

In addition to new charges for the current month, payments for current month credit invoices and prior month credit invoices are recorded in Accounts Receivable. As you review the General Ledger report, note that the payments posted to this account clear the outstanding Accounts Receivable balance from November. The General Ledger report follows.

GO TO ▶
Refer to Hour 18, "Reconciling the Bank Accounts and General Journal Entries," to learn how to balance the General Ledger to the monthly bank statement.

The ending balance in this General Ledger account agrees with the report of open invoices generated from the customer ledger cards. These reports verify that Accounts Receivable is in balance.

The final report to review is the bank deposit report that can be generated from a computerized accounting system. On this report, you can track all the deposits made to the checking account in the current month. This information may be needed to reconcile the bank statement. Note that the simple cash receipts journal for Caricatures by Ed also details the amounts of the bank deposits.

Open Invoice Report.

John Carter DDS
CUSTOMER OPEN INVOICE REPORT
For The Period Ending 12/31/00

NAME / DATE	TT	REF NO	DUE DATE	DISC DATE	DISC AMOUNT	INV AMOUNT	OPEN BALANCE
ELISAMAXWE - Elisa Maxwell							
12/16/00	CI	00001208	12/16			540.00	540.00
					Total Due:		540.00
FRANBIRKHE - Fran Birkhead							
12/14/00	CI	00001204	12/14			592.00	592.00
					Total Due:		592.00
JACKHENSEL - Jack Hensely							
12/04/00	CI	00001201	12/04			440.00	440.00
					Total Due:		440.00
JOYCEMARTI - Joyce Martin							
12/20/00	CI	00001205	12/20			290.00	290.00
					Total Due:		290.00
KENNETHGRA - Kenneth Graun							
12/05/00	CI	00001203	12/05			2,360.00	2,360.00
					Total Due:		2,360.00
KEVINFLIGH - Kevin Flight							
12/14/00	CI	00001210	12/14			365.00	365.00
					Total Due:		365.00
LAURAGONZA - Laura Gonzales							
12/18/00	CI	00001213	12/18			425.00	425.00
					Total Due:		425.00
MARILYNCAP - Marilyn Caponegri							
12/20/00	CI	00001206	12/20			62.00	62.00
					Total Due:		62.00
MARYSMITH - Mary Smith							
12/14/00	CI	00001202	12/14			276.00	276.00
					Total Due:		276.00
ROBERTGONZ - Robert Gonzales							
12/07/00	CI	00001209	12/07			572.00	572.00
					Total Due:		572.00

John Carter DDS
CUSTOMER OPEN INVOICE REPORT
For The Period Ending 12/31/00

NAME / DATE	TT	REF NO	DUE DATE	DISC DATE	DISC AMOUNT	INV AMOUNT	OPEN BALANCE
SYBILTIEDE - Sybil Tiede							
12/18/00	CI	00001212	12/18			386.00	386.00
					Total Due:		386.00
TAMIVARIN - Tami Varin							
12/07/00	CI	00001211	12/07			1,689.00	1,689.00
					Total Due:		1,689.00
WILLIAMCAP - William Caponegri							
12/20/00	CI	00001207	12/20			62.00	62.00
					Total Due:		62.00
					TOTAL OPEN INVOICES:		8,059.00

Accounts Receivable General Ledger.

John Carter DDS Inc.
GENERAL LEDGER REPORT
FOR THE PERIOD 12/1/00 TO 12/31/00

DATE	TT-R	REF NO	DESCRIPTION	DEBIT	CREDIT
			1100 Accounts Receivable		
			Beginning Balance:	14,300.00	
12/04/00	CI-N	00001201	Jack Hensley	440.00	0.00
12/04/00	CI-N	00001202	Mary Smith	276.00	0.00
12/04/00	CR-N	00001255	Dental Care Inc.	0.00	3,450.00
12/05/00	CI-N	00001203	Kenneth Graun	2,360.00	0.00
12/07/00	CI-N	00001209	Robert Gonzales	572.00	0.00
12/07/00	CI-N	00001210	Kevin Flight	365.00	0.00
12/07/00	CI-N	00001211	Tammi Varin	1,689.00	0.00
12/10/00	CR-N	00000990	Premier Dental Service	0.00	3,750.00
12/11/00	CR-N	00000876	ABC Dental Insurance	0.00	4,800.00
12/11/00	CR-N	00000892	Carol Collins	0.00	472.00
12/14/00	CI-N	00001204	Fran Birkhead	592.00	0.00
12/15/00	CI-N	00001208	Elisa Maxwell	540.00	0.00
12/16/00	CR-N	00000756	Eve Slovak	0.00	600.00
12/16/00	CR-N	00000777	Premier Dental Service	0.00	955.00
12/16/00	CR-N	00001635	Tom Parisian	0.00	273.00
12/18/00	CI-N	00001213	Laura Gonzales	425.00	0.00
12/20/00	CI-N	00001205	Joyce Martin	290.00	0.00
12/20/00	CI-N	00001206	Marilyn Caponegri	62.00	0.00
12/20/00	CI-N	00001207	William Caponegri	62.00	0.00
12/22/00	CI-N	00001212	Sybil Tiedemann	386.00	0.00
			Ending Balance:	8,059.00	
			TOTALS:	8,059.00	14,300.00

Bank Deposit Report.

John Carter DDS
BANK DEPOSIT REPORT
Merchants Bank
1000 Checking Account
12/1/00 To 12/31/00

DEPOSIT DATE	DESCRIPTION	AMOUNT
12/01/00	DEPOSIT	522.00
12/04/00	DEPOSIT	675.00
12/04/00	DEPOSIT	935.00
12/06/00	DEPOSIT	2,762.00
12/08/00	DEPOSIT	485.00
12/10/00	DEPOSIT	3,750.00
12/11/00	DEPOSIT	4,800.00
12/11/00	DEPOSIT	472.00
12/11/00	DEPOSIT	422.00
12/14/00	DEPOSIT	3,450.00
12/15/00	DEPOSIT	600.00
12/16/00	DEPOSIT	955.00
12/16/00	DEPOSIT	3,416.00
12/18/00	DEPOSIT	273.00
12/19/00	DEPOSIT	632.00
12/20/00	DEPOSIT	975.00
12/23/00	DEPOSIT	2,545.00
12/29/00	DEPOSIT	1,875.00
	TOTAL DEPOSITS:	29,544.00

This report can be compared to the customer sales journal to see how items entered there are also included on this report.

Studying the various reports generated from Carter's accounting system should help you understand how entries from the cash receipts and sales journals are entered and distributed to the General Ledger accounts and the customer ledgers. It should also demonstrate how that information can be retrieved from the accounting system to check and verify balances at the end of the month.

JUST A MINUTE

If you are working for a company that has a large volume of Credit Sales, check the customer's ledger card balances against the Accounts Receivable balance after each day's sales are posted. If there is an error, you only have to go through one day's transactions to find it. Waiting until the end of the month could mean sorting through a month's worth of postings.

STATEMENTS TO CUSTOMERS

Once Accounts Receivable is in balance, all the patients that have an open invoice on Carter's books will receive a billing statement. With a computerized system, the computer generates the statements; otherwise, they would be typed or handwritten.

TIME SAVER

If the statements are typed or handwritten, make an extra copy for the customer's file. If the customer claims he or she did not receive the statement, it is easier to make a photocopy and send out a duplicate than to retype the statement.

The following is a sample of a statement from Carter's computerized accounting system:

John Carter DDS
82 Apple Grove
Starcrest, AZ

Mr. William Caponegri
597 Harrison
Starcrest, AZ

12/05/00	Cleaning	$62.00

Balance Due		$62.00

Some companies simply mail out a photocopy of the customer's ledger cards that show charges and payments as billing statements. It doesn't matter how the statements are generated as long as they have been checked against the Accounts Receivable records to make sure that the balances you are billing are correct.

HOUR'S UP!

This is the first hour that deals with the month-end accounting procedures. See if you can answer the following questions before continuing on to the next lesson.

1. The Trial Balance is a report that lists all the accounts in the General Ledger with their year-to-date balances.

   a. True

   b. False

2. The General Ledger report for Accounts Receivable will show both debit and credit postings each month.

   a. True

   b. False

3. At the end of the year, a sole proprietor's taxable Income is based on:

   a. The bank balance

   b. The Draw account

   c. The net profit

4. The year-to-date figures on a Profit and Loss Statement cover the financial data from the first day of the current year through the last day of the current month.

   a. True

   b. False

5. Entries in the cash receipts or sales journal for cash transactions are posted as follows:

   a. Debit Cash, credit Income

   b. Debit Accounts Receivable, credit Income

   c. Debit Income, credit Cash

6. At the end of the month, a report that lists the open invoices contains information on all the sales for that month.

    a. True

    b. False

7. The amount of the bank deposits for the current month can be found in:

    a. The General Ledger Cash account

    b. The checkbook

    c. The cash receipts journal

    d. All of the above

8. The Balance Sheet reports from a computerized system automatically consolidate and total balances in some accounts.

    a. True

    b. False

9. The math computation to determine the sales tax when it is included in the price of the merchandise is:

    a. Sales × sales tax rate

    b. Total sales ÷ sales tax rate + 100%

    c. Total sales ÷ sales tax rate

10. Customer ledgers should be balanced with Accounts Receivable how often?

    a. Every week

    b. Twice a month

    c. At the end of each month

QUIZ

HOUR 16

Cash Disbursements Journal

Just as the Cash Receipts Journal processes the incoming revenue, the Cash Disbursements Journal is used to track the outgoing revenue. Every cost that a business incurs flows through this journal where it is categorized and posted to the proper General Ledger account.

The Cash Disbursements Journal works with the check register and is updated on a daily, weekly, or monthly basis depending on the size of the business and the volume of expenditures.

BALANCING ACCRUAL ACCOUNTS

At the end of each month, all the accrual accounts should be checked to make sure they reflect the correct balances. The following are the accrual accounts that should be checked:

- Accounts Payable
- Sales Tax Collected
- Payroll Taxes Payable

If all the bills from the previous month have been paid on time, Accounts Payable should have a zero balance at the end of the month.

Make sure all the checks issued during the month have been posted to the General Ledger. If Accounts Payable still has a balance, it could mean that an invoice was not paid or that a check written for an invoice set up in Accounts Payable was posted incorrectly.

CHAPTER SUMMARY

LESSON PLAN:

In this hour you will learn about ...

- Balancing accrual accounts
- Paying taxes
- Petty cash funds
- Posting disbursements to the General Ledger
- Temporary posting distributions

GO TO ▶
Refer to Hour 9, "Cash Disbursements," for an outline of the procedures for setting up and paying the bills in Accounts Payable.

If an invoice was left unpaid for a reason, that invoice will become a part of the current month's Accounts Payable.

Caricatures by Ed doesn't have a balance in Accounts Payable. Ed's biggest expense is the rent he pays on the mall space, and because that is due on the first of each month, it is expensed as it is paid.

Carter does have invoices set up in Accounts Payable each month, so that account has to be checked.

It only takes a few minutes to look at the account balances and even less time to determine that all is in order. The procedure should be done before invoices and taxes are posted into the accrual accounts for the current month. If there is an outstanding balance in one of the accrual accounts, it can be traced and corrected before more postings are made that may confuse or compound the error.

If a check was posted to the wrong account, the error can be corrected with a simple entry. For example, if a check was posted to Office Expense instead of Accounts Payable, the entry to correct it is as follows:

Date	Ref. No.	Account	Amount
12-31	GJ-31	6300 Office Expense	(142.00)
		2000 Accounts Payable	142.00
			-0-

Office Expense is credited. This removes the amount that is actually a duplicate of the amount posted there at the end of the previous month when the invoice was set up in Accounts Payable. Accounts Payable is debited, as it should have been when the check was originally posted.

TIME SAVER

 When setting up invoices in Accounts Payable, mark each invoice with the words "Accounts Payable" and the date. That way, when the checks are being written, you are reminded to code the check to be posted to Accounts Payable rather than the expense the invoice covers.

PAYING TAXES

The only accrual that Ed has is sales tax collected. That payment is due on or before the fifteenth of the month following the sales period. At the end of each month, the balance remaining in Ed's Sales Tax Collected account is the tax collected for the current month's sales.

At the end of the month, the Sales Tax Collected account on Ed's books should be as follows:

Date	Ref. No.	Description	Debit	Credit
2100		Sales Tax Collected		
11-30	SJ-11	November Sales		91.50
12-15	CD-15	Check #2231	91.50	
12-31	SJ-12	December Sales		140.92
		Ending Balance		140.92

As you can see the prior month's sales tax collected has been paid to the state. The balance that remains in the account is the tax collected on the current month's sale that is not due to be paid until the middle of January.

John Carter, DDS, doesn't have to collect or pay sales tax because dental services are exempt from sales tax. However, Carter does have payroll taxes to be paid. His federal taxes should have been deposited on the fifteenth of the month, and that deposit should have cleared the accounts for Federal Withholding Tax, Social Security Tax, and Medicare Tax.

GO TO ▶
Refer to Hour 13, "Posting Payroll, Computing Taxes, and Conforming to Federal and State Rules and Regulations," for instructions on computing and depositing payroll taxes.

The check written from Carter's account for the federal tax deposit is a little different from the other checks you have reviewed in previous hours. Up to this point, you have only seen samples of checks that were posted to one account in the General Ledger.

The following sample from Carter's computerized accounting system is the Vendor Payment Journal, also known as a Cash Disbursement Journal. It shows how the check for the federal tax deposit was posted.

This check is a total of three account balances that make up the federal taxes accrued for the November payroll. Note that there is no posting to the payroll tax expense account because that account was debited at the end of November when the tax accruals were set up and posted.

GO TO ▶
Refer to Hour 22, "End-of-the Year Payroll Reports and Other Tax Reports," to learn how to close out the payroll and file all the final reports for the current year.

With the posting of this check, the only payroll accrual account that has a balance is State Withholding Tax Payable. Currently that account has a balance for October and November. The state withholding tax for December will be added to this account, and the total will be paid out when the final quarterly tax report for the current year is filed.

```
                            John Carter DDS
                     VENDOR PAYMENT JOURNAL
                        12/ 1/00 To 12/31/00

DATE      TT  ID          NAME                    REF NO       AMOUNT
12/07/00  VC  MERCHANTSB  Merchants Bank          Ck 422        4,238.22
          FTD November P/R

          1000 Checking Account                  4,238.22 cr
          2200 Federal Withholding Tax Payable   3,317.52 dr
          2210 Social Security Tax Payable          471.20 dr
          2212 Medicare Withholding Tax Pay         449.50 dr


                          TOTAL PAYMENTS:                      4,238.22

                          VP - Payments                           0.00
                          VC - Checks                          4,238.22
```

PETTY CASH FUNDS

If you look back on the Balance Sheet for John Carter, DDS, you will see that there is an account called Petty Cash. The balance in that account is $50.

Petty cash is a fund that is kept on hand in most offices to pay for any small Expenses that come up during the month. Postage due on a piece of mail, office supplies, coffee, or batteries for the smoke detector may all be paid out of the petty cash fund. Receipts for all these expenditures should be kept so that the account can be balanced and reimbursed at the end of each month.

Assume that Carter's bookkeeper has the following receipts for petty cash payments at the end of December.

Christmas Decorations	$6.00
Postage Due on a Letter	.55
Book Purchase	29.95
Total Expenditures	$36.50

Once the total of these Expenses is deducted from the original amount in the petty cash fund, the bookkeeper verifies that the remaining cash on hand is $13.50.

In order to bring the petty cash fund back up to the original amount, a check is written and cashed for the difference, or the total Expenses of $36.50.

Like any other check, this check to reimburse the petty cash fund must be posted, allocating the Expenses to the proper accounts in the General Ledger.

The Christmas decorations and postage are general office Expenses. The book is on a new dental procedure and, is therefore, an educational tool.

When the check is issued, it is posted as follows:

John Carter DDS
VENDOR PAYMENT JOURNAL
12/20/00 To 12/31/00

DATE	TT ID	NAME	REF NO	AMOUNT
12/30/00	VC 150 Reimbursement	Petty Cash Fund	ck # 433	36.50
	1000 Checking Account		36.50 cr	
	6140 Office Supplies & Postage		6.55 dr	
	6180 Educational Expense		29.95 dr	
		TOTAL PAYMENTS:		36.50
		VP - Payments		0.00
		VC - Checks		36.50

John Carter, DDS, Vendor Payment Journal Petty Cash Fund.

In reviewing the particulars of this check you may wonder why there is no amount posted to the Petty Cash account when this check is described as a reimbursement to that account. There is no posting to the Petty Cash account because that balance in the General Ledger has not actually changed. At the beginning of the month, the balance was $50, and now at the end of the month, with this reimbursement, the balance is still $50—no adjustment to this account is necessary.

This check does reduce the Cash in Checking balance by $36.50, so that account is credited for that amount. It also increases the Office Expense account by $6.55 and the Educational Expense account by $29.95, so those accounts are debited.

Caricatures by Ed has a minimal number of Expenses each month. The following is a list of the checks Brown wrote from his business account during the month of December.

Date	Ck No.	Vendor	Amount	Description
12-1	2229	La Mesa Mall	$ 500.00	Rent
12-8	2230	The Art Company	82.00	Supplies
12-15	2231	Nevada Revenue Dept.	91.50	Sales tax
12-18	2232	Alphagraphics	25.00	Flyers
12-23	2233	Edward Brown	1,250.00	Draw
12-27	2234	The Art Company	17.00	Supplies
Total Checks			$1,965.50	

The entry to post all of Ed's disbursements for the month of December can be written up and posted to the General Ledger as follows:

Date	Ref. No.	Account	Amount
12-31	CDJ-31	1000 Cash in Checking	(1,965.50)
		6360 Rent	500.00
		6520 Supplies	99.00
		2100 Sales Tax Collected	91.50
		5100 Advertising	25.00
		3220 Draw	1,250.00
			-0-

GO TO ▷
Refer to Hour 9, "Cash Disbursements," for instructions on and samples of disbursements as they are posted to the General Ledger accounts.

Being a larger, more involved business operation, John Carter, DDS, issues more checks for Accounts Payable and current month Expenses.

Also, because Carter's accounting system is computerized, there are a number of reports that can be accessed detailing his monthly disbursements.

The primary report to study in this hour is the Cash Disbursements Journal or Vendor Payment Journal for the month of December. Refer to the following figure.

As you review this journal, you should note that the report shows how each check was posted. The computer posts the checks just as you would if you were entering them in a manual system.

Also observe that at the beginning of the month there were checks written that were posted to Account 2000, Accounts Payable. As you learned a little earlier in this hour, these checks should have cleared the balance in Accounts Payable. The following report of the Accounts Payable account in the General Ledger shows that after these checks were posted, the account balance is zero.

John Carter DDS Inc.
VENDOR PAYMENT JOURNAL
12/1/00 To 12/31/00

DATE	TT ID	NAME	REF NO	AMOUNT
12/01/00	VC 125	Direct Deposit Payroll Service	00000415	5,745.18
	P/R ending 11-30-00			
	1000 Cash in Checking		5,745.18 cr	
	9999 Temporary Distribution		5,695.18 dr	
	6140 Office Supplies & Postage		50.00 dr	
12/01/00	VC 152	Starcrest Professional Offices	00000416	1,500.00
	December Rent			
	1000 Cash in Checking		1,500.00 cr	
	5650 Rent		1,500.00 dr	
12/05/00	VC 151	Dental Services, Inc.	00000417	4,004.00
	Invoice # 34562			
	1000 Cash in Checking		4,004.00 cr	
	2000 Accounts Payable		4,004.00 dr	
12/05/00	VC 176	Niagra Dental Supplies	00000418	622.00
	Invoice #99			
	1000 Cash in Checking		622.00 cr	
	2000 Accounts Payable		622.00 dr	
12/05/00	VC 175	A to Z Office Supplies	00000419	356.75
	Acct. 367			
	1000 Cash in Checking		356.75 cr	
	2000 Accounts Payable		356.75 dr	
12/05/00	VC 158	PRO Subscription Service	00000420	86.25
	House Ideas			
	1000 Cash in Checking		86.25 cr	
	2000 Accounts Payable		86.25 dr	
12/05/00	VC 153	Allied Insurance Brokers	00000421	71.00
	Policy # 009899			
	1000 Cash in Checking		71.00 cr	
	2000 Accounts Payable		71.00 dr	
12/07/00	VC MERCHANTSB	Merchants Bank	00000422	4,238.22
	FTD November Payroll			
	1000 Cash in Checking		4,238.22 cr	
	2200 Federal Withholding Tax Payable		3,317.52 dr	
	2210 Social Security Tax Payable		471.20 dr	
	2212 Medicare Withholding Tax Payable		449.50 dr	
12/14/00	VC 125	Direct Deposit Payroll Service	00000423	5,745.18
	Payroll Ending 12/14/00			
	1000 Cash in Checking		5,745.18 cr	
	9999 Temporary Distribution		5,695.18 dr	
	6140 Office Supplies & Postage		50.00 dr	
12/15/00	VC 153	Allied Insurance Brokers	00000424	328.00
	# 37562 Health Insurance			
	1000 Cash in Checking		328.00 cr	
	6230 Insurance - Employee Group		328.00 dr	
12/15/00	VC 159	Southwest Gas Company	00000425	116.00

John Carter, DDS, Vendor Payment Journal.

John Carter, DDS, Vendor Payment Journal.

John Carter DDS Inc.
VENDOR PAYMENT JOURNAL
12/1/00 To 12/31/00

DATE	TT ID	NAME	REF NO	AMOUNT
	Acct. 625			
	1000 Cash in Checking		116.00 cr	
	6050 Utilities - Gas & Electric		116.00 dr	
12/15/00	VC 160	Arizona Light & Power	00000426	83.50
	Account 900088			
	1000 Cash in Checking		83.50 cr	
	6050 Utilities - Gas & Electric		83.50 dr	
12/15/00	VC MERCHANTSB	Merchants Bank	00000427	1,027.77
	Account # 0077733			
	1000 Cash in Checking		1,027.77 cr	
	2300 Loan Payable - Merchants Bank		694.44 dr	
	6510 Interest Expense		333.33 dr	
12/15/00	VC 157	City of Starcrest	00000428	50.00
	Business License 76433			
	1000 Cash in Checking		50.00 cr	
	6240 License Fees		50.00 dr	
12/15/00	VC 156	U. S. West	00000429	87.30
	555-5555			
	1000 Cash in Checking		87.30 cr	
	6030 Telephone		87.30 dr	
12/15/00	VC 176	Niagra Dental Supplies	00000430	74.95
	Invoice # 329			
	1000 Cash in Checking		74.95 cr	
	5100 Dental Supplies		74.95 dr	
12/18/00	VC 175	A to Z Office Supplies	00000431	52.00
	Toner			
	1000 Cash in Checking		52.00 cr	
	6140 Office Supplies & Postage		52.00 dr	
12/18/00	VC 179	Jenkins Printing Co.	00000432	185.00
	Invoice# 6669			
	1000 Cash in Checking		185.00 cr	
	5150 Brochures and Catalogues		185.00 dr	
12/30/00	VC 150	Petty Cash Fund	00000433	36.50
	Reimbursement			
	1000 Cash in Checking		36.50 cr	
	6140 Office Supplies & Postage		6.55 dr	
	6180 Professional Fees		29.95 dr	
	TOTAL PAYMENTS:			**24,409.60**
	VP - Payments			0.00
	VC - Checks			24,409.60

General Ledger Report For Accounts Payable.

John Carter DDS
GENERAL LEDGER REPORT
FOR THE PERIOD 12/1/00 TO 12/31/00

DATE	TT-R	REF NO	DESCRIPTION	DEBIT	CREDIT
2000 Accounts Payable					
			Beginning Balance:		5,140.00
12/05/00	VC-N	00000417	Dental Services, Inc.	4,004.00	0.00
12/05/00	VC-N	00000418	Niagara Dental Supplies	622.00	0.00
12/05/00	VC-N	00000419	A to Z Office Supplies	356.75	0.00
12/05/00	VC-N	00000420	Publishers Clearing House	86.25	0.00
12/05/00	VC-N	00000421	Allied Insurance Brokers	71.00	0.00
			Ending Balance:		0.00
			TOTALS:	5,140.00	0.00

This verifies that all the prior month's bills are paid and that the account is now ready for the Expenses that will be posted there for December bills (scheduled to be paid in the month of January).

Temporary Posting Distributions

Going back to Carter's Vendor Payment Journal, there is another important item to take note of: It is the introduction of an account you have not seen before. That account is Temporary Distribution (Account 9999)

This account is included in computerized accounting systems to allow financial data to be posted that will be reviewed and distributed to the proper accounts at a later time. This account could also be added to a manual system and used the same way.

Rather than skipping over a check that doesn't have all the information needed to post it properly, you post it to the checking account and to the Temporary Distribution account. This ensures that you will not forget to go back and get the information to post it properly. It also allows you to keep the checking account balance in order.

In this case, the net amount of the payroll checks is posted to this account. This is because Carter uses a payroll service that computes the paychecks and deposits them directly into the employees' bank accounts. Carter pays a fee of $50 for each payroll the company processes, and that amount is included in the check and is charged to office expense.

At the end of each month, the payroll service provides a detailed report of the wages and taxes. When this report is received, Carter's bookkeeper will review the information and make an adjusting entry to distribute the wages and taxes properly.

In this hour, you have seen how the disbursements are handled and posted for a small business using a manual accounting system and for a larger business with a computerized system.

Once again, you have reviewed a number of reports from the computerized accounting system for John Carter, DDS. These reports should be studied and reviewed so that you become familiar with all the ways the accounting information can be presented. The same information can be taken from a manual system, but it would take a little more time and effort.

GO TO ▶
Refer to Hour 18, "Reconciling the Bank Accounts and General Journal Entries," to review the adjustments that are made at the end of each month, including the Accounts Payable entry.

GO TO ▶
Refer to Hour 17, "Payroll Journal and Employee Expense Accounts," to review the end-of-the-month adjustments for payroll and taxes.

HOUR'S UP!

Review and answer these questions about the end-of-the-month procedures for cash disbursements.

1. The report that verifies the Accounts Payable balance comes from:
   a. Customer ledgers
   b. General ledger
   c. Vendor ledgers

2. The Petty Cash account is debited when the reimbursement check is issued.
   a. True
   b. False

3. At the end of the month, the accrual accounts should be checked to make sure they reflect the correct balances.
   a. True
   b. False

4. In a computerized accounting system, entries are posted differently than in a manual system.
   a. True
   b. False

5. The new account introduced in this hour is:
   a. Petty Cash
   b. Bank Deposits
   c. Temporary Distributions

6. The federal tax deposit should zero out all the payroll accrual accounts.
   a. True
   b. False

7. To correct a check for office supplies posted as an expense rather than as Accounts Payable, the entry is:
   a. Debit Cash, credit Accounts Payable
   b. Credit Office Expense, debit Accounts Payable
   c. Debit Accounts Payable, credit Cash

8. If you don't have the information needed to post a check, you should skip it.

   a. True

   b. False

9. Which of the following accounts is not posted when the federal tax deposit check is entered:

   a. Medicare Tax Payable

   b. State Withholding Tax Payable

   c. Federal Withholding Tax Payable

10. Accounts Payable should have a zero balance after all the bills from the prior month have been paid.

   a. True

   b. False

QUIZ

HOUR 17

Payroll Journal and Employee Expense Accounts

CHAPTER SUMMARY

LESSON PLAN:

In this hour you will learn about ...

- Employee expense accounts
- Using a payroll service
- Posting to the General Ledger

You have already received a lot of information about employees, payroll, and payroll taxes. The Payroll Journal is the section of the accounting system designed to distribute wages and payroll taxes to accounts in the General Ledger.

If the payroll is being done in-house, this journal is used each payday to record and issue the paychecks. If a payroll service is employed, the entries in the Payroll Journal will most likely be monthly totals supplied by the service.

In addition to this last bit of information about processing payroll, this hour introduces and explains how workers are reimbursed for Expenses incurred in the course of representing the business that employs them.

EMPLOYEE EXPENSE ACCOUNTS

Employee Expenses are reported, reimbursed, and recorded into the accounting system in a number of ways. Whenever a worker incurs Expenses on behalf of his or her employer, the employee is entitled to a reimbursement.

Salespeople very often have expense accounts to cover normal Expenses such as travel and meals when they are out trying to sell their employers' products. At the end of a specified time period, the employee submits the Expenses, along with receipts to substantiate them, and receives reimbursement from the employer.

Some companies provide their employees with a set amount each month as an advance against Expenses. Still other companies provide employees with expense allowances. This is usually a predetermined, mutually agreed upon amount to cover auto Expenses while on company business.

For example, a real estate management company might give its property managers a monthly allowance to cover the Expenses of traveling from property to property to meet with potential tenants, collect rents, or supervise repairs.

An allowance is different from an expense reimbursement in three ways. First of all, the employee does not get additional funds if Expenses exceed the allowance. Second, the employee does not have to report his or her Expenses to the employer. Third, the allowance is considered to be Income to the employee. At the end of the year, it is reported to the IRS.

GO TO ▶
Refer to Hour 22, "End-of-the-Year Payroll Reports and Other Tax Reports," to learn how expense allowances are reported to the employee and the federal and state taxing authorities.

It is up to the employee to keep the necessary receipts and records to report deductions to offset the additional Income.

With a regular employee expense account, the amount of the company reimbursement checks is considered to be an expense to the business and is handled accordingly.

Consider the following scenario: Acme Hardware has an outside salesman who goes out to contractors and maintenance companies around the state and tries to sell hardware, tools, and building supplies.

At the beginning of each month, the salesman receives a check for $500 as an advance against Expenses. A special account is set up in the Chart of Accounts and the company's General Ledger to record this check.

The account is in the Assets section of the Balance Sheet and is called Employee Advances (Account 1110). It is in the Assets section because the company expects to recover the advance amount at the end of the month. At the same time, a ledger is established for the employee, and the amount of the advance check is recorded there also.

As the month ends, the employee turns in his expense report along with receipts to substantiate the Expenses listed on the report. The following is a sample of a typical expense report completed by an employee:

When this expense report is submitted, the accountant checks it for accuracy and verifies that there are receipts to back up all the Expenses the employee has reported.

Wk. Ending	Gas/Auto	Meals	Ofc. Supplies	Lodging	P.R. Items	Misc. Exp.	Total
12/01/2000	$22.00	$15.00	$0.00	$0.00	$17.00	$0.00	$54.00
12/09/2000	$24.00	$52.00	$12.00	$110.00	$0.00	$5.00	$203.00
12/16/2000	$27.00	$6.00	$7.50	$110.00	$0.00	$16.00	$166.50
12/23/2000	$24.00	$68.00	$0.00	$0.00	$12.00	$0.00	$104.00
12/29/2000	$18.00	$14.00	$0.00	$0.00	$0.00	$24.00	$56.00
Dec. Total	$115.00	$155.00	$19.50	$220.00	$29.00	$45.00	$583.50

Henry Jordan Expense Report for December 2000

Employee Expense Report.

As you can see, the sample report shows that Henry Jordan's Expenses for the month of December total $583.50. That exceeds his original advance check by $83.50.

Once the figures on the report are double-checked, the Expenses are recapped and coded for posting. Look at the Chart of Accounts you created in Hour 1, and Hour 2 to see if you can determine which accounts will be posted to record these Expenses.

The entry that the accountant writes up to record Jordan's Expenses is as follows:

Date	Ref. No.	Account	Amount
12-31	AJ12-1	1000 Cash in Checking	(583.50)
		5100 Advertising	29.00
		5150 Auto Expenses	115.00
		6280 Misc. Expense	45.00
		6300 Office Expense	19.50
		6540 Travel	220.00
		6550 Meals	155.00
			-0-

The accounts that are posted are the ones that most closely fit the reported Expenses. For instance, the heading "P.R. Items" on the expense report is for flyers the salesman had printed with information on discounted merchandise. This is another form of advertising, so the expense was charged to that account.

This entry is also like the one you reviewed in the last hour for petty cash expenditures. In this example, the employee receives a check for $583.50. This is actually his advance for the next month ($500), plus a reimbursement for the $83.50 he spent from his own pocket. However, the account for Employee Advances is not posted because there is no change in that account. The balance in that account remains at $500.

Now what if the employee's Expenses for the month were less than the original amount of the advance? If the employee turned in a report for Expenses of $450, then that is the amount of the check that would be issued to him. That amount plus the $50 he has left from the previous month's advance, totals $500. Again, the balance in the Employee Advance account does not change.

The number of employee expense accounts doesn't matter. They all can be handled as outlined in the previous examples.

USING A PAYROLL SERVICE

Of our two sample companies, only one of them, John Carter, DDS, has employees. As you learned in the last hour, Carter employs a payroll service that issues checks and deposits them directly into the employees' accounts.

Twice a month, checks are issued to the payroll service to cover the net amount of the paychecks plus the service's processing fee. The check issued to cover the paychecks is then posted to Temporary Distributions (Account 9999).

GO TO ▶
Refer to Hour 16, "Cash Disbursements Journal," to an introduction and explanation to the Temporary Distributions account.

At the end of the month, the payroll service issues a report on the payroll processed during that month. When Carter's bookkeeper gets the report, she checks the information on it and prepares the proper payroll and tax entries.

There are many different payroll services across the country, and the reports issued may vary in design, but the information they provide will be in accordance with what is needed to satisfy federal and state requirements.

Many banks offer payroll services to their customers and this gives you the added convenience of having your payroll accounts and operating accounts in one location. Accounting firms often process payroll for their clients and if the firm does not offer this service it can most likely recommend a good alternative.

Usually a variety of reports are issued by the payroll services. One lists each individual employee and details the payroll checks issued to each one during that particular month. The report also totals wages and taxes, and usually automatically figures the amount of the federal tax deposit and, if applicable, state withholding tax and unemployment tax.

PROCEED WITH CAUTION

Always double-check the payroll figures and the tax deposit amount to verify its accuracy. Ultimately, the responsibility for depositing the correct tax amount remains with the employer.

Some payroll services prepare the quarterly reports for the client. Others simply supply the information needed for the reports based on the payroll checks they have processed.

At the end of December, Carter's payroll service provided a number of reports on the current month and year-to-date payroll. Since you are still working on the month-end procedures, the following example is for the month of December only.

John Carter DDS   December 2000 Payroll Report

Date	Employee	Gross Wages	SS Tax	Medicare Tax	FWH	SWH	Net Check
12/01/2000	John Carter	$5,850.00	$0.00	$84.83	$1,392.76	$139.28	$4,233.13
12/15/2000	John Carter	$5,850.00	$0.00	$84.83	$1,392.76	$139.28	$4,233.13
Dec. Total		$11,700.00	$0.00	$169.66	$2,785.52	$278.56	$8,466.26
12/01/2000	Judy Carter	$500.00	$31.00	$7.25	$36.00	$3.60	$422.15
12/15/2000		$500.00	$31.00	$7.25	$36.00	$3.60	$422.15
Dec. Total		$1,000.00	$62.00	$14.50	$72.00	$7.20	$844.30
12/01/2000	Mary Jones	$1,400.00	$86.80	$20.30	$230.00	$23.00	$1,039.90
12/15/2000		$1,400.00	$86.80	$20.30	$230.00	$23.00	$1,039.90
Dec. Total		$2,800.00	$173.60	$40.60	$460.00	$46.00	$2,079.80
Grand Total		$15,500.00	$235.60	$224.76	$3,317.52	$331.76	$11,390.36

Federal Tax Deposit   4,238.22 Due January 15, 2001

Monthly Payroll Report.

In this example, the employees are paid on a semimonthly schedule, with two paychecks each month. The checks are issued on the 1st and the 15th of the month. All the employees are salaried, so there are no hourly computations on the report.

The most important item you should note on this report is that John Carter has no Social Security tax deducted from his payroll for the month of December. A quick calculation of Carter's gross wages multiplied by the number of payroll periods in the year tells you that his salary has surpassed the wage limit for Social Security tax. In this particular year, the wage limit was $76,200.

JUST A MINUTE

Remember that the wage limit on Social Security tax changes from year to year.

Gross Wages	5,850.00
Number of Pay Periods	× 24
Total Wages	140,400.00
2000 Wage Limit	−76,200.00
Excess Wages	64,200.00

GO TO ▶
Refer to Hour 12, "Payroll Taxes: Employee/Employer," for basic information on payroll taxes and calculations.

With this information, you can verify the amount that the payroll service has reported for the federal tax deposit.

Total Wages	15,500.00
Less Carter's Wages	−11,700.00
Social Security Wages	3,800.00

Federal Tax Deposit Computation:

$3,800.00 \times .124 =$	471.20	Social Security Tax
$15,500.00 \times .029 =$	449.50	Medicare Tax
	920.70	
	3,317.52	Federal Withholding Tax
	4,238.22	Total Tax Deposit

Although Carter's wages for December are not subject to Social Security tax, they are still subject to Medicare tax.

JUST A MINUTE

Medicare tax is payable on all wages—there is no wage limit on this tax.

POSTING TO THE GENERAL LEDGER

With the information the payroll service has provided, Carter's bookkeeper can now post the payroll and taxes to the proper accounts.

Keep in mind that the net amount of the paychecks has already been posted to the Cash in Checking account as a credit, so only the debit that remains in Temporary Distribution has to be allocated to the proper accounts.

Taking the information from the payroll service report, the entry to post the December payroll for John Carter, DDS, is written up as follows:

Date	Ref. No.	Account	Amount
12-31	PR12-31	9999 Temporary Distribution	(11,390.36)
		6000 Salaries & Wages	15,500.00
		2200 FWH Tax Payable	(3,317.52)
		2210 SS Tax Payable	(235.60)
		2212 Medicare Tax Payable	(224.76)
		2220 SWH Tax Payable	(331.76)
			-0-

To post and redistribute December payroll

If you look back on the sample report in the last hour, you will see that there were two separate entries to the Temporary Distribution account from the Cash Disbursements Journal. Those two postings equal the amount that is reversed by the previous entry and bring that account back to zero.

The last entry to be made for December payroll is the employer's portion of the taxes that needs to be posted to the payroll accrual accounts and the expense account.

GO TO ▶ Refer to Hour 13, "Posting Payroll, Computing Taxes, and Conforming to Federal and State Rules and Regulations," for examples and instructions for posting the employer's portion of payroll taxes.

GO TO ▶
Refer to Hour 22, "End-of-the-Year Payroll Reports and Other Tax Reports," for instructions on preparing wage statements for employees.

Both the entries are entered into the computer for posting. You can then access a report from the computer showing the entries as they were entered and posted.

The interesting thing to note when you review a report from a computerized accounting system is that the information is presented very much like the standard manual entries. Whenever you study a report from a computerized system, you can see that the computerized accounting system is designed to present the data the same way it would appear in a handwritten entry in a manual accounting system.

The following is a report of the last two payroll entries from Carter's accounting system:

Computer Report Of Payroll Entries.

John Carter DDS Inc.
GENERAL JOURNAL REPORT
12/1/00 TO 12/31/00

Date: 12/31/00   Ref No: PR12-31
Desc: To redistribute December Payroll

GL ACCOUNT / NAME	DEBIT	CREDIT
9999 Temporary Distribution		11,390.36
6000 Salaries & Wages	15,500.00	
2200 Federal Withholding Tax Payable		3,317.52
2210 Social Security Tax Payable		235.60
2212 Medicare Withholding Tax Payable		224.76
2220 State Withholding Taxes Payable		331.76
Total:	15,500.00	15,500.00

Date: 12/31/00   Ref No: PRT12-31
Desc: To record Employer Tax

GL ACCOUNT / NAME	DEBIT	CREDIT
2210 Social Security Tax Payable		235.60
2212 Medicare Withholding Tax Payable		224.74
6490 Taxes - Payroll	460.34	
Total:	460.34	460.34

GENERAL JOURNAL TOTAL:	15,960.34	15,960.34

Since it is the end of the year as well as the end of the month, the payroll service provides Carter with a report of the individual employee payroll ledgers. These payroll ledgers will be used to issue the end-of-the-year tax statements.

Hour's Up!

This hour presented lessons in end-of-the-month tasks for employee expense accounts and Payroll Journals. The following questions are based on these lessons.

1. Gross wages are usually posted to the General Ledger account Salaries & Wages as:

    a. Debits

    b. Credits

2. Using a payroll service relieves the employer of the responsibility of depositing payroll taxes.

    a. True

    b. False

3. Expenses taken from an employee's expense report are posted as business Expenses to the employer.

    a. True

    b. False

4. A check to reimburse an employee for auto Expenses is posted as follows:

    a. Credit Cash in Checking, debit Employee Advances

    b. Credit Cash in Checking, debit Auto Expense

    c. Credit Employee Advances, debit Auto Expense

5. The wage limit for Medicare tax changes from year to year.

    a. True

    b. False

6. Social Security tax is posted to the accrual accounts as a:

    a. Debit

    b. Credit

7. An expense allowance is considered to be Income to the employee.

    a. True

    b. False

8. Information for the employees' W-2 forms is taken from:

   a. The payroll tax worksheet

   b. Employee payroll ledgers

   c. The General Ledger

9. A computerized accounting system presents data much like a manual accounting system.

   a. True

   b. False

10. The federal tax deposit is computed by adding employees' deductions for Social Security, Medicare, and federal withholding taxes.

    a. True

    b. False

Reconciling the Bank Accounts and General Journal Entries

CHAPTER SUMMARY

LESSON PLAN:

In this hour you will learn about …

- Balancing the bank accounts
- Adjustments
- Posting to the General Ledger

All the transactions have been processed through the Cash Receipts Journal, the Cash Disbursements Journal, and the Payroll Journal. The month is drawing to a close and all of this data will be consolidated and presented on the financial statements.

Now is the time to review the work that you have done during the current month and make sure everything is in order and in balance.

BALANCING THE BANK ACCOUNTS

Before financial statements can be issued, the balance in the operating account must be checked and verified; at the end of the month, go over the checkbook register. Make sure all deposits are recorded and added to the balance, and that all checks have been deducted from the balance.

Once you are satisfied that everything is properly recorded in the checkbook, compare the balance in the checkbook with the balance in the Cash in Checking account in the General Ledger.

Everything in the checkbook should have been posted to the General Ledger: deposits posted as cash receipts or sales, and checks posted as disbursements. If all these items were posted correctly, the balance in the checkbook should agree with the balance for Cash in Checking in the General Ledger.

GO TO ▶
Refer to Hour 5, "Organization and Proper Accounting Procedures," for instructions on keeping the operating account up-to-date and in balance.

The bank statement usually doesn't arrive until after the first of the month, and the books won't actually be closed out before the accounts are reconciled. However, it is wise to check the balances at the end of the month. If the checkbook and the General Ledger don't agree, you will have to find out why.

If the checkbook balance doesn't agree with the General Ledger balance, you can look for the discrepancy by doing the following:

- If the checkbook balance is more than the General Ledger balance, recheck the deposits to make sure they were all posted and recorded for the correct amounts.

- If the checkbook balance is less than the General Ledger balance, review the checks to make sure they were all posted and recorded for the correct amounts.

- If all the checks and deposits are posted correctly, go back through the checkbook and make sure your addition and subtraction calculations are correct. Then, if you are managing a manual accounting system, you will also have to check the math in the General Ledger.

TIME SAVER

If the discrepancy is a number that can be divided by 9, look for a transposition error, such as 98.00 recorded, added, or subtracted as 89.00.

The procedures outlined can be used for any size company. However, in a small company such as Caricatures by Ed, chances of an error are slim because there is not a lot of financial activity.

Ed has a balance of $2,768 in his checking account at the end of December. After all his sales and checks are posted to Cash in Checking, the General Ledger for this account is as follows:

Date	Ref. No.	Description	Debit	Credit
1000 Cash in Checking				
12-1-00		Beginning Balance	1,774.50	
12-31-00	SJ12-1	December Sales	2,959.00	
12-31-00	CD12-2	December Disbursements		1,965.50
			-----------	-----------
12-31-00		Ending Balance	2,768.00	

As you can see, the balance in the General Ledger agrees with the checkbook balance. This indicates that all the postings were done, and posted correctly.

When the bank statement arrives, Ed prepares a worksheet that enables him to reconcile his checkbook and General Ledger to the bank statement. Before you study the bank reconciliation worksheet, take another look at the financial activity for this small business that was presented in prior hours. Ed's cash receipts were as follows:

Cash Receipts Journal

December 2000

Date	Sales	Sales Tax	Total Cash	Bank Deposit
12-2	546.67	27.33	574.00	
12-3	236.19	11.81	248.00	822.00 (12-4)
12-9	407.62	20.38	428.00	
12-10	500.95	25.05	526.00	954.00 (12-11)
12-16	264.76	13.24	278.00	
12-17	354.28	17.72	372.00	650.00 (12-18)
12-23	271.42	13.58	285.00	285.00 (12-26)
12-30	236.19	11.81	248.00	248.00 (1-2-01)
	2,818.08	140.92	2,959.00	2,959.00

You will also need to review the Cash Disbursements or the listing of checks for Caricatures by Ed for the month of December.

Ed's Cash Disbursements for December were as follows:

Date	Ck No.	Vendor	Amount	Description
12-1	2229	La Mesa Mall	$ 500.00	Rent
12-8	2230	The Art Company	82.00	Supplies
12-15	2231	Nevada Revenue Dept.	91.50	Sales Tax
12-18	2232	Alphagraphics	25.00	Flyers
12-23	2233	Edward Brown	1,250.00	Draw
12-27	2234	The Art Company	17.00	Supplies
Total Checks			$1,965.50	

The following worksheet has been designed to verify the cash accounts and can be used by any size business. This reconciliation is based on the information presented for Ed's financial activity in the month of December.

Sample Bank Reconciliation Worksheet.

	Balance 11-30-00	Deposits	Disbursed	Balance 12-31-00
1 Balance per Bank Stmt	185650	271100	193900	262850
Deposits in Transit				
11-30-00	— 0 —	— 0 —		
12-31-00		24800		24800
O/S Checks				
11-30-00	‹8200›		‹8200›	
12-31-00			10850	‹10850›
	177450	295900	196550	276800
Balance per Check Book & General Ledger				276800

Outstanding Checks

2231   91.50
2234   17.00
        108.50

Although there are other ways to do a bank reconciliation, it is recommended that it be done this way for a few reasons. Using this type of worksheet gives you the correct total of deposits and disbursements for the month. If your balance doesn't agree with the bank's balance, you can easily determine if the discrepancy is in the deposits or the checks.

The *Deposit in Transit* of $248 is the last deposit that Ed had for the month of December. This deposit is added into the bank's deposits because it has already been posted as part of the Income realized in December.

STRICTLY DEFINED

A **Deposit in Transit** is a bank deposit that has been posted in the accounting system for the month but that did not reach the bank in time to be included on the monthly statement.

Clearly showing the Deposit in Transit on the worksheet is a reminder to keep that deposit receipt and to make sure the bank includes it on the next month's statement.

The same is true for the outstanding checks. These are checks written in December and posted as disbursements on Ed's books. Although they have not yet cleared the bank account, they are added to the disbursements and then listed separately on the worksheet. If these checks do not appear on the next bank statement, the information needed to follow up on them is readily available.

GO TO ▶
Refer to Hour 10, "The Importance of Work Papers, Receipts, and Other Records," for information on what to keep and how to keep it.

The bank statements and the reconciliation worksheets should be kept together in a separate file that can be easily accessed if questions arise on deposits or checks.

GENERAL JOURNAL ENTRIES

General Journal Entries are used to make adjustments to the General Ledger. They can be made at any time during the month, but they are used mostly at the end of the month when all the accounts are being checked and verified.

STRICTLY DEFINED

General Journal Entries are used to correct or adjust balances in the General Ledger. As the name implies, these entries cover a wide range of adjustments and all the accounts.

POSTING TO THE GENERAL LEDGER

Often once the bank reconciliation is done, the Cash in Checking account in the General Ledger must be adjusted. This can be due to a posting error, bank service charges, or other bank charges such as check printing.

If an adjustment needs to be made, the amount and the reason should be noted on the reconciliation worksheet. For example, if a bank charged $15 for check printing in December, an adjustment would have to be made to record this charge.

Even though the bank statement is not received until after the first of the following month, adjustments necessitated by the bank statement should be posted on the books for the month that the statement covers.

JUST A MINUTE

Although the month has ended, it is not closed out and the financial statements are not issued until all adjustments that affect the financial data in December are posted.

The General Journal Entry or Adjusting Entry to post a bank charge for check printing should be written up as follows:

Date	Ref. No.	Account	Amount
12-31	AJ-1	1000 Cash in Checking	(15.00)
		6300 Office Expense	15.00

			-0-

To record check printing charges

Because checks are considered to be office supplies, the expense is posted to the Office Expense account.

There are no adjustments to be made on Ed's books for the month of December. His bank account is in balance with the bank statement, and he has no equipment to be depreciated.

The other business you have been studying, John Carter, DDS, does have adjustments that must be made before the month can be closed out.

Carter's operating account has been reconciled using the same type of worksheet that Ed used. There were no adjustments to be made to Carter's checking account. However, Carter also has a substantial amount in a savings account—when he receives the bank statement on that account, an adjustment will have to be made for the interest earned on the savings.

Depending on the type of savings account, interest is reported either monthly or quarterly. Carter's account is one that receives interest on a quarterly basis.

The entry to post the interest to the General Ledger on Carter's savings account would be written up as follows:

Date	Ref. No.	Account	Amount
12-31-00	AJ-1	1050 Savings Account	312.00
		4200 Interest Income	(312.00)

To record quarterly interest per bank statement

The other adjustment that needs to be made on Carter's books is the monthly depreciation adjustment.

Since Carter's dental practice is only 3 years old, all the Assets on his books were acquired at the same time. If you look back on his Balance Sheet for November, you will see that his Assets are divided into three categories: Leasehold Improvements is the cost that was incurred in modifying the rented space in a professional building to suit the needs of Carter's dental practice, Equipment contains the more expensive items needed to service patients, and Furniture & Fixtures is comprised of desks and the furnishings for the reception area.

GO TO ▶
Refer to Hour 4, "Depreciable Assets, Prepaid Expenses, and Other Accounts," to find examples of depreciation schedules and instructions on how and why Assets are depreciated.

Of course, Carter purchased other things, including a computer and software programs, but his accountant elected to expense those items in the year they were purchased.

FYI The IRS has a number of publications that explain depreciation and the election to expense equipment. For a complete list of these publications, visit the Web site, www.irs.gov

The following Depreciation Schedule shows each category and the Assets covered under that designation.

General Journal Report Depreciation Expense.

JOHN CARTER DDS   DEPRECIATION SCHEDULE

DATE	DESCRIPTION	COST	LIFE	MO. DEP.	ACC. 1998	ACC. 1999	ACC. 2000	TOTAL DEP.
	EQUIPMENT:							
1-98	Dental chairs (2)	$6,050.00	5 years	$100.83	$1,209.96	$1,209.96	$1,209.96	$3,629.88
1-98	X-Ray Equipment	$5,000.00	5 years	$83.33	$999.96	$999.96	$999.96	2,999.88
1-98	Drills & Lights	$2,300.00	5 years	$38.00	$456.00	$456.00	$456.00	$1,368.00
	Total Equipment	**$13,350.00**		**$222.16**	**$2,665.92**	**$2,665.92**	**$2,665.92**	**$7,997.76**
	Leasehold Improvements:							
1-98	**Leasehold Improvements**	**$25,600.00**	10 years	**$213.33**	**$2,559.96**	**$2,559.96**	**$2,559.96**	**$7,679.88**
	Furniture & Fixtures							
1-98	Desks (3)	$1,500.00	7 years	$17.85	$214.20	$214.20	$214.20	$642.60
1-98	Waiting Room Chairs (6)	$1,200.00	7 years	$14.28	$171.36	$171.36	$171.36	$514.08
1-98	Tables & Lamps	$900.00	7 years	$10.71	$128.52	$128.52	$128.52	$385.56
	Total Furniture & Fixtures	**$3,600.00**		**$42.84**	**$514.08**	**$514.08**	**$514.08**	**$1,542.24**
	TOTALS	**$42,550.00**		**$478.33**	**$5,739.96**	**$5,739.96**	**$5,739.96**	**17219.88**

After this entry is entered into the computer, you can look at the accounts that were posted in the General Ledger and see what the balances are at the end of December.

By comparing the General Ledger balances in the Accumulated Depreciation accounts to the information on the depreciation schedule, you can see how the information on the schedule is transferred into the accounting system.

The following General Ledger report shows the balances in the Asset and Accumulated Depreciation accounts for John Carter, DDS, at the end of December.

General Ledger Report of Asset and Accumulated Depreciation Accounts.

John Carter DDS Inc.
GENERAL JOURNAL REPORT
12/1/00 TO 12/31/00

Date: 12/31/00   Ref No: AJ-2
Desc: To record monthly depreciation expense.

GL ACCOUNT / NAME	DEBIT	CREDIT
1401 A.D. Leasehold Improvements		213.33
1501 A.D. Furniture & Fixtures		42.84
1551 A.D. Equipment		222.16
6530 Depreciation Expense	478.33	
Total:	478.33	478.33
GENERAL JOURNAL TOTAL:	478.33	478.33

These reports are yet another example of how each piece of accounting information joins with the other data to form the complete financial picture of a business enterprise.

The last posting to be done on Carter's books is the Accounts Payable entry. Here is a listing of the bills that were incurred in December that will not be paid out of the checking account until January:

Dental Services, Inc.	$2,763.00
Niagra Dental Supplies	478.75
A to Z Office Supplies	132.00
Allied Insurance Brokers	71.00

	$3,444.75

Once this entry is posted, you can examine one of the accounts in the General Ledger and see how this entry has been recorded there. On the following page is the General Ledger report for Dental Supplies (Account 5100).

As you look over this report, you should take note of the beginning balance, which is the balance that is reported on the company's Profit and Loss Statement for November 30, 2000.

You will also see that check #430 was posted to this account on December 15. This check is listed on the Vendor Payment Report. Finally, the entry for the December invoice being set up in Accounts Payable is recorded. The new balance in this account will be the balance of this expense for the month ending December 31, 2000.

GO TO ▶
Refer to Hour 21, "The Monthly Profit and Loss Statement," for information on how all the data from the General Ledger comes together to produce the end-of-the-month financial statement.

End-of-the-month general Journal Entries vary from business to business. You have already studied the inventory adjustments that a manufacturing company or retail business makes. The adjustments depend on the type of business that is being operated.

The thing to remember is that you can make as many entries as you need to capture all the information relevant to the current month.

General Ledger Report for Account 5100.

John Carter DDS Inc.
GENERAL LEDGER REPORT
FOR THE PERIOD 12/1/00 TO 12/31/00

DATE	TT-R	REF NO	DESCRIPTION	DEBIT	CREDIT
1400 Leasehold Improvements					
			Beginning Balance:	25,600.00	
				0.00	0.00
			Ending Balance:	25,600.00	
1401 A.D. Leasehold Improvements					
			Beginning Balance:		7,466.55
12/31/00	GJ-N	AJ-2	To record monthly depreciation	0.00	213.33
			Ending Balance:		7,679.88
1500 Furniture & Fixtures					
			Beginning Balance:	3,600.00	
				0.00	0.00
			Ending Balance:	3,600.00	
1501 A.D. Furniture & Fixtures					
			Beginning Balance:		1,499.40
12/31/00	GJ-N	AJ-2	To record monthly depreciation	0.00	42.84
			Ending Balance:		1,542.24
1550 Equipment					
			Beginning Balance:	13,350.00	
				0.00	0.00
			Ending Balance:	13,350.00	
1551 A.D. Equipment					
			Beginning Balance:		7,775.60
12/31/00	GJ-N	AJ-2	To record monthly depreciation	0.00	222.16
			Ending Balance:		7,997.76
			TOTALS:	0.00	478.33

HOUR'S UP!

Answer the following questions to test your knowledge of Bank Reconciliation and general Journal Entries.

1. General Journal Entries can be made only at the end of the current month.

    a. True

    b. False

2. The bank reconciliation worksheet should include a listing of outstanding checks.

    a. True

    b. False

3. The Depreciation Schedule verifies the amounts posted in:

   a. Depreciation Expense

   b. Accumulated Depreciation

   c. Both

4. The entry to post interest on the savings account is:

   a. Credit Cash in Checking, debit Interest Income

   b. Credit Sales, debit Cash in Savings

   c. Debit Cash in Savings, credit Interest Income

5. All businesses have depreciation Expenses.

   a. True

   b. False

6. A Deposit in Transit is a deposit that has not been posted in the General Ledger.

   a. True

   b. False

7. The balance in the operating account should be checked and verified before the financial statements are issued.

   a. True

   b. False

8. If the checkbook balance is more than the General Ledger balance of Cash in Checking, review the checks to be sure they were all posted.

   a. True

   b. False

9. Deposits recorded in the checkbook should be posted to the General Ledger as:

   a. General Journal Entries

   b. Cash receipts or sales

   c. Cash disbursements

10. A discrepancy amount that can be divided by 9 is likely to be:

   a. A debit posted as a credit

   b. An addition error

   c. A transposition error

QUIZ

Hour 19

The Trial Balance

Chapter Summary

LESSON PLAN:

In this hour you will learn about ...

- Reviewing the General Ledger accounts
- How the financial statements evolve
- Formatting the Profit and Loss Statements

Financial statements and many of the other reports that are generated by an accounting system are carefully reviewed by business owners and managers; the Trial Balance is a report that they rarely see. The Trial Balance is a report that is generated for the accountant.

This report enables the accountant to do a final review of the year-to-date financial data before it is transferred to the Balance Sheet and the Profit and Loss statements.

Reviewing the General Ledger Accounts

The Trial Balance is a report that lists all of the accounts in the General Ledger and their year-to-date balances. With all the information consolidated onto one report, you can review each account balance and check it against other reports and information. For example, the total in the Salaries & Wages account can be verified by looking back at the totals on the employee ledger cards.

In a computerized system, the Trial Balance can be printed out quickly and easily. In a manual system, like that of Caricatures by Ed, the accountant has to go through the General Ledger, make sure that all the accounts are totaled, and then transfer the balances to the Trial Balance. The accountant also adds columns to the Trial Balance to record the current month's transactions because that information is needed to produce the financial statements that are done manually.

The following Trial Balance worksheet is a sample of one that could be made up for Caricatures by Ed. The figures are based on the November financial statements and the December transactions.

Manual Trial Balance for Caricatures by Ed.

Caricatures By Ed

Trial Balance December 31, 2000

Acct #	Description	Balance 11-30-00	Transactions December 2000 Debit	Transactions December 2000 Credit	Balance 12-31-00
1000	Cash in Checking	177450	295900	<196550>	276800
1050	Cash on Hand	10000			10000
2100	Sales Tax Collected	<9150>	9150	<14092>	<14092>
3210	Capital	<50000>			<50000>
3220	Draw	796900	125000		921900
3040	Retained Earnings	<925200>		<219408>	<1144608>
		-0-	430050	430050	-0-
4000	Sales	<1830000>		<281808>	<2111808>
5100	Advertising	57400	2500		59900
5150	Auto Expense	52600			52600
6300	office Expense	-0-			-0-
6360	Rent	550000	50000		600000
6520	Supplies	244800	9900		254700
	Net Profit	<925200>	62400	<281808>	<1144608>

December Profit 2194.08

TIME SAVER

For a manual system, make up a form based on the sample on four-column paper listing all the accounts in your General Ledger. The form can then be photocopied, and the copies can be used as a Trial Balance worksheet each month.

A lot of information is contained on this sample, so take some extra time to study it. Verifying the source of this information will require that you look back on Hour 15, "Cash Receipts Journal"; Hour 16, "Cash Disbursements Journal"; and Hour 18, "Reconciling the Bank Accounts and the General Journal Entries," for the prior month's financial statements, cash receipts, cash disbursements, and adjustments. All of these balances and transactions would be in Ed's General Ledger.

The Trial Balance worksheet is done on four-column paper, and the General Ledger accounts are listed in the same order as they appear in the General Ledger and the financial statements.

The first numerical column to be filled in is for the beginning balances or the balances from the financial statements issued on November 30, 2000.

Columns 2 and 3 are used to record the totals posted to each account during the month of December. Debits are recorded in Column 2, and credits are posted in Column 3. Note that some of the accounts, such as Cash in Checking and Sales Tax Collected, have both debits and credits posted in December.

The debit posted to Cash in Checking is the total of all the bank deposits that resulted from Ed's cash receipts or sales journal in December. The credits in this account resulted from the checks that were written and posted as cash disbursements.

In the Sales Tax Collected account, the debit is the check that was written to pay the sales tax for the prior month. The credit is the sales tax collected for the month of December.

The Draw account had one entry posted in December for the check that Ed wrote to himself to draw money out of the business account.

The current month's profit has been added to the Retained Earnings account. Because this is a manual system, and because it is also Ed's first year in business the net profit is also the Retained Earnings. If desired, you could show the profit for the first 11 months as Retained Earnings and the current month profit as a separate figure.

GO TO ▶
Refer to Hour 16, "Cash Disbursements Journal," for instructions on paying taxes and posting the payments to the General Ledger accounts.

PROCEED WITH CAUTION

In a computerized accounting system, the net profit is automatically posted to the Balance Sheet when the financial statements are printed. Only in a manual system does the accountant have to manually insert the current month's net profit into the Balance Sheet.

The December sales have been posted to the Income account, and the Expenses are posted to the expense accounts. This information will be used to produce the current month totals on the Profit and Loss Statement.

Column 4 has the year-to-date balances or the final balances in the General Ledger accounts. This column of figures will be presented on the Balance Sheet and on the year-to-date section of the Profit and Loss Statement. This column is the total of the first three columns.

For instance, if you take all the information recorded in the Cash in Checking row, it equals the final balance for that account.

Cash in Checking:

1,774.50	(Column 1: Balance 11-30-00)
+2,959.00	(Column 2: December Debit Transactions)
−1,965.50	(Column 3: December Credit Transactions)

2,768.00	(Column 4: Balance 12-31-00)

Once all the information is set forth on the worksheet, it is separated into the Balance Sheet section and the Profit and Loss section.

The columns are added in each section to make sure they are in balance. In the Balance Sheet section, columns 1 and 4 should add up to zero. Columns 2 and 3 should add up to the same totals for debits and credits. Remember, debits should always equal credits, resulting in a zero balance when they are added together.

Since this is Ed's first year in business, the total of Column 1 in the Profit and Loss section should be the same as the Retained Earnings in the Balance Sheet section.

JUST A MINUTE

If a business has been in existence for more than a year, the Balance Sheet section will have designations for retained Earnings (prior years) and net profit (current year).

Columns 2 and 3 in the Profit and Loss section are totaled; the sum of these two columns should be the Net Profit posted in the Balance Sheet section. The year-to-date Column 4 will have the same total as the Retained Earnings in the Balance Sheet section.

Essentially, once figures are entered into a computerized accounting system, the computer automatically compiles all the information needed for the financial statements, separating the current month's information from the year-to-date information. However, going through the process manually gives you a better understanding of how it all works.

This is important because it gives you the basic knowledge you need to manage any accounting system. If you enter information into a computer incorrectly, it will take that incorrect information and process it as if it were accurate. Using a computer does not ensure accuracy. Knowing what financial data has to be entered and how to enter it is what enables the computer to produce accurate reports.

Remember, the worksheet presented in this hour is a suggested format. It is designed to show you how information and totals are cross-checked and verified. You may want to devise your own format for a manual Trial Balance worksheet.

The Trial Balance report printed from John Carter's computerized accounting system presents the information in a different format. Again, remember that the balances shown for each account are the year-to-date balances for that account. You have seen the reports for the current month's transactions and Carter's financial statements for the previous month.

In a computerized system, information is easily accessed. If any of the information on the Trial Balance report raises a question, you can go to the General Ledger report for that specific account and check on the postings.

You have already seen samples of the General Ledger reports for various accounts in Carter's accounting system. You have also reviewed the information that was posted to some of these accounts by looking at the reports for cash receipts, sales, cash disbursements, and general Journal Entries.

JUST A MINUTE

Often the Trial Balance is used as a reference tool. It is a one-page report that can be printed quickly and easily, and it contains information that can be used for posting Accounts Payable and federal tax deposits.

The Trial Balance for John Carter, DDS, that reflects all the transactions and accounts you have been studying is shown in the following figure.

Trial Balance.

John Carter DDS Inc.
TRIAL BALANCE
December 31, 2000

GL ACCOUNT/NAME	DEBIT	CREDIT
1000 Cash in Checking	26,537.10	
1050 Savings Account	42,312.00	
1080 Petty Cash	50.00	
1100 Accounts Receivable	8,059.00	
1400 Leasehold Improvements	25,600.00	
1401 A.D. Leasehold Improvements		7,679.88
1500 Furniture & Fixtures	3,600.00	
1501 A.D. Furniture & Fixtures		1,542.24
1550 Equipment	13,350.00	
1551 A.D. Equipment		7,997.76
2000 Accounts Payable		3,444.75
2200 Federal Withholding Tax Payable		3,317.52
2210 Social Security Tax Payable		471.20
2212 Medicare Withholding Tax Payable		449.50
2220 State Withholding Taxes Payable		995.28
2300 Loan Payable-Merchants Bank		25,000.16
3040 Retained Earnings		28,328.94
3210 Capital		10,000.00
4000 Fees - Patients		351,903.00
4200 Interest Income		1,512.00
5100 Dental Supplies	10,804.70	
5150 Brochures and Catalogues	4,585.00	
5230 Laboratory Fees	68,483.00	
5650 Rent	18,000.00	
6000 Salaries & Wages	186,000.00	
6030 Telephone	1,015.30	
6050 Utilities - Gas & Electric	2,409.50	
6140 Office Supplies & Postage	1,942.55	
6160 Dues & Subscriptions	560.00	
6180 Educational Expense	919.95	
6220 Insurance - General	3,547.00	
6230 Insurance - Employee Group	3,936.00	
6240 License Fees	300.00	
6490 Taxes - Payroll	10,891.21	
6510 Interest Expense	3,999.96	
6530 Depreciation Expense	5,739.96	
TOTALS:	442,642.23	442,642.23

One thing to note as you review Carter's Trial Balance report is that the debit and credit columns are totaled, and those totals are the same. In other words, debits equal credits.

How the Financial Statements Evolve

The best example of how the financial statements evolve from the General Ledger is shown with the manual worksheet sample for Caricatures by Ed. However, you can look at the computerized Trial Balance and see how the financial information there is lined up in order and ready to be transferred to the Balance Sheet and the Profit and Loss Statement.

In the manual system, the accountant must physically take the information from the Trial Balance and place it in the proper places on the Balance Sheet and the Profit and Loss Statement. Carter's computerized system requires only a few keystrokes to print out the reports. The thing to remember with both systems is the necessary time and effort that goes into compiling the data that has been entered into both systems.

Work papers were prepared so that the information could be laid out and checked for accuracy before it was entered into the system. After the entries were posted, more checks and balances were done to verify that all was correct and in order.

All the lessons in this book have stressed the importance of following the proper accounting procedures because doing so eliminates errors.

FORMATTING THE PROFIT AND LOSS STATEMENT

The financial statements can be formatted in a number of different ways. The format that you have seen so far is the most common one. The current month's figures and the year-to-date figures are presented side by side, with no other additional information.

Some companies—especially small businesses, such as Caricatures by Ed—may print only the year-to-date figures on the Profit and Loss Statement.

It is usually up to the business owner or manager to determine what kind of information should be reflected on the Profit and Loss Statement. As you learned earlier, the financial statements provide crucial data needed to run a successful business.

Many companies like to compare the current year's financial data with the prior year's data. This gives them a gauge by which they can determine whether the business is improving year by year or is falling behind.

Some companies want the Profit and Loss Statement to include percentages. A restaurant, for instance, needs to know what its food costs are, and that can be presented on the Profit and Loss Statement. An additional column is added to display the percentages.

What percentage of the profits is going for each expense can be displayed on the Income statement. Using the information on Carter's Trial Balance, you can figure the percentage of his Income that is being spent on dental supplies.

GO TO ▶
Refer to Hour 21, "The Monthly Profit and Loss Statement," for information on tailoring the financial statements to a company's specific needs.

Divide the cost of the dental supplies ($10,804) by the gross Income ($351,903) to discover that Carter is paying out 3 percent of his Income for Dental Supplies. Using the same formula, you will find that approximately 19 percent is being spent on lab fees.

Companies can also have budget information included in the financial statements. In this format, the expense totals can be compared to the budget to see if they are over or under what was projected.

Start out with a standard format for the financial statements, and add percentages and comparisons as needed or requested.

HOUR'S UP!

The Trial Balance is an important part of the accounting system. See how much you have learned about it by answering the following questions.

1. The Trial Balance is taken from:
   a. The check register
   b. The Cash Receipts Journal
   c. The General Ledger

2. The Trial Balance is sometimes used as a reference tool.
   a. True
   b. False

3. A debit to Cash in Checking means that a check was posted.
   a. True
   b. False

4. The Trial Balance reflects year-to-date financial data.
   a. True
   b. False

5. If a question arises about a balance listed on the Trial Balance, you can check on it by:
   a. Looking at the postings in the General Ledger
   b. Calling the bank
   c. Reviewing the cash receipts

6. A computerized accounting system automatically corrects data entry errors.

   a. True

   b. False

7. A work paper for a manual Trial Balance can include both the current month and the year to date information.

   a. True

   b. False

8. The most common format for Profit and Loss Statements is:

   a. Current month and year-to-date figures

   b. Prior year and year-to-date figures

   c. Current year and budget figures

9. The balance in Cash in Checking at the end of the month reflects all the transactions that went through the operating account.

   a. True

   b. False

10. A Profit and Loss Statement can be formatted to include:

   a. Percentages

   b. Budget information

   c. Prior year's data

   d. All of the above

QUIZ

PART V

Financial Statements

Hour 20

The Monthly Balance Sheet

At this point, all the cash receipts, sales, disbursements, and payroll information have been entered into your accounting system.

You have also reconciled the bank statements with the General Ledger cash accounts, entered adjustments such as interest Income and depreciation Expenses, and set up your Accounts Payable for payment and posted it to the General Ledger.

The Trial Balance has been prepared and reviewed and found to be in good order as well. It's time to issue the financial statements. The first report to be prepared is the monthly Balance Sheet.

In this hour, you will see how all the financial data that has been processed for Caricatures by Ed and John Carter, DDS, comes together and is presented on the Balance Sheet.

Producing the Balance Sheet

In a manual system such as the one used by Caricatures by Ed, the accounting information must be taken from the Trial Balance worksheet and put onto the Balance Sheet.

Although the monthly transactions affect the Balance Sheet accounts, they are not reported separately—instead, they are included in the year-to-date balances.

GO TO ▶
Refer to Hour 19, "The Trial Balance," for information on the working Trial Balance for a manual accounting system.

Based on the working Trial Balance for Caricatures by Ed, the following Balance Sheet has been issued for December 31, 2000:

Caricatures by Ed

Balance Sheet

December 31, 2000

Assets:	
Cash in Checking	$ 2,768.00
Cash on Hand	100.00

Total Assets	$ 2,868.00
Liabilities:	
Sales Tax Collected	140.92

Total Liabilities	140.92
Equity:	
Capital	500.00
Draw	(9,219.00)
Retained Earnings	11,446.08

Total Liabilities & Equity	$2,868.00

GO TO ▶
Refer to Hour 3, "Chart of Accounts Becomes the General Ledger," to find a listing of the accounts, along with a chart showing accounts that are normally credits and accounts that are normally debits.

One thing should be noted on this Balance Sheet. Although it has been explained in other lessons, it bears repeating: The account balances in the Assets section of the Balance Sheet are debits. The account balances in the Liability and Equity sections are credits, with the exception of the Draw account.

The balance for Ed's Draw account is shown in brackets. Don't let that confuse you—remember that this is done because it is a debit in an area normally considered to hold credit balances. The brackets indicate that the balance of that account is being subtracted from the other balances in that section of the Balance Sheet.

Ed's Balance Sheet is a simple statement because his business is a small one-man retail operation. His only liability is the sales tax he collects; he has no payroll or payroll taxes.

John Carter, DDS, has a more detailed Balance Sheet report because his dental practice is a larger business with employees, taxes, and other Assets and Liabilities.

As you review the Balance Sheet for John Carter, DDS, you will be able to relate the information it contains with many of the entries and adjustments studied earlier. You will see how the December adjustments have changed the balances you originally reviewed on Carter's November Balance Sheet.

You can go back and review the entries that increased or decreased balances in specific accounts. This will give you a better understanding of how these financial reports evolve.

Take note of the following:

- Increase in Savings Account
- Decrease in Accounts Receivable
- Increase in Accumulated Depreciation accounts
- Decrease in Accounts Payable
- Increase in Payroll Taxes Payable
- Decrease in Loan Payable–Merchants Bank

Keep in mind that the federal tax deposit cleared the November balances. These balances were replaced by the taxes for the December payroll. All the employees are salaried and earn the same amount each pay period; therefore, the taxes for November and December are the same. The Payroll Taxes Payable account has increased because of the state withholding taxes that are paid quarterly rather than monthly.

The following Balance Sheet is for John Carter, DDS, and reports the balances as of December 31, 2000.

Carter's Balance Sheet was, of course, printed as a computerized report from his accounting system. Ed's Balance Sheet was typed up using the information from the working Trial Balance.

How the reports were produced is less important than the fact that the net result is the same. Both reports contain verified accurate information from the individual accounting systems.

TIME SAVER

For a manual accounting system, the format for the Balance Sheet can be typed up and photocopied so that, at the end of the month, the figures can simply be inserted on the preprinted form.

Balance Sheet Report.

John Carter DDS Inc.
BALANCE SHEET
December 31, 2000

ASSETS

CURRENT ASSETS

Cash in Checking	$	26,537.10
Savings Account		42,312.00
Petty Cash		50.00
Accounts Receivable		8,059.00

TOTAL CURRENT ASSETS		$	76,958.10

Leasehold Improvements	$	25,600.00
A.D. Leasehold Improvements		(7,679.88)

PROPERTY AND EQUIPMENT

Furniture & Fixtures	3,600.00
A.D. Furniture & Fixtures	(1,542.24)
Equipment	13,350.00
A.D. Equipment	(7,997.76)

TOTAL PROPERTY AND EQUIPMENT	$	7,410.00
TOTAL ASSETS	$	102,288.22

John Carter DDS Inc.
BALANCE SHEET
December 31, 2000

LIABILITIES AND EQUITY

CURRENT LIABILITIES

Accounts Payable	$	3,444.75
PAYROLL TAXES PAYABLE		5,233.50
CURRENT PORTION LONG-TERM DEBT		25,000.16

TOTAL CURRENT LIABILITIES	$	33,678.41

EQUITY

Retained Earnings	$	28,328.94
Capital		10,000.00
NET INCOME (LOSS)		30,280.87

TOTAL EQUITY	$	68,609.81
TOTAL LIABILITIES AND EQUITY	$	102,288.22

THE BALANCE SHEET AS A MANAGEMENT TOOL

Carter's Balance Sheet gives you a good overall view of his financial condition. Knowing how to interpret the financial information on the Balance Sheet report will help you understand why these reports are so important.

Managers and financial professionals use the Balance Sheet information to make business decisions. A banker, for instance, would look at Carter's Balance Sheet and see that even though the company has an outstanding loan, the corporation is stable enough to take on another liability. That is because the Balance Sheet shows that Carter's current Assets are more than two times greater than the total of his current and long-term Liabilities.

The other positive thing that stands out on Carter's Balance Sheet is that his property and equipment still have a good amount of useful life. That is, these depreciable Assets will not have to be replaced in the near future.

Still another point in Carter's favor is the fact that the current year's profit exceeds his retained earnings for the last two years. This is a sign of constant and substantial growth.

As for Carter himself, looking at the Balance Sheet as the manager of his own dental office, he might consider expanding the practice by hiring another dentist or a dental assistant who could take care of routine things like cleanings, freeing up his time for more expensive procedures.

Overall, the Balance Sheet shows the solvency of a company. Even a small enterprise such as Caricatures by Ed can use the information on the Balance Sheet to make management decisions.

For example, based on the financial picture presented on his report, Ed can see that working in the mall only two days a week is a profitable part-time business. He has only invested $500 to get the business started, and now at the end of his first year, he may consider adding some inventory, such as picture frames that could be sold with his drawings.

GO TO ▶
Refer to Hour 21, "The Monthly Profit and Loss Statement," to review the Income statements and learn how this information is used.

All the financial reports contain valuable information. While the Profit and Loss Statement is also used to make management decisions, it presents the financial picture in another way and focuses on other details.

By now you should have a good grasp of the Balance Sheet, its components, and how it is used. With this knowledge, you can produce this report from the accounting data of any type of business.

HOUR'S UP!

Here are some questions about the Balance Sheet that you should be able to answer without looking back on this hour's lesson.

1. Which of the following accounts appears in the Liabilities section of the Balance Sheet?

   a. Cash on Hand

   b. Accounts Payable

   c. Leasehold Improvements

2. The Balance Sheet contains year-to-date financial data.

   a. True

   b. False

3. Which of the following accounts appears in the Assets section of the Balance Sheet?

   a. Capital

   b. Payroll Taxes Payable

   c. Equipment

4. Long-term debts such as bank loans can be found in the Assets section of the Balance Sheet.

   a. True

   b. False

5. Which of the following is included in Payroll Taxes Payable on the Balance Sheet?

   a. Federal withholding tax

   b. Social Security tax

   c. State withholding tax

   d. All of the above

6. The Balance Sheet reflects the financial stability of a company.

   a. True

   b. False

7. Accounts Receivable can be found in what section of the Balance Sheet?

    a. Assets

    b. Liabilities

    c. Equity

8. If the Current Assets on the Balance Sheet are greater than all the Liabilities, the company is considered a good banking risk.

    a. True

    b. False

9. The Accumulated Depreciation accounts can be found in what section of the Balance Sheet?

    a. Assets

    b. Liabilities

    c. Equity

10. The current month's Accounts Payable should be included on the Balance Sheet.

    a. True

    b. False

QUIZ

Hour 21

The Monthly Profit and Loss Statement

LESSON PLAN:

In this hour you will learn about ...

- Issuing the Profit and Loss Statement
- Using the Profit and Loss Statement
- Tailoring the statement to specific needs

The Profit and Loss Statement is the second half of the monthly financial statements. This is the report that tracks the overall success or failure of the daily business operation.

The Profit and Loss Statement, or the Income statement, as it is often called, is a simple, straightforward report. It is this report that provides the infamous *bottom line* of the business enterprise.

STRICTLY DEFINED

The **bottom line** is the net profit or loss that appears on the Income statement. This amount is the last figure on the report—hence, it is called the bottom line.

While all the information on the Profit and Loss Statement is related to the information on the Balance Sheet, it is structured to provide a more detailed accounting of the day-to-day business operations.

Again, all the transactions and adjustments reviewed and posted in previous hours have been compiled into the final account balances reported on the Profit and Loss Statement.

ISSUING THE PROFIT AND LOSS STATEMENT

The remainder of the financial data included on the Trial Balance prepared for Caricatures by Ed can now be transferred to the Profit and Loss Statement for this small business.

As you examine this report, you can refer back to the Trial Balance to see how the current month and year-to-date figures were used to make up the Profit and Loss Statement.

Caricatures by Ed

Income Statement as of December 31, 2000

	December 1 through December 31, 2000	January 1 through December 31, 2000
Income:		
Sales	$2,818.08	$21,118.08
Total Income	$2,818.08	$21,118.08
Expenses:		
Advertising Expense	25.00	599.00
Auto Expense	-0-	526.00
Rent Expense	500.00	6,000.00
Supplies	99.00	2,547.00
Total Expenses	$ 624.00	$ 9,672.00
Net Profit (Loss)	$2,194.08	$11,446.08

GO TO ▶ Refer to Hour 22, "End-of-the-Year Payroll and Other Tax Reports," to learn how a sole proprietor's financial information is used on his or her personal tax return.

The information on Ed's Profit and Loss Statement as of December 31, 2000, will be used to complete his personal tax return.

As you move on to the December statement for John Carter, DDS, you will once again be able to make the connections between this final report and the transactions and adjustments you learned about in previous hours.

The figure on the following page is the Income Statement or Profit and Loss Statement for John Carter, DDS, for the period ending December 31, 2000.

Using the petty cash reimbursement as an example, you can look at Carter's Income statement and see that the amount paid out of Petty Cash for a book and posted as an Educational Expense is indeed shown as an expense in that account for the month of December. Payroll taxes is another expense that can be tracked back to entries for the month of December.

Income Statement.

		December 01, 2000 To December 31, 2000		January 01, 2000 To December 31, 2000
John Carter DDS Inc. **INCOME STATEMENT** **For The Period**				
INCOME				
Fees - Patients	$	23,303.00	$	351,903.00
Interest Income		312.00		1,512.00
Total INCOME	$	23,615.00	$	353,415.00
EXPENSES				
Dental Supplies	$	553.70	$	10,804.70
Brochures and Catalogues		185.00		4,585.00
Laboratory Fees		2,763.00		68,483.00
Rent		1,500.00		18,000.00
Salaries & Wages		15,500.00		186,000.00
Telephone		87.30		1,015.30
Utilities - Gas & Electric		199.50		2,409.50
Office Supplies & Postage		290.55		1,942.55
Dues & Subscriptions		0.00		560.00
Educational Expense		29.95		919.95
Insurance - General		71.00		3,547.00
Insurance - Employee Group		328.00		3,936.00
License Fees		50.00		300.00
Taxes - Payroll		460.34		10,891.21
Interest Expense		333.33		3,999.96
Depreciation Expense		478.33		5,739.96
Total EXPENSES	$	22,830.00	$	323,134.13
Total NET OPERATING INCOME (LOSS)	$	785.00	$	30,280.87
NET INCOME (LOSS) BEFORE TAX	$	785.00	$	30,280.87
NET INCOME (LOSS)	$	785.00	$	30,280.87

Relating the financial data back to the monthly entries and adjustments has been stressed over and over again. That's because it is a vital part of understanding accounting in general. If you are able to look at a financial statement and know the source of the reported data, you have mastered a big part of the accounting process.

Once you know the basics and the principles of accounting, you will be to apply them to any type business. If you step into an accounting position at an existing business, you can do it with confidence.

Each business has its own patterns and routines, and an accountant—or any employee, for that matter—who is new to the company will have to learn the specific procedures of the operation. However, the accounting system will conform to the accepted standards.

Every business deals with banks, taxing entities, vendors, and customers. Standard procedures are not only expected, but also mandatory for a business enterprise to function. The accounting system must follow a standard course from the first transaction to the financial statements.

USING THE PROFIT AND LOSS STATEMENT

You should also look back on the financial statements for both companies to see if there are notable differences in Income and net profit.

Comparing Carter's November statement to the one just issued for December, you will find that the Income for December is $5,000 less than in the previous month. However, the Expenses have dropped only $2,000. These differences are then reflected in the net profit that is $3,000 less than that of November.

Any time there is a significant drop in Income, it bears analyzing and investigating. Most likely, in this case the difference in Income can be attributed to the time of the year. December is a busy month with holidays, shopping, and the end of the year looming close. Patients might tend not to schedule dental work in December, but to put it off until the new year.

JUST A MINUTE

Since Carter's dental practice is 3 years old, copies of his financial statements would be available for the prior years, and you could look back to see if the month of December is typically a month when Income is lower.

As far as Carter's Expenses, they would not drop by as large a margin as his Income, even though he was seeing fewer patients. His largest Expenses, payroll, rent, and utilities would stay the same. Again, looking back at prior years' statements would tell whether there is a reason for concern.

On the other hand, Caricatures by Ed experienced a substantial increase in sales in the month of December, while his Expenses have actually decreased. Logic will dictate that the reason for this is also the time of year. While Carter's Income took a dip because of the holidays, the sales of a retail business would be higher.

TAILORING THE INCOME STATEMENT TO SPECIFIC NEEDS

Hour 19, "The Trial Balance," introduced you to other formats that can be used for Profit and Loss Statements. One of them was the comparative statement.

In January, Ed will begin his second year in business. This will give him an opportunity to compare his financial data from the prior year to that of the current year. If desired, an additional column can be set up on the Income statement to list the Income and Expenses from the same month of the prior year. With the information laid out like this, it will be easy for Ed to see if the business is growing or staying constant.

Comparative statements are standard for some companies. The managers of retail and manufacturing companies are especially interested in this type of Income statement. Obviously, the ability to compare sales from one year to another is a valuable management tool. Computerized accounting systems can be programmed to issue statements in this format.

GO TO ▶

Refer to Hour 24, "Accounting Software Programs," to learn about the different features of computerized accounting programs and how to use them.

The other statement format introduced in Hour 19 was one in which percentages are displayed showing how much of the total Income is expended for each expense. This is a very common format used by many companies. It allows management to track Expenses in an explicit manner, relating each one back to the total Income.

The percentages show how the current month's Expenses connect with the current month's Income. Another set of percentages shows how the year-to-date Expenses connect to the Income for the year.

As an example of this format, study the following report based on Carter's financial data.

Looking at this percentage format, you can see that the biggest expense Carter has is payroll. This is not unusual for a personal service business such as a dental practice. The core of the business is the professional who is performing the service.

The percentages for other Expenses such as rent and utilities are fairly low for this dental practice. In other businesses, rent and utilities might have much larger percentages in relation to sales. A restaurant, for instance, may find that a more expensive, prestigious location is a wise expenditure because the ambiance contributes to the diners' enjoyment and brings them back more often.

Income Statement for John Carter, DDS, Percentage Format.

	John Carter DDS Inc. INCOME STATEMENT For The Period				
	December 01, 2000 To December 31, 2000	Pct%		January 01, 2000 To December 31, 2000	Pct%
INCOME					
Fees - Patients	$ 23,303.00	98.68	$	351,903.00	99.57
Interest Income	312.00	1.32		1,512.00	0.43
Total INCOME	$ 23,615.00	100.00	$	353,415.00	100.00
EXPENSES					
Dental Supplies	$ 553.70	2.34	$	10,804.70	3.06
Brochures and Catalogues	185.00	0.78		4,585.00	1.30
Laboratory Fees	2,763.00	11.70		68,483.00	19.38
Rent	1,500.00	6.35		18,000.00	5.09
Salaries & Wages	15,500.00	65.64		186,000.00	52.63
Telephone	87.30	0.37		1,015.30	0.29
Utilities - Gas & Electric	199.50	0.84		2,409.50	0.68
Office Supplies & Postage	290.55	1.23		1,942.55	0.55
Dues & Subscriptions	0.00	0.00		560.00	0.16
Educational Expense	29.95	0.13		919.95	0.26
Insurance - General	71.00	0.30		3,547.00	1.00
Insurance - Employee Group	328.00	1.39		3,936.00	1.11
License Fees	50.00	0.21		300.00	0.08
Taxes - Payroll	460.34	1.95		10,891.21	3.08
Interest Expense	333.33	1.41		3,999.96	1.13
Depreciation Expense	478.33	2.03		5,739.96	1.62
Total EXPENSES	$ 22,830.00	96.68	$	323,134.13	91.43
Total NET OPERATING INCOME (LOSS)	$ 785.00	3.32	$	30,280.87	8.57
NET INCOME (LOSS) BEFORE TAX	$ 785.00	3.32	$	30,280.87	8.57
NET INCOME (LOSS)	$ 785.00	3.32	$	30,280.87	8.57

Also take note of how the percentages of certain Expenses increase or decrease when that expense is compared on a year-to-date basis. The payroll percentage, for example, is 65.64 percent for the month of December because the Income figure is lower than usual. The payroll percentage for the year goes down considerably when it is applied to the total Income.

The various formats that can be used for the Profit and Loss Statement provide specific information for specific businesses.

The initial process to tailor the statements to the needs of the company may take some extra time and effort. Nevertheless, it is worth the additional work because the information is so valuable. Also, once the format is put into place in the accounting system, it will be easy to manage.

HOUR'S UP!

You have now progressed through the final accounting report for the month. Try to answer these questions relating to the Profit and Loss Statement.

1. The current month's percentage reported for an expense is always the same as the year-to-date percentage.

    a. True

    b. False

2. The information for the Income statement can be taken directly from the Trial Balance.

    a. True

    b. False

3. Which of the following accounts can be found on the Profit and Loss Statement?

    a. Accounts Payable

    b. Cash on Hand

    c. Telephone Expense

4. Every expense on the Profit and Loss Statement can be traced back to the month's transactions and adjustments.

    a. True

    b. False

5. The principles of accounting cannot be applied to every business.

    a. True

    b. False

6. The amount a company has paid out for hospitalization insurance can be found in which of the following accounts?

    a. Insurance–Employees' Group

    b. Insurance–General

    c. Office Expense

7. A reduction in Income from one month to another should always be investigated.

    a. True

    b. False

8. Tailoring a statement to the specific needs of a company is often a waste of time and effort.

   a. True

   b. False

9. The bottom line is:

   a. Net profit or loss

   b. Total Expenses

   c. Net Income

10. Which of the following statements gives an overall look at the day-to-day business operation?

    a. Balance Sheet

    b. Accounts Receivable

    c. Profit and Loss statement

HOUR 22

End-of-the-Year Payroll Reports and Other Tax Reports

CHAPTER SUMMARY

LESSON PLAN:

In this hour you will learn about ...

- W-2s for employees
- 1099s for vendors
- Completing the Federal Unemployment Tax Report
- Personal and business tax returns

At the end of the calendar year, a number of tax reports must be completed and filed. Unless your business is incorporated and the corporation operates on a fiscal year that ends sometime other than December 31, which only means that the corporation tax return is not due at this time. All the other tax reports are due in accordance with the regulations set forth by the IRS.

As everyone is aware, personal tax returns are due on April 15 each year. To give everyone time to gather the information needed for their personal tax returns, the government has set deadlines for employers to follow.

Employees must receive their yearly statement of wages and taxes no later than January 31. This is the same date that the payroll reports for the last quarter of the year are due. The payroll reports for the quarter ending December 31 are done in exactly the same way as the reports for the other three quarters of the year.

In addition to wages, companies are required to report to the IRS any miscellaneous payments that exceed $600 made to individuals or companies. This includes the allowances given to employees to defray Expenses. These payments are reported to the IRS on Form 1099.

In this hour, you will learn how to complete and file the various reports and forms that must be issued at the end of the year.

GO TO ▶ Refer to Hour 14, "Payroll Tax Reports," for instructions and samples for quarterly payroll reports.

W-2s FOR EMPLOYEES

If your payroll is done by a payroll service, the W-2s and the end-of-the-year payroll tax reports will most likely be issued as part of the service. However, as you have been told repeatedly, the accountant still must have a working knowledge of these reports and forms, as well as the rules and regulations that go along with them.

The information for the W-2s comes from the employee payroll ledgers. John Carter, DDS, has three employees, and the following payroll ledgers have been completed for each one of them.

John Carter Payroll Ledger.

John Carter DDS   555-55-5555   1111 N. Mason Avenue, Starcrest, AZ 85755

Date	Gross Wages	SS Tax	Medicare Tax	FWH	SWH	Net Check
1st Qtr.	$35,100.00	$2,176.20	$508.98	$8,356.56	$835.68	$23,222.58
2nd Qtr.	$35,100.00	$2,176.20	$508.98	$8,356.56	$835.68	$23,222.58
3rd Qtr.	$35,100.00	$372.00	$508.98	$8,356.56	$835.68	$25,026.78
4th Qtr.	$35,100.00	$0.00	$508.98	$8,356.56	$835.68	$25,398.78
T-2000	$140,400.00	$4,724.40	$2,035.92	$33,426.24	$3,342.72	$96,870.72

Judy Carter Payroll Ledger.

Judy Carter   666-66-6666   1111 N. Mason Avenue, Starcrest, AZ 85755

Date	Gross Wages	SS Tax	Medicare Tax	FWH	SWH	Net Check
1st Qtr.	$3,000.00	$186.00	$43.50	$216.00	$21.60	$2,532.90
2nd Qtr.	$3,000.00	$186.00	$43.50	$216.00	$21.60	$2,532.90
3rd Qtr.	$3,000.00	$186.00	$43.50	$216.00	$21.60	$2,532.90
4th Qtr.	$3,000.00	$186.00	$43.50	$216.00	$21.60	$2,532.90
T-2000	$12,000.00	$744.00	$174.00	$864.00	$86.40	$10,131.60

Mary Jones		777-77-7777	255 S. 49th St. Starcrest, AZ 85755			
Date	Gross Wages	SS Tax	Medicare Tax	FWH	SWH	Net Check
1st Qtr.	$8,400.00	$520.80	$121.80	$1,380.00	$138.00	$6,239.40
2nd Qtr.	$8,400.00	$520.80	$121.80	$1,380.00	$138.00	$6,239.40
3rd Qtr.	$8,400.00	$520.80	$121.80	$1,380.00	$138.00	$6,239.40
4th Qtr.	$8,400.00	$520.80	$121.80	$1,380.00	$138.00	$6,239.40
T-2000	$33,600.00	$2,083.20	$487.20	$5,520.00	$552.00	$24,957.60

Mary Jones Payroll Ledger.

As you look over these employee ledgers, you should be able to see how the figures correspond with the monthly Payroll Journal from Carter's payroll service that you reviewed earlier.

The payroll figures in the preceding samples are totaled by quarter because that information is needed to prepare the quarterly reports. Each ledger also has a total for the year, and that is the information that will be transferred to the employees' individual W-2 forms.

The sample W-2s that follow were completed using the information from the sample employee ledgers.

GO TO ▶

Refer to Hour 17, "Payroll Journal and Employee Expense Accounts," for samples and instructions for posting information from the Payroll Journal.

Mary Jones W-2.

a Control number		OMB No. 1545-0008		
b Employer identification number 00-000000			1 Wages, tips, other compensation 33,600.00	2 Federal income tax withheld 5,520.00
c Employer's name, address, and ZIP code John Carter, DDS Inc. 82 Apple Grove Starcrest, AZ 85755			3 Social security wages 33,600.00	4 Social security tax withheld 2,083.20
			5 Medicare wages and tips 33,600.00	6 Medicare tax withheld 487.20
			7 Social security tips	8 Allocated tips
d Employee's social security number 777-77-7777			9 Advance EIC payment	10 Dependent care benefits
e Employee's name, address, and ZIP code Mary Jones 255 S. 49th St. Starcrest, AZ 85755			11 Nonqualified plans	12 Benefits included in box 1
			13 See instrs. for box 13	14 Other
			15 Statutory employee ☐ Deceased ☐ Pension plan ☐ Legal rep. ☐ Deferred compensation ☐	
16 State Employer's state I.D. no. AZ 00-0000	17 State wages, tips, etc. 33,600.00	18 State income tax 552.00	19 Locality name 20 Local wages, tips, etc.	21 Local income tax

Form **W-2** Wage and Tax Statement **2000**
Copy B To Be Filed With Employee's FEDERAL Tax Return

Department of the Treasury—Internal Revenue Service
This information is being furnished to the Internal Revenue Service.

Judy Carter W-2.

a Control number		OMB No. 1545-0008		
b Employer identification number 00–000000			**1** Wages, tips, other compensation 12,000.00	**2** Federal income tax withheld 864.00
c Employer's name, address, and ZIP code John Carter DDS Inc. 82 Apple Grove Starcrest, AZ 85755			**3** Social security wages 12,000.00	**4** Social security tax withheld 744.00
			5 Medicare wages and tips 12,000.00	**6** Medicare tax withheld 174.00
			7 Social security tips	**8** Allocated tips
d Employee's social security number 666–66–6666			**9** Advance EIC payment	**10** Dependent care benefits
e Employee's name, address, and ZIP code Judy Carter 1111 N. Mason Avenue Starcrest, AZ 85755			**11** Nonqualified plans	**12** Benefits included in box 1
			13 See instrs. for box 13	**14** Other
		15 Statutory employee ☐	Deceased ☐	Pension plan ☐ Legal rep. ☐ Deferred compensation ☐
16 State Employer's state I.D. no. AZ 00–0000	**17** State wages, tips, etc. 12,000.00	**18** State income tax 86.40	**19** Locality name **20** Local wages, tips, etc.	**21** Local income tax

Form **W-2** Wage and Tax Statement **2000**
Copy B To Be Filed With Employee's FEDERAL Tax Return

Department of the Treasury—Internal Revenue Service
This information is being furnished to the Internal Revenue Service.

John Carter W-2.

a Control number		OMB No. 1545-0008		
b Employer identification number 00–000000			**1** Wages, tips, other compensation 140,400.00	**2** Federal income tax withheld 33,426.24
c Employer's name, address, and ZIP code John Carter DDS Inc. 82 Apple Grove Starcrest, AZ 85755			**3** Social security wages 76,200.00	**4** Social security tax withheld 4,724.40
			5 Medicare wages and tips 140,400.00	**6** Medicare tax withheld 2,035.92
			7 Social security tips	**8** Allocated tips
d Employee's social security number 555–55–5555			**9** Advance EIC payment	**10** Dependent care benefits
e Employee's name, address, and ZIP code John Carter 1111 N. Mason Avenue Starcrest, AZ 85755			**11** Nonqualified plans	**12** Benefits included in box 1
			13 See instrs. for box 13	**14** Other
		15 Statutory employee ☐	Deceased ☐	Pension plan ☐ Legal rep. ☐ Deferred compensation ☐
16 State Employer's state I.D. no. AZ 00–0000	**17** State wages, tips, etc. 140,400.00	**18** State income tax 3,342.72	**19** Locality name **20** Local wages, tips, etc.	**21** Local income tax

Form **W-2** Wage and Tax Statement **2000**
Copy B To Be Filed With Employee's FEDERAL Tax Return

Department of the Treasury—Internal Revenue Service
This information is being furnished to the Internal Revenue Service.

The W-2s for Mary Jones and Judy Carter are similar in that the information on the payroll ledger is transferred as is directly to the W-2 form.

However, you must pay particular attention to John Carter's W-2. His is a little different because, during the year, he reached the maximum amount for Social Security tax.

Boxes 1, 3, and 5 on the forms for Mary and Judy contain their individual earnings amounts, which is also their total earnings.

On John Carter's W-2, box 3 for Social Security Wages is $76,200 because that is the maximum amount subject to Social Security tax for this calendar year.

Take some time to study the employee ledgers and make sure you understand how the information on the ledgers is reported on the W-2s.

At the end of the year, the IRS sends employers a limited number of W-2 forms. Additional forms can be purchased at an office supply store or can be ordered from the IRS. Some forms can also be obtained online from the IRS Web site at www.irs.gov.

PROCEED WITH CAUTION

If you want to order additional forms from the IRS, do it several weeks in advance. It takes time to process and mail the orders, and you must have the forms in time to meet the filing deadlines.

The W-2s are usually carbonized multiple forms with two forms to a page. The top page goes to the Social Security Administration, and the individual forms on this page are continuous and cannot be separated. This page is also printed in red ink.

All the other copies can be separated for mailing to the individual employees. On each copy, a notation on the bottom tells you who is supposed to receive that copy. For example, one will read, "Copy D for Employer"; another will read, "Copy C for Employees' Records."

These notations are important because the copies of the W-2s must be distributed accordingly to the federal government, the state government, and the employees.

The top pages that are mailed to the Social Security Administration are sent with another form, W-3: "Transmittal of Wages and Tax Statements." A sample of the transmittal that would be sent with the W-2s for Carter's company follows.

W-3: Transmittal of Wages and Tax Statement.

DO NOT STAPLE OR FOLD

a Control number	33333	For Official Use Only ▶ OMB No. 1545-0008		

b		941	Military	943	1 Wages, tips, other compensation	2 Federal income tax withheld
Kind of Payer	▶	☒	☐	☐	186,000.00	39,810.00
		CT-1 ☐	Hshld. emp ☐	Medicare govt emp ☐	3 Social security wages 121,800.00	4 Social security tax withheld 7551.60

c Total number of Forms W-2 3	d Establishment number 1	5 Medicare wages and tips 186,000.00	6 Medicare tax withheld 2,697.12

e Employer identification number 00-000000	7 Social security tips	8 Allocated tips

f Employer's name	9 Advance EIC payments	10 Dependent care benefits
John Carter DDS Inc.		
	11 Nonqualified plans	12 Deferred compensation
82 Apple Grove Starcrest, AZ 85755	13	
	14	
g Employer's address and ZIP code		
h Other EIN used this year	15 Income tax withheld by third party payer

i Employer's state I.D. no. 00-0000		

Contact person Judy Carter	Telephone number (520) 555-5555	Fax number ( )	E-mail address

Under penalties of perjury, ... that I have examined this return and accompanying documents ... and to the best of my knowledge and belief they are true, correct, and complete.

Signature ▶   Title ▶   Date ▶

Form **W-3** Transmittal of Wage and Tax Statements **2000** Department of the Treasury Internal Revenue Service

Send this entire page with the entire Copy A page of Form(s) W-2 to the Social Security Administration. Photocopies are NOT acceptable. Do NOT send any remittance (cash, checks, money orders, etc.) with Forms W-2 and W-3.

An Item To Note

Separate instructions. See the separate **2000 Instructions for Forms W-2 and W-3** for information on completing this form.

Purpose of Form

Use this form to transmit Copy A of **Form(s) W-2, Wage and Tax Statement.** Make a copy of Form W-3, and keep it with Copy D (For Employer) of Form(s) W-2 for your records. Use Form W-3 for the correct year. **File Form W-3 even if only one Form W-2 is being filed.** If you are filing Form(s) W-2 on magnetic media or electronically, **do not** file Form W-3.

When To File

File Form W-3 with Copy A of Form(s) W-2 by February 28, 2001.

Where To File

Send this entire page with the entire Copy A page of Form(s) W-2 to:

> **Social Security Administration Data Operations Center Wilkes-Barre, PA 18769-0001**

Note: *If you use "Certified Mail" to file, change the ZIP code to "18769-0002." If you use an IRS approved private delivery service, add "ATTN: W-2 Process, 1150 E. Mountain Dr." to the address and change the ZIP code to "18702-7997." See* **Circular E**, *Employer's Tax Guide (Pub. 15), for a list of IRS approved private delivery services.*

For Privacy Act and Paperwork Reduction Act Notice, see the 2000 Instructions for Forms W-2 and W-3.

Note that the W-3 transmittal looks like the W-2 form. The figures entered on the W-3 are the totals taken from the W-2s.

The Social Security Administration keeps earnings records on all wage earners. Once the wage and tax data is processed by the Social Security Administration, the information is sent on to the IRS.

One very important thing to remember is that the totals on your W-3 must balance with the total on your W-2 forms and on your quarterly reports. In other words, the wages and taxes reported on the four quarterly 941s must add up to the same figures reported on the W-2s. Be sure to double-check these figures to make sure they all agree.

TIME SAVER

 Most tax reports, including the W-2 forms, can be submitted electronically. Information on electronic filing can be obtained from the IRS. Companies with more than 250 employees are required to file electronically.

State and local taxing entities have their own transmittal forms that must be completed and sent along with copies of W-2s.

PROCEED WITH CAUTION

The IRS shares its information with state governments. The state or local tax authorities may impose penalties if you fail to submit the required information.

1099s FOR VENDORS

Some years ago, the IRS decided that some taxpayers were neglecting to report all of their Income. Legislation was then passed requiring that payments made to nonemployees be reported at the end of the year on Form 1099.

1099s are used to report employee allowances, nonemployee compensation, rental Income, interest payments, and any other miscellaneous payments that exceed $600 during the calendar year. Some states have their own reporting requirements that may be lower than $600.

To conform to these reporting requirements, you should obtain a tax identification number or Social Security number from any vendor or nonemployee to whom you make payments during the year. If the vendor is a corporation, you do not need to report the 1099 Income, but every other company or individual that received $600 or more from you or your business must be included in the 1099 reporting.

The filing date for 1099s is February 28 of each year. This gives you an extra month to gather this information and complete and file the reports.

The 1099 form does not have as many copies as the W-2 form. You can obtain these forms from the IRS or purchase them at an office supply store.

One copy of the form goes to the payee, and the other copy is sent directly to the IRS with the transmittal form, Form 1096. Samples of these forms can be found in Appendix B, "Sample Forms."

GO TO ▶
Refer to Hour 14 for worksheets and instructions for filing the annual federal unemployment tax report.

COMPLETING THE FEDERAL UNEMPLOYMENT TAX REPORT

The federal unemployment tax is reported annually on Form 940. There is also a Form 940EZ that can be used by certain employers.

The information needed to file Form 940 is taken from the quarterly report worksheet.

A sample of the federal unemployment Form 940 is included in Appendix B.

PERSONAL AND BUSINESS TAX RETURNS

You have studied two sample companies as they went through the end-of-the-month and the end-of-the-year accounting process.

One company, John Carter, DDS, is a corporation. Because this corporation ends its year in accordance with the calendar year, the tax return is due on March 15. The tax return for any corporation is due on the fifteen of the third month after the end of its year. For instance, if a corporation operates on a fiscal year that ends June 30 each year, the tax return is due on or before September 15.

JUST A MINUTE

Extensions can be sent to the IRS requesting permission to file a tax return after the due date. A tax professional should be consulted for the necessary forms and information on requirements.

For the most part, the information needed to prepare the tax return for Carter's corporation will be taken from the financial reports issued by his computerized system. Both federal and state tax returns must be filed. A tax professional should be retained to file these corporate tax reports. As an officer and an employee of the corporation, John Carter, DDS, received a W-2 form. This will be used to file his personal Income tax return.

The other business owner, Ed Brown, will also file a personal tax return (Form 1040). As a sole proprietor, the profits of Caricatures by Ed will be reported on Schedule C of Ed's personal Income tax return.

GO TO ▶

Refer to Hour 14 for information on how a sole proprietor reports business Income and pays taxes on that Income.

The end of the year is a busy time for the accounting department in any size business. While the day-to-day business activities continue for the month of January, all the tax reports must be worked on and filed.

This is why organization and record keeping are so important. If you have kept good records on payroll, employees, and vendors during the year, you can handle all the reports and paperwork that the end of the year necessitates with a minimum amount of effort and stress.

Hour's Up!

You have now studied and reviewed the year-end tax reports and should be ready to answer the following questions.

1. The total wages and taxes reported on the W-2s must agree with the amounts reported on the quarterly reports.
   a. True
   b. False

2. A 1099 must be filed for any vendor, other than a corporation, that was paid more than $600 during the year.
   a. True
   b. False

3. W-2s must be filed and sent to employees on or before what date?
   a. February 28
   b. January 31
   c. February 10

4. The IRS has a Web site where you can obtain information and tax forms.
   a. True
   b. False

5. The transmittal used for W-2s is form number:
   a. W-4
   b. 941
   c. W-3

6. The main copies of the W-2 reports are sent directly to the IRS.

    a. True

    b. False

7. State and local taxing authorities usually have their own transmittals for their copies of W-2s.

    a. True

    b. False

8. The annual federal unemployment tax report is form number:

    a. 940

    b. 941

    c. 1040

9. 1099s must be filed and sent to vendors on or before:

    a. January 31

    b. February 10

    c. February 28

10. The information needed to complete the W-2s is taken from:

    a. Vendor ledgers

    b. Employee ledgers

    c. Payroll journals

Hour 23

Closing the Books at the End of the Year

CHAPTER SUMMARY

LESSON PLAN:

In this hour you will learn about ...

- What happens to the General Ledger
- Customer accounts
- Vendor accounts

All the tax reports have been completed and filed. Once the corporate tax return is done, if there is tax due, your tax professional will instruct you to do a General Journal Entry. The tax is posted in the year that the liability was incurred.

A sole proprietor will not have any tax to post to his books because any tax due is his personal expense.

If you are using a computerized accounting system, make sure that all your files are backed up on a disk before attempting to close the books.

WHAT HAPPENS TO THE GENERAL LEDGER

The Balance Sheet accounts are not closed. Those balances are all carried over to the next year. The only difference is that the net profit for the year that is being closed out goes into the new year as Retained Earnings.

For Caricatures by Ed, there are only a few accounts on the Balance Sheet. After the books are closed for the year, Ed's Balance Sheet will remain as it was on the financial statements issued on December 31, 2000.

The same is true for the larger company, John Carter, DDS. Every account in the Balance Sheet section of the General Ledger is carried over to the new year.

Think about the accounts that are in the Balance Sheet section, and this will make perfect sense to you. There is

GO TO ▶

Refer to Hour 20, "The Monthly Balance Sheet," for information on Balance Sheets for sample companies, a corporation, and a sole proprietor.

the cash account—you wouldn't close the checking account and open a new one to pay bills and deposit revenue for the new year. You just keep operating with the same account. The ending cash balance for December 31, 2000, becomes the beginning cash balance for January 1, 2001.

The same is true for the other Assets. They are the Assets of the business, and their value doesn't change until the accumulated depreciation is posted for the first month of the new year.

All the Liabilities are also carried over. For example, the balance on Carter's bank loan remains the same until it is reduced by the payment made for January 2001.

The accounts that do change are the accounts in the Profit and Loss section of the General Ledger. All these accounts are zeroed out, and the net profit for the year 2000 is added to Retained Earnings. The year 2000 becomes the prior year, and the year 2001 becomes the current year.

In a manual system, you will have to physically go through each account in the Profit and Loss section of the General Ledger and post a debit to offset the credit balances, and post credits to offset the debits, so that each account becomes a zero balance. The difference between these debits and credits is the net profit, which is then posted to the Retained Earnings account.

Take a look at the closing entry for Caricatures by Ed that follows:

Date	Ref. No.	Account	Amount
12-31-00	AJ-3	4000 Sales	21,118.08
		5100 Advertising	(599.00)
		5150 Auto Expense	(526.00)
		6360 Rent	(6,000.00)
		6520 Supplies	(2,547.00)
		3040 Retained Earnings	(11,446.08)

			-0-

To close books for the year 2000

The balance in the Sales account was a credit of $21,118.08 at the end of December. To close it out, a debit for the same amount is posted. Each expense account had a debit balance, so a credit in the same amount was posted to each of them to close them out. The remaining balance is, of course, the amount of the net profit for the year, and that is posted to the Retained Earnings account.

Once the books are closed out, you can simply draw a line under the zero balance and continue to use the same sheet to post the first transactions of the new year.

If there are a lot of entries on the ledger sheets, you can remove the ones that have been closed out and file them with the Trial Balance worksheet. Then set up new ledger sheets for the new year's postings.

In Carter's computerized accounting system, the same process takes place. Only instead of the accountant going through each account, the computer automatically zeroes out all the accounts in the Profit and Loss section and posts the profit to Retained Earnings.

Before doing the year-end closing in a computerized system, you should print out a General Ledger report. If you have printed out a General Ledger report each month, you can just print out another one for December. If you have not printed them out on a monthly basis, you should print one out for the entire year before closing out the system.

PROCEED WITH CAUTION

Make sure you have a backup copy of the current year's data before doing a year-end closing in a computerized accounting system. Once the year is closed, it cannot be opened again.

CUSTOMER ACCOUNTS

All the customers' accounts are part of your Accounts Receivable. Accounts Receivable is a Balance Sheet account; therefore, these accounts are not closed out at the end of the year.

Actually, the customer ledgers retain all the information that has ever been posted to them. This can be 1 year's transactions or 10 years' transactions.

If you want to remove a customer ledger, you must first zero out the account balance. If it is a credit balance, you can issue a check to the customer. Once the check is posted, the customer ledger can be cleared off.

The entry to post such a check is different from the Accounts Receivable entries you have reviewed so far. Assume that one of Carter's patients had a ledger balance of $100 and paid that amount. A week or so later, the patient's dental insurance also paid the bill.

The patient now has a $100 credit on the ledger card, so a check is written to refund the overpayment and close out the patient's balance.

The entry would be written up as follows:

Date	Ref. No.	Account	Amount
1-1-01	CK# 482	1000 Cash in Checking	(100.00)
		1100 Accounts Receivable	100.00

To clear patient account

At first glance, this entry may be confusing because Accounts Receivable is usually debited only when a sale occurs. However, in this case, Accounts Receivable was debited when the original fee was posted.

Later, when the check from the patient came in, Accounts Receivable was credited, clearing the original balance. But when the insurance check came in, Accounts Receivable had to be credited again, which resulted in the credit balance on the patient's ledger.

The refund check is simply offsetting that second credit. A look at the patient's ledger may make the procedure a little easier to understand.

John Carter, DDS
82 Apple Grove
Starcrest, AZ

Mrs. Jane Finerson
3345 E. Maple Ave.
Starcrest, AZ

Date	Description	Amount	ROA	Balance
10-10-00	Porcelain Filling	100.00		100.00
10-15-00	Finerson Ck# 987		100.00	-0-
11-1-00	Dental Care Ck# 33		100.00	(100.00)
1-1-01	Our Check # 482	100.00		-0-

Once the patient ledger has a zero balance, you can remove it from a manual accounting system, if desired.

Many computerized systems will not allow you to delete a ledger once it has been posted. This is a safeguard built into the computerized systems.

VENDOR ACCOUNTS

Just as a bank loan would not be forgiven just because one year ended and another began, a vendor account balance is carried over into the next year or accounting period. Again, vendor accounts are part of another Balance Sheet account, Accounts Payable.

Vendor ledgers remain in the accounting system for as long as the company does business with that particular vendor. The information posted on the vendor ledgers is often needed for reference. Manufacturing and retail companies routinely look back at the invoices recorded on the vendor ledgers to check prices on goods received.

The payment terms and tax identification numbers should also be recorded on the vendor ledgers. In February, when the 1099s are due to be issued, the vendor ledgers provide the information needed to complete these tax reports.

TIME SAVER

It is a good idea to set up a vendor ledger for any person who may require a 1099 form at the end of the year. All the information needed for the 1099 can be recorded on the ledger card.

In a manual system, you can simply remove any ledger that no longer will be used. But, as with customer ledgers, many computerized systems will not allow you to delete a vendor ledger once it has been created and amounts have been posted to it.

Keeping ledgers with no balance in the accounting system will not affect the accounting process. You will find that reports can be generated that will bypass ledgers without a balance.

MOVING FROM ONE YEAR TO THE NEXT

During the month of January, you will be moving back and forth between the old year and the new year. The business operation does not stop and start again—it keeps going.

GO TO ▶
Refer to Hour 24, "Accounting Software Programs," to learn about some of the features of computerized accounting programs.

In a manual system, you can simply skip a few spaces and record transactions in the Profit and Loss section of the General Ledger while you are gathering all the information needed to close out the prior year.

In a computerized system, you can keep the prior year open and post entries there as long as necessary. At the same time, you will be posting entries into the first month of the new year.

Don't think that you must rush through the year-end closing so that you can start the new year. Take as much time as you need to make sure that everything that belongs in the old year is posted and in balance.

GO TO ▶
Refer to Hour 10, "The Importance of Work Papers, Receipts, and Other Records," for instructions for proper retention of all types of accounting records.

Closing out the old year involves more than just closing the books for the year. All the paperwork generated during the old year must be moved from one file to another to make room for the new year's paperwork. Take care not to put the previous year's records too far out of reach because they may be needed for reference.

Keeping a set of books for any size business requires knowledge, skill, and organization. All through the year, it is your attention to detail that makes all the pieces fit together so that the financial data can be properly maintained and reported.

As everything from the old year is sorted and boxed for storage, there is a sense of accomplishment that you can and should enjoy.

QUIZ

HOUR'S UP!

You have now learned about the end-of-the-year closing procedures. Test what you have learned by answering these questions.

1. Vendor ledgers are not closed at the end of the year.
   a. True
   b. False

2. Always back up your computerized accounting files before doing a year-end closing.
   a. True
   b. False

3. When the closing entry is posted in a manual system, the offsetting amount is posted to:

    a. Cash in Checking

    b. Accounts Receivable

    c. Retained Earnings

4. A sole proprietor's Income tax liability should be posted in his accounting system.

    a. True

    b. False

5. A vendor ledger can be deleted from a computerized accounting system at any time.

    a. True

    b. False

6. Which of the following account balances is carried over to the new year?

    a. Salaries & Wages

    b. Accounts Receivable

    c. Depreciation Expense

7. The business operation stops when the year-end closing takes place.

    a. True

    b. False

8. How is a check to refund a credit balance on a customer ledger posted?

    a. Credit Cash, debit Accounts Receivable

    b. Credit Accounts Receivable, debit Sales

    c. Credit Accounts Receivable, debit Cash

9. Many computerized accounting systems will not allow you to delete a ledger once it has been posted.

    a. True

    b. False

10. Customer ledgers are closed out at the end of the year.

    a. True

    b. False

QUIZ

HOUR 24

Accounting Software Programs

CHAPTER SUMMARY

LESSON PLAN:

In this hour you will learn about ...

- Setting up a computer program
- Modifying programs to specific needs
- Converting a manual system to a computer program

In the preceding hours of this book, you have learned how to set up and maintain a manual system. You have also been introduced to a computerized accounting system. The procedures for managing both are basically the same.

An accounting software program can be a real time saver. It also gives you the ability to store more information and access it in many different ways.

Although a software program may save you time in the long run, there is a certain amount of time that must be initially invested in the program. Setting up and managing a manual accounting system will help you decide if you need to invest the time and money into a computer and an accounting software program.

If you have a small business, you may want to stay with a manual accounting system. Perhaps you are not computer-literate or don't know what type of accounting program will best suit your needs. Many small businesses simply run their operation out of a business checking account and use a professional accounting firm to reconcile the account and prepare reports.

That is fine as long as you understand the basic principles of accounting, are knowledgeable enough to recognize potential problems, and are able to use the financial reports to obtain the necessary management information.

Of course, any business that operates on an accrual basis needs more than a checking account to take care of its transactions.

JUST A MINUTE

Accounts Receivable and Accounts Payable are part of an accounting system that operates on an accrual basis.

If your business requires the maintenance of customer ledgers and vendor accounts, you should really consider a computerized system. Although ledgers can be handled in a manual system, there are more steps to follow, which means more time and work. You have already seen how efficiently the computerized system handled these accounts for the sample company John Carter, DDS.

Do some research before deciding on an accounting software program. Some programs are more user-friendly; some programs offer better technical support, which is important. When looking at the software programs on the market, you should consider the ones that are a level higher than what you think you might need. Some programs are more for keeping household records than doing business accounting.

The type of computer you will use to run the program will also determine the software you purchase. Go to the computer software supplier or your local office supply store, and look over the available programs. If possible, ask for a demonstration of the program.

While all the accounting programs operate basically the same, some have features that may be more desirable for your type of business. For example, if you have a large customer base, you will want a program that has exceptionally good reporting features for your Accounts Receivable. If you have a business that adheres to a strict budget, make sure you purchase a software program that allows you to input the budget figures and make them a part of your financial reports.

GO TO ▶
Refer to Hour 21, "The Monthly Profit and Loss Statement," to find information on financial reports that can be tailored for your particular business needs.

All the accounting software programs come with reference guides. Look through the guide and determine how easy it is to understand. The guides also include samples of the reports that can be printed from the program. Review these to see if they provide the right kind of information for your business and customers.

If you will use the program to process payroll, find out how much the necessary updates for tax rates and wages limits will cost you each year.

Once you have chosen a program and installed it on your computer, take the time to look through the program and become familiar with the features.

SETTING UP A COMPUTER PROGRAM

Most of the software programs come with a tutorial that will take you through the features, using sample companies much like the ones you reviewed in this book.

When you feel comfortable with features of your program, you can begin the setup process. After you enter the business name, address, and tax identification number, the program will ask you to choose your accounting periods. This is a crucial step because once you choose the accounting periods, they cannot be changed.

You can delete your company and start all over, but you can't change the accounting periods in a company that has already been entered.

In most systems, the program will display the months in a calendar year. The first accounting period will be January 1 through January 31, the second will be February 1 through February 28, and so on.

It doesn't matter which month of the year you are physically in. If you are going to operate your business on a calendar year, which is highly recommended for a new accounting system, choose these standard accounting periods. You can start entering information for any month of this calendar year.

If your business does operate on a fiscal year, you can choose the month your year begins, and the program will adjust the choices to a different 12-month period.

GO TO ▶
Refer to Hour 3, "Chart of Accounts Becomes the General Ledger," for instructions for beginning your business year in the middle of the calendar year.

With that task completed, you will be asked to choose a Chart of Accounts for your business. The program has Charts of Accounts built into it for a variety of business endeavors. You can highlight any of the business types and then preview the program's prescribed Chart of Accounts for that kind of operation. Do this until you find the Chart of Accounts that best suits your needs.

None of the Charts of Accounts is going to exactly what you want and need, but once you choose the Chart of Accounts, you can modify it.

TIME SAVER

As long as you find a business category close to your own, you can use the system for a while before changing the program's built-in Chart of Accounts. The Chart of Accounts can be modified at any time.

The next screen the computer program brings up will ask you to enter your bank account information. You don't have to fill in every blank on this screen, but you will have to put in the name of the bank where all your revenue is being deposited.

That account will be designated as your main bank account, or Account 1000 in your Chart of Accounts. Most programs will not allow you to proceed unless this information is entered.

After the main bank account is entered, you can enter your savings accounts or other bank accounts if you desire, although that information is not required for the program to operate.

If at any time during this setup process you make a big mistake, you can go back to the opening screen, delete your company, and then put it in again. Also, much of the information you put in (except for the accounting periods) can be modified later.

MODIFYING PROGRAMS TO SPECIFIC NEEDS

Before you begin entering accounting data, go through the Chart of Accounts on the program and make sure that all the accounts you need are there.

If you will want statements with budget comparisons, the budget information will have to be entered. This should also be done before any other accounting data is put into the program.

JUST A MINUTE

Some reporting features, such as percentage comparisons, are automatically calculated by the computer program and need no input from the user.

If you have vendors, set up the vendor accounts in the program. The same goes for customer accounts. All of this information should be entered before the transactions or year-to-date data.

As you go along, vendors and customers can be easily added, but all existing ledgers should be set up initially.

If you have employees, set up the employee ledgers in the program. If your ledgers have balances, follow the program's instructions for entering them on the ledger cards. Once this is done, you can print out a report and verify it against your old ledger cards.

CONVERTING A MANUAL SYSTEM TO A COMPUTERIZED SYSTEM

The accounting data should be entered into the computerized system from the Trial Balance.

If you don't have a Trial Balance worksheet, sit down and write one up before you go to the computer. It is vital that you put the information in correctly.

Make sure that everything is balanced. If you have customer ledgers, the balance in your Accounts Receivable account must tally with the total of the ledgers. Obviously, the same holds true for vendor ledgers and the balance in Accounts Payable.

When you go into the accounting program, you will be able to set the date for your posting. Don't start in the middle of a month—you want to enter the year-to-date information at the end of a month. For example, if it is June 1, you will enter the totals for the month ending May 31. Setting the date of May 31 allows you to post this information in the accounting period beginning May 1 and ending May 31.

You will post the information from your Trial Balance as a General Journal Entry. Most programs will not allow you to save the entry to the General Ledger unless it is in balance.

After the data is entered and saved, run a Trial Balance from the computer and compare it to your manual worksheet. Then run a General Ledger report to make sure all your opening balances are correct for each General Ledger account.

A computerized system will ask you if you want to include accounts with zero balances. If you have General Ledger accounts that you don't need, you don't have to worry about eliminating them right away. If there's nothing posted in them, they will not print out on the reports.

After this done, you can run financial statements for the month. Look them over carefully to make sure they are set up the way you want them.

The method outlined is a shortcut, or a quick way to get your information in the computer so that you can start working in the current month, posting current transactions.

If so desired, you can do a Trial Balance for each month of the year and enter the information into each corresponding month in the software

GO TO ▶
Refer to Hour 19, "The Trial Balance," for instructions on preparing a worksheet for a Trial Balance from a manual system.

program. This is not usually necessary. You should already have financial reports for the prior months from your manual system.

Remember that the preceding guidelines are just that: guidelines. The software program you purchase may have set up requirements that vary from these. Study the manual and reference materials that come with the program. If needed, call the technical service departments for assistance. It's important to get the software installed and set up correctly.

As you have seen in earlier hours, accounting software programs operate just like a manual accounting system. If you have studied all the lessons in this book, you will have no trouble applying them to a computerized system.

HOUR'S UP!

You have now reviewed the recommended process for selecting and using an accounting software program. Answering the following questions will help you retain this information.

1. An accounting software program should come with good technical support.
    a. True
    b. False

2. A computerized system saves time and work in handling customer accounts.
    a. True
    b. False

3. What kind of reports do you need if you have a large customer base?
    a. Cash flow reports
    b. Accounts Payable reports
    c. Accounts Receivable reports

4. Accounting periods in a software program can be changed at any time during the year.
    a. True
    b. False

5. What things should you look for in an accounting software program?

   a. A user-friendly program

   b. Inexpensive updates

   c. A higher-level program

   d. All of the above

6. An accounting software program gives you the ability to access more information in more ways.

   a. True

   b. False

7. An accounting system that operates on a calendar year is recommended for most new business enterprises.

   a. True

   b. False

8. What day of the month should you use when entering year-to-date financial information into a computerized system?

   a. The first day of the month

   b. The last day of the month

   c. The 15th of the month

9. Payroll software requires annual updating.

   a. True

   b. False

10. The financial data from a manual system should be entered in the computerized system from what report?

   a. Bank statement

   b. Profit and Loss Statement

   c. Trial Balance

QUIZ

APPENDIX A
Twenty-Minute Recap

HOUR 1: THE CHART OF ACCOUNTS/BALANCE SHEET ACCOUNTS

In this hour, you learn how to set up the accounts that will be used in the Balance Sheet section of the accounting system to record financial data. Because each account is established in the Chart of Accounts, you will find an explanation of its purpose and use in the accounting system. You will also learn how these accounts are presented on the Balance Sheet section of the financial statements.

HOUR 2: PROFIT AND LOSS STATEMENT ACCOUNTS

This hour takes you further into the accounting structure and introduces all the accounts needed to record the day-to-day business activities. These accounts are presented in the order in which they will appear on the Profit and Loss Statement, and each one is explained as it is established. At the end of this hour, you will have completed a standard Chart of Accounts.

HOUR 3: CHART OF ACCOUNTS BECOMES THE GENERAL LEDGER

In this hour, you learn how the accounts established in the two previous hours are transferred into the General Ledger, where the information is actually posted. Accounting periods and opening entries are presented, as is detailed information on debits and credits. The lesson goes on to explain how all the accounts in the General Ledger offset each other to maintain order and balance.

HOUR 4: DEPRECIABLE ASSETS, PREPAID EXPENSES, AND OTHER ACCOUNTS

Now that you have studied the standard accounts needed by most companies, this hour takes you a step further. You learn about the Assets that can be depreciated, as well as why, how, and when they are written off. You also learn about prepaid accounts and their use in certain circumstances. The hour concludes by providing information on miscellaneous accounts that are used by companies with specific needs.

HOUR 5: ORGANIZATION AND PROPER ACCOUNTING PROCEDURES

Information on the operating account or the business checking account is presented in this hour. Suggestions for banking and keeping the account updated are included. This hour also stresses the importance of setting up files and keeping the paperwork generated by the business in good order. It includes suggestions for types of filing systems, supplies, and ways to keep the workload under control.

HOUR 6: DAILY SALES TRANSACTIONS

This is the first hour that deals with daily business transactions; it concentrates on Income and the Income accounts. This is all the revenue generated by sales or services. Cash sales and Credit Sales are covered, as are the procedures for establishing customer accounts, collecting sales tax, and posting sales or any type of Income to the General Ledger.

HOUR 7: COST OF SALES OR SERVICES

All the Expenses directly related to sales or services are presented in this hour. You will find information on purchases and instructions for handling inventory and adjusting it at the end of each month. Vendors and vendor accounts are also covered, which leads into the information for Accounts Payable and posting all these purchases and other Expenses to the General Ledger.

HOUR 8: DISCOUNTS, ALLOWANCES, AND OTHER ADJUSTMENTS

This hour focuses on the special handling required by discounts, refunds, and other adjustments. It begins with the adjustments that apply to the Income from sales and services. The hour continues with information on purchase discounts. The final part of this lesson deals with customer accounts that have become uncollectable and must be deleted from the accounting system. In each part of this hour, samples and instructions are provided for posting these adjustments to the General Ledger.

HOUR 9: CASH DISBURSEMENTS

Specific information on writing checks and keeping the checkbook in order is presented in this hour. The lesson also provides instructions for posting checks to the various expense accounts in the General Ledger. This hour builds on the information in previous hours for Accounts Payable; it gives more information on how this account is used to make sure that all the Expenses that relate to one particular month are recorded so that they can be included on the financial statements.

HOUR 10: THE IMPORTANCE OF WORK PAPERS, RECEIPTS, AND OTHER RECORDS

This hour stresses the need for retaining records in good order. It offers suggestions on how this is done and gives information on the length of time that each type of record needs to be kept. The hour continues with information on paying bills and reconciling vendor statements and the records that must be maintained for these tasks. Finally, this hour introduces and explains the reports that must be completed and retained for sales tax reporting.

HOUR 11: SALARY AND WAGES

Hiring employees is a big step for any business, and it requires advance planning and research. This hour provides information that will familiarize you with the items that should be in place before that first employee is hired. The required government forms are presented and explained. Information on the different types of wages is also included.

HOUR 12: PAYROLL TAXES: EMPLOYEE/EMPLOYER

Becoming an employer entails a lot of record keeping for the accounting system. An introduction and explanation of all the taxes associated with employees is presented in this hour. This includes the employee and employer portions of Social Security and Medicare taxes, as well as the federal and state withholding taxes and unemployment taxes.

HOUR 13: POSTING PAYROLL, COMPUTING TAXES, AND CONFORMING TO FEDERAL AND STATE RULES AND REGULATIONS

In this hour, you learn about the requirements for remitting payroll taxes to the federal government. A special section shows you how to compute your tax Liabilities and explains tax accrual accounts. Posting taxes to the General Ledger using these accrual accounts is also covered. The hour ends with information on deadlines for paying the various types of taxes and the penalties for failure to honor the deadlines.

HOUR 14: PAYROLL TAX REPORTS

Quarterly payroll tax reports are introduced and explained in this hour. This lesson includes detailed instructions for compiling the information needed for the reports and gives more instructions on how to calculate the taxes on worksheets that can be used to complete the forms. Reports for both the federal government and state taxing entities are presented.

HOUR 15: CASH RECEIPTS JOURNAL

The Cash Receipts Journal is used to record all the revenue that comes into the business during the month. Examinations of the books for two different companies will help explain the end-of-the-month tasks and procedures associated with the cash receipts. In this hour, you learn how the information in this journal is reviewed and adjusted in the General Ledger. Information on balancing the customer accounts and sending out statements to the customers is also reviewed.

HOUR 16: CASH DISBURSEMENTS JOURNAL

Balancing Accounts Payable, paying taxes, and reconciling vendor statements and petty cash funds are all explained in this hour. A new account, Temporary Postings, is also introduced, and its function and purpose are outlined. In addition, this hour includes sample reports and examples of how all of these items are processed and posted to the General Ledger.

HOUR 17: PAYROLL JOURNAL AND EMPLOYEE EXPENSE ACCOUNTS

The end-of-the-month tasks related to payroll and employee ledgers are presented and explained in this hour. Employee expense accounts are introduced, and the procedures for handling the different types of reimbursements and allowances are described in detail. This hour also outlines how all of these employee-related items are posted to the General Ledger, along with samples that can be studied.

HOUR 18: RECONCILING THE BANK ACCOUNTS AND GENERAL JOURNAL ENTRIES

In this hour, you learn how to verify the balance in the operating account with the balance in the General Ledger cash account and the balance on the bank statement. A sample worksheet shows you how to analyze and compare the information in the General Ledger with the bank statement. The lesson continues with instructions on making the various end-of-the-month adjustments for corrections and Expenses such as depreciation.

HOUR 19: THE TRIAL BALANCE

In this hour, you will see samples of the Trial Balance, the report that lists all the accounts in the General Ledger with their year-to-date balances. This report is used to review the account balances before they are transferred to the Balance Sheet and the Profit and Loss Statement. Information is also presented on how the financial statements evolve from the Trial Balance and the General Ledger, as well as how to format this information to the needs of various types of businesses.

HOUR 20: THE MONTHLY BALANCE SHEET

A monthly Balance Sheet is presented for two different sample companies. The process for producing a manual report is described, and a computerized report sample is explained and reviewed. This hour also provides information on how the Balance Sheet is used by management and other interested parties.

HOUR 21: THE MONTHLY PROFIT AND LOSS STATEMENT

Using the two sample companies, Profit and Loss Statements are presented and explained. The process for producing this statement manually is also outlined. The hour continues with information on how to tailor this report to the specific needs of various companies.

HOUR 22: END-OF-THE-YEAR PAYROLL REPORTS AND OTHER TAX REPORTS

In this hour, you learn about the end-of-the-year payroll reports that must be completed and filed. Employee W-2s and 1099s are presented and explained. The hour also describes the process for compiling information needed for corporate and personal tax returns that comes from the accounting system.

HOUR 23: CLOSING THE BOOKS AT THE END OF THE YEAR

Information and procedures for closing out the year in the accounting system is presented in this hour. As the old year ends, the new year begins; this hour gives suggestions that will help you understand it all. It also explains the effects that the year-end close has on the accounts in the General Ledger.

HOUR 24: ACCOUNTING SOFTWARE PROGRAMS

In this final hour, you learn how to apply what you have learned in the preceding hours to a computerized accounting system. Included are suggestions on how to choose a software program and how to enter your accounting data into the program so that it works well for your business.

Sample Forms

SAMPLE COMPANY
BALANCE SHEET
September 30, 2000

ASSETS

CURRENT ASSETS

Checking Account	$	26,537.10		
Petty Cash		50.00		
Accounts Receivable		17,059.00		
Inventory		42,312.00		
TOTAL CURRENT ASSETS			$	85,958.10

PROPERTY AND EQUIPMENT

Land	$	50,000.00		
Buildings		250,000.00		
A/D - Buildings		(12,500.00)		
Equipment		23,350.00		
A/D - Equipment		(2,350.00)		
Furniture and Fixtures		7,680.00		
A/D - Furniture & Fixtures		(2,100.00)		
TOTAL PROPERTY AND EQUIPMENT			$	314,080.00
TOTAL ASSETS			$	400,038.10

SAMPLE COMPANY
BALANCE SHEET
September 30, 2000

LIABILITIES AND EQUITY

CURRENT LIABILITIES

Accounts Payable	$	7,997.76		
PAYROLL TAXES PAYABLE		5,687.35		
CURRENT PORTION LONG-TERM DEBT		25,000.00		
TOTAL CURRENT LIABILITIES			$	38,685.11

EQUITY

Retained Earnings	$	58,349.55		
Capital		50,000.00		
NET INCOME (LOSS)		253,003.44		
TOTAL EQUITY			$	361,352.99
TOTAL LIABILITIES AND EQUITY			$	400,038.10

Balance Sheet.

Income Statement.

SAMPLE COMPANY
INCOME STATEMENT
For The Period

January 01, 2000
to
September 30, 2000

SALES		
Sales	$	451,903.00
Total SALES	$	451,903.00
COST OF SALES		
Purchases	$	78,483.00
Total COST OF SALES	$	78,483.00
Total GROSS PROFIT	$	373,420.00
SELLING EXPENSES		
Freight and Delivery	$	9,675.00
Total SELLING EXPENSES	$	9,675.00
GENERAL & ADMINISTRATIVE		
Salaries and Wages	$	86,000.00
Utilities		5,956.50
Insurance - Employee Group		3,936.00
Interest Expense		4,000.00
Office Expense		3,942.55
Taxes - Payroll		5,891.21
Telephone		1,015.30
Total GENERAL & ADMINISTRATIVE	$	110,741.56
Total NET OPERATING INCOME (LOSS)	$	253,003.44
NET INCOME (LOSS) BEFORE TAX	$	253,003.44
NET INCOME (LOSS)	$	253,003.44

TYA MANUFACTURING
CHART OF ACCOUNTS

Chart of Accounts—
manufacturing
company.

ACCOUNT NUMBER	NAME	TYPE	BALANCE SHEET SECTION / INCOME STATEMENT SECTION
1000	Checking Account	Asset	CURRENT ASSETS
1080	Petty Cash	Asset	CURRENT ASSETS
1098	Undeposited Cash	Asset	CURRENT ASSETS
1099	Cash Transfers	Asset	CURRENT ASSETS
1100	Accounts Receivable	Asset	CURRENT ASSETS
1190	Allowance for Bad Debts	Asset	CURRENT ASSETS
1200	Inventory - Raw Materials	Asset	CURRENT ASSETS
1210	Inventory - Finished Goods	Asset	CURRENT ASSETS
1220	Inventory - W.I.P.	Asset	CURRENT ASSETS
1350	Prepaid Expenses	Asset	PREPAID EXPENSES
1500	Land	Asset	PROPERTY AND EQUIPMENT
1510	Buildings	Asset	PROPERTY AND EQUIPMENT
1511	A/D - Buildings	Asset	PROPERTY AND EQUIPMENT
1570	Equipment	Asset	PROPERTY AND EQUIPMENT
1571	A/D - Equipment	Asset	PROPERTY AND EQUIPMENT
1580	Furniture and Fixtures	Asset	PROPERTY AND EQUIPMENT
1581	A/D - Furniture & Fixtures	Asset	PROPERTY AND EQUIPMENT
1650	Vehicles	Asset	PROPERTY AND EQUIPMENT
1651	A/D - Vehicles	Asset	PROPERTY AND EQUIPMENT
1680	Other Fixed Assets	Asset	PROPERTY AND EQUIPMENT
1681	A/D - Other Fixed Assets	Asset	PROPERTY AND EQUIPMENT
1800	Utility Deposits	Asset	OTHER ASSETS
1810	Other Assets	Asset	OTHER ASSETS
1900	Organization Costs	Asset	OTHER ASSETS
1901	Accum Amortization - Org Costs	Asset	OTHER ASSETS
2000	Accounts Payable	Liability	CURRENT LIABILITIES
2100	Loan Payable - Bank of USA	Liability	CURRENT LIABILITIES
2105	Credit Card Payable-VISA	Liability	CURRENT LIABILITIES
2110	401K Payable	Liability	CURRENT LIABILITIES
2120	Customer Security Deposits	Liability	CURRENT LIABILITIES
2190	Sales Taxes Payable	Liability	CURRENT LIABILITIES
2200	Federal Withholding Tax Payable	Liability	PAYROLL TAXES PAYABLE
2210	Social Security Tax Payable	Liability	PAYROLL TAXES PAYABLE
2212	Medicare Withholding Tax Payable	Liability	PAYROLL TAXES PAYABLE
2220	State Withholding Taxes Payable	Liability	PAYROLL TAXES PAYABLE
2280	Accrued FUTA	Liability	PAYROLL TAXES PAYABLE
2290	Accrued SUTA	Liability	PAYROLL TAXES PAYABLE
3010	Common Stock	Equity	EQUITY
3040	Retained Earnings	Equity	EQUITY
3110	Partners Capital #1	Equity	EQUITY
3160	Partners Drawing #1	Equity	EQUITY
4000	Sales	Income	SALES
4180	Payment Discounts	Income	SALES
4190	Sales Returns & Allowances	Income	SALES
4200	Purchases	Expense	DIRECT MATERIALS
4210	Purchase Discounts Expense	Expense	DIRECT MATERIALS
4420	Equipment Rental	Expense	FACTORY OVERHEAD
4430	Insurance - Employee Group	Expense	FACTORY OVERHEAD
4440	Insurance - General	Expense	FACTORY OVERHEAD
4450	Misc Expense	Expense	FACTORY OVERHEAD

continues

continued

*Chart of Accounts—
manufacturing
company.*

**TYA MANUFACTURING
CHART OF ACCOUNTS**

ACCOUNT NUMBER	NAME	TYPE	BALANCE SHEET SECTION / INCOME STATEMENT SECTION
4460	Office Expense	Expense	FACTORY OVERHEAD
4470	Outside Services	Expense	FACTORY OVERHEAD
4480	Rent Expense	Expense	FACTORY OVERHEAD
4490	Repairs & Maintenance	Expense	FACTORY OVERHEAD
4500	Supplies	Expense	FACTORY OVERHEAD
5050	Commissions	Expense	SELLING EXPENSES
5100	Advertising	Expense	SELLING EXPENSES
5150	Brochures and Catalogs	Expense	SELLING EXPENSES
5230	Travel	Expense	SELLING EXPENSES
5660	Freight and Delivery	Expense	SELLING EXPENSES
6000	Salaries & Wages	Expense	GENERAL & ADMINISTRATIVE
6010	Employer Social Security Expense	Expense	GENERAL & ADMINISTRATIVE
6015	Employer Medicare Expense	Expense	GENERAL & ADMINISTRATIVE
6100	Auto Expense	Expense	GENERAL & ADMINISTRATIVE
6120	Bank Service Charges	Expense	GENERAL & ADMINISTRATIVE
6160	Depreciation Expense	Expense	GENERAL & ADMINISTRATIVE
6180	Dues & Subscriptions	Expense	GENERAL & ADMINISTRATIVE
6200	Equipment Rental Expense	Expense	GENERAL & ADMINISTRATIVE
6220	Utilities	Expense	GENERAL & ADMINISTRATIVE
6230	Insurance - Employee Group Expense	Expense	GENERAL & ADMINISTRATIVE
6240	Insurance - General Expense	Expense	GENERAL & ADMINISTRATIVE
6255	401K Expense	Expense	GENERAL & ADMINISTRATIVE
6260	Interest Expense	Expense	GENERAL & ADMINISTRATIVE
6270	Legal & Accounting	Expense	GENERAL & ADMINISTRATIVE
6280	Miscellaneous Expense	Expense	GENERAL & ADMINISTRATIVE
6300	General Office Expense	Expense	GENERAL & ADMINISTRATIVE
6340	Postage Expense	Expense	GENERAL & ADMINISTRATIVE
6360	General Rent Expense	Expense	GENERAL & ADMINISTRATIVE
6440	Supplies Expense	Expense	GENERAL & ADMINISTRATIVE
6480	Taxes - Real Estate	Expense	GENERAL & ADMINISTRATIVE
6490	Taxes - Payroll	Expense	GENERAL & ADMINISTRATIVE
6500	Taxes - Other	Expense	GENERAL & ADMINISTRATIVE
6520	Telephone	Expense	GENERAL & ADMINISTRATIVE
6540	Travel & Entertainment	Expense	GENERAL & ADMINISTRATIVE
6550	Bad Debts	Expense	GENERAL & ADMINISTRATIVE
6560	Fines & Penalties	Expense	GENERAL & ADMINISTRATIVE
7100	Finance Charge Income	Other Income	OTHER INCOME
7210	Federal Income Tax	Expense	INCOME TAXES
7220	State Income Tax	Expense	INCOME TAXES
9999	Temporary Distribution	Expense	OTHER EXPENSES

TYA NON PROFIT
CHART OF ACCOUNTS

ACCOUNT NUMBER	NAME	TYPE	BALANCE SHEET SECTION / INCOME STATEMENT SECTION
1000	Cash in Bank	Asset	UNRESTRICTED FUND
1050	Savings Account	Asset	UNRESTRICTED FUND
1080	Petty Cash	Asset	UNRESTRICTED FUND
1098	Undeposited Cash	Asset	UNRESTRICTED FUND
1099	Cash Transfers	Asset	UNRESTRICTED FUND
1100	Receivables	Asset	UNRESTRICTED FUND
1190	Allowance for Bad Debts	Asset	UNRESTRICTED FUND
1200	Inventories	Asset	UNRESTRICTED FUND
1400	Prepaid Expenses	Asset	PREPAID EXPENSES
1500	Cash - Restricted Fund	Asset	RESTRICTED FUND
1510	Investments	Asset	RESTRICTED FUND
1520	Grants Receivable	Asset	RESTRICTED FUND
1600	Cash - Building Fund	Asset	BUILDING FUND
1602	Investments - Building Fund	Asset	BUILDING FUND
1604	Pledges Receivable	Asset	BUILDING FUND
1610	Land	Asset	BUILDING FUND
1615	Buildings	Asset	BUILDING FUND
1620	A/D - Buildings	Asset	BUILDING FUND
1645	Equipment	Asset	BUILDING FUND
1650	A/D - Equipment	Asset	BUILDING FUND
1655	Furniture & Fixtures	Asset	BUILDING FUND
1660	A/D - Furniture & Fixtures	Asset	BUILDING FUND
1665	Vehicles	Asset	BUILDING FUND
1670	A/D - Vehicles	Asset	BUILDING FUND
1800	Cash - Endowment Fund	Asset	ENDOWMENT FUNDS
1850	Investments - Endowment Fund	Asset	ENDOWMENT FUNDS
2000	Accounts Pay - Unrestricted	Liability	UNRESTRICTED FUND LIABILITIES
2100	Employee Health Ins Payable	Liability	UNRESTRICTED FUND LIABILITIES
2103	Research Grants	Liability	RESTRICTED FUND LIABILITIES
2105	Dental Insurance Payable	Liability	UNRESTRICTED FUND LIABILITIES
2110	401K Payable	Liability	UNRESTRICTED FUND LIABILITIES
2120	Customer Security Deposits	Liability	UNRESTRICTED FUND LIABILITIES
2150	Designated Future Periods	Liability	UNRESTRICTED FUND LIABILITIES
2200	Federal Withholding Tax Payable	Liability	UNRESTRICTED FUND LIABILITIES
2210	Social Security Tax Payable	Liability	UNRESTRICTED FUND LIABILITIES
2212	Medicare Withholding Tax Payable	Liability	UNRESTRICTED FUND LIABILITIES
2500	Accounts Payable - Restricted	Liability	RESTRICTED FUND LIABILITIES
2800	Accounts Payable - Endowment	Liability	ENDOWMENT FUNDS LIABILITIES
3000	Fund Balance (Central)	Equity	FUND BALANCES
3010	Unrestricted - Not Designated	Equity	FUND BALANCES
3030	Unrestricted - Designated	Equity	FUND BALANCES
3040	Equity	Equity	FUND BALANCES
3100	Restricted Fund Balance	Equity	FUND BALANCES
3110	Building Fund Balance	Equity	FUND BALANCES
3150	Endowment Fund Balance	Equity	FUND BALANCES
4000	Contributions - Unrestricted	Income	SUPP & REV - UNRESTRICTED
4010	Special Events	Income	SUPP & REV - UNRESTRICTED
4020	Legacies & Bequests	Income	SUPP & REV - UNRESTRICTED
4030	Campaigns	Income	SUPP & REV - UNRESTRICTED
4040	Membership Dues	Income	SUPP & REV - UNRESTRICTED

Chart of Accounts—nonprofit organization.

continues

continued

continued

*Chart of Accounts—
nonprofit organiza-
tion.*

**TYA NON PROFIT
CHART OF ACCOUNTS**

ACCOUNT NUMBER	NAME	TYPE	BALANCE SHEET SECTION / INCOME STATEMENT SECTION
4050	Investment Income	Income	SUPP & REV - UNRESTRICTED
4070	Real Gain on Invest - Unrestricted	Income	SUPP & REV - UNRESTRICTED
4080	Miscellaneous	Income	SUPP & REV - UNRESTRICTED
4090	Transfer from Other Funds - Unrestricted	Income	SUPP & REV - UNRESTRICTED
4280	Sales Discounts	Income	SUPP & REV - UNRESTRICTED
4500	Contributions - Restricted	Income	SUPPORT & REV - RESTRICTED
4510	Investment Income - Unrestricted	Income	SUPPORT & REV - RESTRICTED
4520	Transfer from Other Funds - Restricted	Income	SUPPORT & REV - RESTRICTED
4600	Contributions - Building	Income	SUPPORT & REV - BUILDING FUNDS
4610	Investment Income - Building	Income	SUPPORT & REV - BUILDING FUNDS
4620	Realized Gain on Sale of Asset	Income	SUPPORT & REV - BUILDING FUNDS
4630	Transfer from Other Funds - Bd	Income	SUPPORT & REV - BUILDING FUNDS
4800	Contributions - Endowment	Income	SUPPORT & REV - ENDOWMENT
4810	Legacies & Bequests - Endowmnt	Income	SUPPORT & REV - ENDOWMENT
4820	Realized Gain on Investments	Income	SUPPORT & REV - ENDOWMENT
5000	Program A - Unrestricted	Expense	PROGRAM A
5010	Salaries & Wages	Expense	PROGRAM A
5015	Employer Social Security	Expense	PROGRAM A
5016	Employer Medicare	Expense	PROGRAM A
5020	Fringe Benefits	Expense	PROGRAM A
5030	Travel	Expense	PROGRAM A
5040	Advertising	Expense	PROGRAM A
5050	Other	Expense	PROGRAM A
5060	Purchases Discounts Expense	Expense	PROGRAM A
5100	Program B - Unrestricted	Expense	PROGRAM B
5200	Program C - Unrestricted	Expense	PROGRAM C
5300	Program D - Unrestricted	Expense	PROGRAM D
5500	Program F - Unrestricted	Expense	PROGRAM F
5600	Program G - Unrestricted	Expense	PROGRAM G
5660	Freight & Delivery	Expense	PROGRAM G
5700	Program H - Unrestricted	Expense	PROGRAM H
5800	Program I - Unrestricted	Expense	PROGRAM I
5900	Transfers to Other Funds - Unrestricted	Expense	TRANSFERS TO OTHER FUNDS
6000	Program A - Restricted	Expense	PROGRAM A
6100	Program B - Restricted	Expense	PROGRAM B
6200	Program C - Restricted	Expense	PROGRAM C
6300	Program D - Restricted	Expense	PROGRAM D
6400	Program E - Restricted	Expense	PROGRAM E
6500	Program F - Restricted	Expense	PROGRAM F
6600	Program G - Restricted	Expense	PROGRAM G
6700	Program H - Restricted	Expense	PROGRAM H
6800	Program I - Restricted	Expense	PROGRAM I
6900	Transfers to Other Funds - Restricted	Expense	TRANSFERS TO OTHER FUNDS
7000	Management & General - Bldg	Expense	EXPENSES - BUILDING FUND
7010	Fund Raising	Expense	EXPENSES - BUILDING FUND
7020	Transfer to Other Funds - Bldg	Expense	EXPENSES - BUILDING FUND
8000	Management & General	Expense	EXPENSES - ENDOWMENT FUND
8010	Transfer to Other Funds	Expense	EXPENSES - ENDOWMENT FUND
9999	Temporary Distribution	Expense	EXPENSES - ENDOWMENT FUND

Chart of Accounts—
contractor.

ACCOUNT NUMBER	NAME	TYPE	BALANCE SHEET SECTION / INCOME STATEMENT SECTION
1000	Checking Account	Asset	CURRENT ASSETS
1050	Savings Account	Asset	CURRENT ASSETS
1060	Payroll Account	Asset	CURRENT ASSETS
1070	Cash - Trustee Account	Asset	CURRENT ASSETS
1080	Petty Cash	Asset	CURRENT ASSETS
1098	Undeposited Cash	Asset	CURRENT ASSETS
1099	Cash Transfers	Asset	CURRENT ASSETS
1100	Accounts Receivable	Asset	CURRENT ASSETS
1120	Mortgages Receivable	Asset	CURRENT ASSETS
1140	Notes Receivable	Asset	CURRENT ASSETS
1190	Allowance for Bad Debts	Asset	CURRENT ASSETS
1200	Inventory - Land	Asset	CURRENT ASSETS
1210	Inventory - Buildings	Asset	CURRENT ASSETS
1220	Construction in Progress	Asset	CURRENT ASSETS
1240	Contracts Receivable	Asset	CURRENT ASSETS
1350	Prepaid Expenses	Asset	PREPAID EXPENSES
1500	Land	Asset	PROPERTY AND EQUIPMENT
1510	Buildings	Asset	PROPERTY AND EQUIPMENT
1511	A/D - Buildings	Asset	PROPERTY AND EQUIPMENT
1570	Equipment	Asset	PROPERTY AND EQUIPMENT
1571	A/D - Equipment	Asset	PROPERTY AND EQUIPMENT
1580	Furniture and Fixtures	Asset	PROPERTY AND EQUIPMENT
1581	A/D - Furniture & Fixtures	Asset	PROPERTY AND EQUIPMENT
1650	Vehicles	Asset	PROPERTY AND EQUIPMENT
1651	A/D - Vehicles	Asset	PROPERTY AND EQUIPMENT
1800	Utility Deposits	Asset	OTHER ASSETS
1810	Other Assets	Asset	OTHER ASSETS
1900	Organization Costs	Asset	OTHER ASSETS
1901	Accum Amortization - Org Costs	Asset	OTHER ASSETS
1910	Escrow Deposits	Asset	OTHER ASSETS
1920	Municipal Tax Liens & Deposits	Asset	OTHER ASSETS
2000	Accounts Payable	Liability	CURRENT LIABILITIES
2100	Employee Health Ins Payable	Liability	CURRENT LIABILITIES
2105	Dental Insurance Payable	Liability	CURRENT LIABILITIES
2110	401K Payable	Liability	CURRENT LIABILITIES
2115	Commissions Payable	Liability	CURRENT LIABILITIES
2120	Customer Security Deposits	Liability	CURRENT LIABILITIES
2130	Escrow Deposits Payable	Liability	CURRENT LIABILITIES
2190	Sales Taxes Payable	Liability	CURRENT LIABILITIES
2200	Federal Withholding Tax Payable	Liability	PAYROLL TAXES PAYABLE
2210	Social Security Tax Payable	Liability	PAYROLL TAXES PAYABLE
2212	Medicare Withholding Tax Payable	Liability	PAYROLL TAXES PAYABLE
2220	State Withholding Taxes Payable	Liability	PAYROLL TAXES PAYABLE
2250	Local Withholding Taxes Payable	Liability	PAYROLL TAXES PAYABLE
2280	Accrued FUTA	Liability	PAYROLL TAXES PAYABLE
2290	Accrued SUTA	Liability	PAYROLL TAXES PAYABLE
2690	Accrued Other Expenses	Liability	OTHER ACCRUED EXPENSES
3010	Common Stock	Equity	EQUITY
3030	Additional Paid in Capital	Equity	EQUITY
3040	Retained Earnings	Equity	EQUITY

continues

continued

Chart of Accounts— contractor.

**TYA CONTRACTIOR
CHART OF ACCOUNTS**

ACCOUNT NUMBER	NAME	TYPE	BALANCE SHEET SECTION / INCOME STATEMENT SECTION
3210	Capital	Equity	EQUITY
3220	Drawing	Equity	EQUITY
4000	Sales	Income	SALES
4280	Sales Discounts	Income	SALES
4290	Sales Returns & Allowances	Income	SALES
4292	Income - Installment Sales	Income	SALES
4294	Rental Income	Income	SALES
4310	Purchases	Expense	COST OF SALES
4410	Purchases Discounts	Expense	COST OF SALES
4430	Purchase Returns & Allowances	Expense	COST OF SALES
4490	Cost of Construction Sold	Expense	COST OF SALES
5000	Roads & Curbs	Expense	LAND AND DEVELOPMENT
5100	Water Mains	Expense	LAND AND DEVELOPMENT
5120	Engineering	Expense	LAND AND DEVELOPMENT
5140	Surveys	Expense	LAND AND DEVELOPMENT
5150	Brochures and Catalogues	Expense	LAND AND DEVELOPMENT
5160	Legal & Municipal Costs	Expense	LAND AND DEVELOPMENT
5180	Fill	Expense	LAND AND DEVELOPMENT
5500	Salary - Foreman	Expense	DIRECT COSTS
5505	Wages - Construction	Expense	DIRECT COSTS
5510	Masonry	Expense	DIRECT COSTS
5525	Carpentry	Expense	DIRECT COSTS
5530	Plumbing	Expense	DIRECT COSTS
5535	Heating & Air	Expense	DIRECT COSTS
5540	Sheet Metal	Expense	DIRECT COSTS
5545	Electrical	Expense	DIRECT COSTS
5550	Appliances	Expense	DIRECT COSTS
5555	Other Subcontractors	Expense	DIRECT COSTS
5600	Miscellaneous Expense - Sales	Expense	DIRECT COSTS
5650	Payroll Taxes - Sales	Expense	DIRECT COSTS
5660	Freight and Delivery	Expense	DIRECT COSTS
5800	Real Estate Taxes	Expense	INDIRECT COSTS
5810	Heat Light & Power	Expense	INDIRECT COSTS
5820	Permits	Expense	INDIRECT COSTS
5830	Occupancy	Expense	INDIRECT COSTS
5840	Cleaning	Expense	INDIRECT COSTS
5850	Landscaping	Expense	INDIRECT COSTS
6000	Salaries & Wages	Expense	GENERAL & ADMINISTRATIVE
6010	Employer Social Security Expense	Expense	GENERAL & ADMINISTRATIVE
6015	Employer Medicare Expense	Expense	GENERAL & ADMINISTRATIVE
6030	Officers Salaries	Expense	GENERAL & ADMINISTRATIVE
6100	Auto Expense	Expense	GENERAL & ADMINISTRATIVE
6120	Bank Service Charges	Expense	GENERAL & ADMINISTRATIVE
6140	Contributions	Expense	GENERAL & ADMINISTRATIVE
6160	Depreciation Expense	Expense	GENERAL & ADMINISTRATIVE
6180	Dues & Subscriptions	Expense	GENERAL & ADMINISTRATIVE
6200	Equipment Rental	Expense	GENERAL & ADMINISTRATIVE
6220	Utilities	Expense	GENERAL & ADMINISTRATIVE
6230	Insurance - Employee Group	Expense	GENERAL & ADMINISTRATIVE
6240	Insurance - General	Expense	GENERAL & ADMINISTRATIVE

continues

continued

*Chart of Accounts—
contractor.*

**TYA CONTRACTIOR
CHART OF ACCOUNTS**

ACCOUNT NUMBER	NAME	TYPE	BALANCE SHEET SECTION / INCOME STATEMENT SECTION
6250	Insurance - Officers Life	Expense	GENERAL & ADMINISTRATIVE
6255	401K Expense	Expense	GENERAL & ADMINISTRATIVE
6260	Interest Expense	Expense	GENERAL & ADMINISTRATIVE
6270	Legal & Accounting	Expense	GENERAL & ADMINISTRATIVE
6280	Miscellaneous Expense	Expense	GENERAL & ADMINISTRATIVE
6295	Occupancy Expense	Expense	GENERAL & ADMINISTRATIVE
6300	Office Expense	Expense	GENERAL & ADMINISTRATIVE
6310	Outside Services	Expense	GENERAL & ADMINISTRATIVE
6340	Postage Expense	Expense	GENERAL & ADMINISTRATIVE
6360	Rent Expense	Expense	GENERAL & ADMINISTRATIVE
6380	Repairs & Maintenance	Expense	GENERAL & ADMINISTRATIVE
6440	Supplies Expense	Expense	GENERAL & ADMINISTRATIVE
6480	Taxes - Real Estate	Expense	GENERAL & ADMINISTRATIVE
6490	Taxes - Payroll	Expense	GENERAL & ADMINISTRATIVE
6500	Taxes - Other	Expense	GENERAL & ADMINISTRATIVE
6520	Telephone	Expense	GENERAL & ADMINISTRATIVE
6540	Travel & Entertainment	Expense	GENERAL & ADMINISTRATIVE
6550	Bad Debts	Expense	GENERAL & ADMINISTRATIVE
6560	Fines & Penalties Expense	Expense	GENERAL & ADMINISTRATIVE
7100	Finance Charge Income	Other Income	OTHER INCOME
7210	Federal Income Tax	Expense	INCOME TAXES
7220	State Income Tax	Expense	INCOME TAXES
9999	Temporary Distribution	Expense	OTHER EXPENSES

General Journal Entry on four-column ledger paper.

TYA Contractor
Journal Entries 7/31/00

	Date	Account	Acct #	Debit	Credit	
1	7/31	Sales	4000		272,000.00	JG-1
2		Cost of Const Sold	4490	1,500.00		
3		Contract Receivable	1240	270,500.00		
4						
5						
6		To record sale by ABC Realty				
7						
8						
9	7/31	Cash in Checking	1000		8,530.00	JG-2
10		Appliances	5550	8,530.00		
11						
12		To record appliances for Monte Vista				
13						
14	7/31	Cash in Checking	1000		42.00	JG-3
15		Auto Expense	6100	17.00		
16		Office Expense	6300	25.00		
17						
18		To record Petty Cash reimbursement				

National Brand 45-504 Eye-Ease® / 45-304 2-Pack / Made in USA

TVA Sample

Amortization Schedule

Prepared By _JC_ 1-1-98
Approved By _____

Date	Description / Life	Mo. Amort.	Acc. Amort. 1999	Acc. Amort. 2000	Acc. Amort. 2001
1-1-99	Goodwill 5,000.00 36 mo.	138 88	1666 56	1666 56	
1-1-99	Org. Costs 2,100.00 36 mo.	58 33	699 96	699 96	

Amortization Schedule on four-column ledger paper.

Application for Employer Identification Number.

Form **SS-4** (Rev. April 2000) Department of the Treasury Internal Revenue Service	**Application for Employer Identification Number** (For use by employers, corporations, partnerships, trusts, estates, churches, government agencies, certain individuals, and others. See instructions.) ▶ **Keep a copy for your records.**	EIN OMB No. 1545-0003

Please type or print clearly.

1 Name of applicant (legal name) (see instructions)

2 Trade name of business (if different from name on line 1)	**3** Executor, trustee, "care of" name
4a Mailing address (street address) (room, apt., or suite no.)	**5a** Business address (if different from address on lines 4a and 4b)
4b City, state, and ZIP code	**5b** City, state, and ZIP code

6 County and state where principal business is located

7 Name of principal officer, general partner, grantor, owner, or trustor—SSN or ITIN may be required (see instructions) ▶

8a Type of entity (Check only one box.) (see instructions)

Caution: *If applicant is a limited liability company, see the instructions for line 8a.*

☐ Sole proprietor (SSN) _____
☐ Partnership   ☐ Personal service corp.
☐ REMIC   ☐ National Guard
☐ State/local government ☐ Farmers' cooperative
☐ Church or church-controlled organization
☐ Other nonprofit organization (specify) ▶ _____
☐ Other (specify) ▶

☐ Estate (SSN of decedent) _____
☐ Plan administrator (SSN) _____
☐ Other corporation (specify) ▶ _____
☐ Trust
☐ Federal government/military   (enter GEN if applicable) _____

8b If a corporation, name the state or foreign country (if applicable) where incorporated

State	Foreign country

9 Reason for applying (Check only one box.) (see instructions)
☐ Started new business (specify type) ▶ _____
☐ Hired employees (Check the box and see line 12.)
☐ Created a pension plan (specify type) ▶

☐ Banking purpose (specify purpose) ▶ _____
☐ Changed type of organization (specify new type) ▶ _____
☐ Purchased going business
☐ Created a trust (specify type) ▶ _____
☐ Other (specify) ▶

10 Date business started or acquired (month, day, year) (see instructions) | **11** Closing month of accounting year (see instructions)

12 First date wages or annuities were paid or will be paid (month, day, year). **Note:** *If applicant is a withholding agent, enter date income will first be paid to nonresident alien. (month, day, year)* . . . . ▶

13 Highest number of employees expected in the next 12 months. **Note:** *If the applicant does not expect to have any employees during the period, enter -0-. (see instructions)* . . . . ▶

Nonagricultural	Agricultural	Household

14 Principal activity (see instructions) ▶

15 Is the principal business activity manufacturing? . . . . ☐ Yes ☐ No
If "Yes," principal product and raw material used ▶

16 To whom are most of the products or services sold? Please check one box.   ☐ Business (wholesale)
☐ Public (retail) ☐ Other (specify) ▶   ☐ N/A

17a Has the applicant ever applied for an employer identification number for this or any other business? . . . . ☐ Yes ☐ No
Note: *If "Yes," please complete lines 17b and 17c.*

17b If you checked "Yes" on line 17a, give applicant's legal name and trade name shown on prior application, if different from line 1 or 2 above.
Legal name ▶   Trade name ▶

17c Approximate date when and city and state where the application was filed. Enter previous employer identification number if known.

Approximate date when filed (mo., day, year)	City and state where filed	Previous EIN

Under penalties of perjury, I declare that I have examined this application, and to the best of my knowledge and belief, it is true, correct, and complete.

Business telephone number (include area code) ( )
Fax telephone number (include area code) ( )

Name and title (Please type or print clearly.) ▶

Signature ▶   Date ▶

Note: *Do not write below this line. For official use only.*

Please leave blank ▶	Geo.	Ind.	Class	Size	Reason for applying

For Privacy Act and Paperwork Reduction Act Notice, see page 4.   Cat. No. 16055N   Form **SS-4** (Rev. 4-2000)

W-4 form.

Form W-4 (2000)

Purpose. Complete Form W-4 so your employer can withhold the correct Federal income tax from your pay. Because your tax situation may change, you may want to refigure your withholding each year.

Exemption from withholding. If you are exempt, complete only lines 1, 2, 3, 4, and 7, and sign the form to validate it. Your exemption for 2000 expires February 16, 2001.

Note: *You cannot claim exemption from withholding if (1) your income exceeds $700 and includes more than $250 of unearned income (e.g., interest and dividends) and (2) another person can claim you as a dependent on their tax return.*

Basic instructions. If you are not exempt, complete the **Personal Allowances Worksheet** below. The worksheets on page 2 adjust your withholding allowances based on itemized deductions, adjustments to income, or two-earner/two-job situations. Complete all worksheets that apply. They will help you figure the number of withholding allowances you are entitled to claim. **However, you may claim fewer (or zero) allowances.**

Child tax and higher education credits. For details on adjusting withholding for these and other credits, see **Pub. 919,** How Do I Adjust My Tax Withholding?

Head of household. Generally, you may claim head of household filing status on your tax return only if you are unmarried and pay more than 50% of the costs of keeping up a home for yourself and your dependent(s) or other qualifying individuals. See line E below.

Nonwage income. If you have a large amount of nonwage income, such as interest or dividends, you should consider making estimated tax payments using **Form 1040-ES,** Estimated Tax for Individuals. Otherwise, you may owe additional tax.

Two earners/two jobs. If you have a working spouse or more than one job, figure the total number of allowances you are entitled to claim on all jobs using worksheets from only one Form W-4. Your withholding usually will be most accurate when all allowances are claimed on the Form W-4 prepared for the highest paying job and zero allowances are claimed for the others.

Check your withholding. After your Form W-4 takes effect, use Pub. 919 to see how the dollar amount you are having withheld compares to your projected total tax for 2000. Get Pub. 919 especially if you used the **Two-Earner/Two-Job Worksheet** on page 2 and your earnings exceed $150,000 (Single) or $200,000 (Married).

Recent name change? If your name on line 1 differs from that shown on your social security card, call 1-800-772-1213 for a new social security card.

Personal Allowances Worksheet (Keep for your records.)

A	Enter "1" for **yourself** if no one else can claim you as a dependent	A _____
B	Enter "1" if: { • You are single and have only one job; or • You are married, have only one job, and your spouse does not work; or • Your wages from a second job or your spouse's wages (or the total of both) are $1,000 or less. } . .	B _____
C	Enter "1" for your **spouse.** But, you may choose to enter -0- if you are married and have either a working spouse or more than one job. (Entering -0- may help you avoid having too little tax withheld.)	C _____
D	Enter number of **dependents** (other than your spouse or yourself) you will claim on your tax return	D _____
E	Enter "1" if you will file as **head of household** on your tax return (see conditions under **Head of household** above) .	E _____
F	Enter "1" if you have at least $1,500 of **child or dependent care expenses** for which you plan to claim a credit . .	F _____
G	**Child Tax Credit:** • If your total income will be between $18,000 and $50,000 ($23,000 and $63,000 if married), enter "1" for each eligible child. • If your total income will be between $50,000 and $80,000 ($63,000 and $115,000 if married), enter "2" if you have two eligible children, enter "2" if you have three or four eligible children, or enter "3" if you have five or more eligible children.	G _____
H	Add lines A through G and enter total here. Note: *This may be different from the number of exemptions you claim on your tax return.* ▶	H _____

For accuracy, complete all worksheets that apply. {	• If you plan to **itemize or claim adjustments to income** and want to reduce your withholding, see the **Deductions and Adjustments Worksheet** on page 2. • If you are **single,** have **more than one job** and your combined earnings from all jobs exceed $34,000, OR if you are **married** and have a **working spouse or more than one job** and the combined earnings from all jobs exceed $60,000, see the **Two-Earner/Two-Job Worksheet** on page 2 to avoid having too little tax withheld. • If **neither** of the above situations applies, **stop here** and enter the number from line H on line 5 of Form W-4 below.

---------------------- **Cut here and give Form W-4 to your employer. Keep the top part for your records.** ----------------------

Form **W-4** Department of the Treasury Internal Revenue Service	**Employee's Withholding Allowance Certificate** ▶ **For Privacy Act and Paperwork Reduction Act Notice, see page 2.**	OMB No. 1545-0010 **2000**

1 Type or print your first name and middle initial	Last name	2 Your social security number

Home address (number and street or rural route)	3 ☐ Single ☐ Married ☐ Married, but withhold at higher Single rate. Note: *If married, but legally separated, or spouse is a nonresident alien, check the Single box.*
City or town, state, and ZIP code	4 If your last name differs from that on your social security card, check here. **You must call 1-800-772-1213 for a new card** . . . ▶ ☐

5	Total number of allowances you are claiming (from line **H** above **OR** from the applicable worksheet on page 2)	5
6	Additional amount, if any, you want withheld from each paycheck	6 $
7	I claim exemption from withholding for 2000, and I certify that I meet **BOTH** of the following conditions for exemption: • Last year I had a right to a refund of **ALL** Federal income tax withheld because I had **NO** tax liability **AND** • This year I expect a refund of **ALL** Federal income tax withheld because I expect to have **NO** tax liability. If you meet both conditions, write "EXEMPT" here . . . . ▶	7

Under penalties of perjury, I certify that I am entitled to the number of withholding allowances claimed on this certificate, or I am entitled to claim exempt status.

Employee's signature
(Form is not valid
unless you sign it) ▶ _____   Date ▶ _____

8 Employer's name and address (Employer: Complete lines 8 and 10 only if sending to the IRS.)	9 Office code (optional)	10 Employer identification number

Cat. No. 10220Q

W-4 form (page 2).

Form W-4 (2000)   Page **2**

Deductions and Adjustments Worksheet

Note: *Use this worksheet only if you plan to itemize deductions or claim adjustments to income on your 2000 tax return.*

1	Enter an estimate of your 2000 itemized deductions. These include qualifying home mortgage interest, charitable contributions, state and local taxes, medical expenses in excess of 7.5% of your income, and miscellaneous deductions. (For 2000, you may have to reduce your itemized deductions if your income is over $128,950 ($64,475 if married filing separately). See **Worksheet 3** in Pub. 919 for details.) . . .	1	$
2	Enter: { $7,350 if married filing jointly or qualifying widow(er) / $6,450 if head of household / $4,400 if single / $3,675 if married filing separately }	2	$
3	**Subtract** line 2 from line 1. If line 2 is greater than line 1, enter -0-	3	$
4	Enter an estimate of your 2000 adjustments to income, including alimony, deductible IRA contributions, and student loan interest	4	$
5	**Add** lines 3 and 4 and enter the total (Include any amount for credits from **Worksheet 7** in Pub. 919.) .	5	$
6	Enter an estimate of your 2000 nonwage income (such as dividends or interest)	6	$
7	**Subtract** line 6 from line 5. Enter the result, but not less than -0-	7	$
8	**Divide** the amount on line 7 by $3,000 and enter the result here. Drop any fraction	8	
9	Enter the number from the **Personal Allowances Worksheet,** line H, page 1	9	
10	**Add** lines 8 and 9 and enter the total here. If you plan to use the **Two-Earner/Two-Job Worksheet,** also enter this total on line 1 below. Otherwise, **stop here** and enter this total on Form W-4, line 5, page 1 .	10	

Two-Earner/Two-Job Worksheet

Note: *Use this worksheet only if the instructions under line H on page 1 direct you here.*

1	Enter the number from line H, page 1 (or from line 10 above if you used the **Deductions and Adjustments Worksheet**)	1	
2	Find the number in **Table 1** below that applies to the **LOWEST** paying job and enter it here	2	
3	If line 1 is **MORE THAN OR EQUAL TO** line 2, subtract line 2 from line 1. Enter the result here (if zero, enter -0-) and on Form W-4, line 5, page 1. **Do not** use the rest of this worksheet	3	

Note: *If line 1 is **LESS THAN** line 2, enter -0- on Form W-4, line 5, page 1. Complete lines 4–9 below to calculate the additional withholding amount necessary to avoid a year end tax bill.*

4	Enter the number from line 2 of this worksheet	4	
5	Enter the number from line 1 of this worksheet	5	
6	**Subtract** line 5 from line 4	6	$
7	Find the amount in **Table 2** below that applies to the **HIGHEST** paying job and enter it here	7	$
8	**Multiply** line 7 by line 6 and enter the result here. This is the additional annual withholding needed . .	8	$
9	**Divide** line 8 by the number of pay periods remaining in 2000. For example, divide by 26 if you are paid every other week and you complete this form in December 1999. Enter the result here and on Form W-4, line 6, page 1. This is the additional amount to be withheld from each paycheck	9	$

Table 1: Two-Earner/Two-Job Worksheet

Married Filing Jointly				All Others			
If wages from **LOWEST** paying job are—	Enter on line 2 above	If wages from **LOWEST** paying job are—	Enter on line 2 above	If wages from **LOWEST** paying job are—	Enter on line 2 above	If wages from **LOWEST** paying job are—	Enter on line 2 above
$0 - $4,000	0	41,001 - 45,000	8	$0 - $5,000	0	65,001 - 80,000	8
4,001 - 7,000	1	45,001 - 55,000	9	5,001 - 11,000	1	80,001 - 100,000	9
7,001 - 13,000	2	55,001 - 63,000	10	11,001 - 17,000	2	100,001 and over	10
13,001 - 19,000	3	63,001 - 70,000	11	17,001 - 22,000	3		
19,001 - 25,000	4	70,001 - 85,000	12	22,001 - 27,000	4		
25,001 - 31,000	5	85,001 - 100,000	13	27,001 - 40,000	5		
31,001 - 37,000	6	100,001 - 110,000	14	40,001 - 50,000	6		
37,001 - 41,000	7	110,001 and over	15	50,001 - 65,000	7		

Table 2: Two-Earner/Two-Job Worksheet

Married Filing Jointly		All Others	
If wages from **HIGHEST** paying job are—	Enter on line 7 above	If wages from **HIGHEST** paying job are—	Enter on line 7 above
$0 - $50,000	$420	$0 - $30,000	$420
50,001 - 100,000	780	30,001 - 60,000	780
100,001 - 130,000	870	60,001 - 120,000	870
130,001 - 250,000	1,000	120,001 - 270,000	1,000
250,001 and over	1,100	270,001 and over	1,100

W-5 form.

2000 Form W-5

Department of the Treasury
Internal Revenue Service

Instructions

A Change To Note

Beginning in 2000, new rules apply to determine who is a foster child for purposes of the earned income credit (EIC). See page 3 for details.

Purpose

Use Form W-5 if you are eligible to get part of the EIC in advance with your pay and choose to do so. See **Who Is Eligible To Get Advance EIC Payments?** below. The amount you can get in advance generally depends on your wages. If you are married, the amount of your advance EIC payments also depends on whether your spouse has filed a Form W-5 with his or her employer. However, your employer cannot give you more than $1,412 throughout 2000 with your pay. You will get the rest of any EIC you are entitled to when you file your tax return and claim the EIC.

If you do not choose to get advance payments, you can still claim the EIC on your 2000 tax return.

What Is the EIC?

The EIC is a credit for certain workers. It reduces the tax you owe. It may give you a refund even if you do not owe any tax.

Who Is Eligible To Get Advance EIC Payments?

You are eligible to get advance EIC payments if **all three** of the following apply.

1. You expect to have at least one qualifying child. If you do not expect to have a qualifying child, you may still be eligible for the EIC, but you **cannot** receive advance EIC payments. See **Who Is a Qualifying Child?** on page 2.

2. You expect that your 2000 earned income and modified AGI (adjusted gross income) will each be less than $27,413. Include your spouse's income if you plan to file a joint return. As used on this form, **earned income** does not include amounts inmates in penal institutions are paid for their work or workfare payments (defined on this page). For most people, **modified AGI** is the total of adjusted gross income plus any tax-exempt interest. But see the 1999 revision of **Pub. 596,** Earned Income Credit, for information about how to figure your 2000 modified AGI if you expect to receive nontaxable payments from a pension, annuity, or an IRA; or you plan to file a 2000 Form 1040.

3. You expect to be able to claim the EIC for 2000. To find out if you may be able to claim the EIC, answer the questions on page 2.

Workfare payments. These are cash payments certain people receive from a state or local agency that administers public assistance programs funded under the Federal Temporary Assistance for Needy Families (TANF) program in return for certain work activities such as **(1)** work experience activities (including work associated with remodeling or repairing publicly assisted housing) if sufficient private sector employment is not available, or **(2)** community service program activities.

How To Get Advance EIC Payments

If you are eligible to get advance EIC payments, fill in the 2000 Form W-5 at the bottom of this page. Then, detach it and give it to your employer. If you get advance payments, you **must** file a 2000 Federal income tax return.

You may have only **one** Form W-5 in effect at one time. If you and your spouse are both employed, you should file separate Forms W-5.

(Continued on page 2)

▼ *Give the lower part to your employer; keep the top part for your records.* ▼

———————— Detach here ————————

Form **W-5**	**Earned Income Credit Advance Payment Certificate**	OMB No. 1545-1342
Department of the Treasury Internal Revenue Service	▶ Use the current year's certificate only. ▶ Give this certificate to your employer. ▶ This certificate expires on December 31, 2000.	**2000**

Print or type your full name	Your social security number

Note: *If you get advance payments of the earned income credit for 2000, you* **must** *file a 2000 Federal income tax return. To get advance payments, you* **must** *have a qualifying child and your filing status must be any status* **except** *married filing a separate return.*

		Yes	No
1	I expect to be able to claim the earned income credit for 2000, I do not have another Form W-5 in effect with any other current employer, and I choose to get advance EIC payments		
2	Do you expect to have a qualifying child?		
3	Are you married?		
4	If you are married, does your spouse have a Form W-5 in effect for 2000 with any employer?		

Under penalties of perjury, I declare that the information I have furnished above is, to the best of my knowledge, true, correct, and complete.

Signature ▶ _____ Date ▶ _____

Cat. No. 10227P

I-9 form.

U.S. Department of Justice
Immigration and Naturalization Service

Employment Eligibility Verification

Please read instructions carefully before completing this form. The instructions must be available during completion of this form. ANTI-DISCRIMINATION NOTICE: It is illegal to discriminate against work eligible individuals. Employers CANNOT specify which document(s) they will accept from an employee. The refusal to hire an individual because of a future expiration date may also constitute illegal discrimination.

Section 1. Employee Information and Verification. To be completed and signed by employee at the time employment begins.

Print Name: Last	First	Middle Initial	Maiden Name
Address (Street Name and Number)		Apt. #	Date of Birth (month/day/year)
City	State	Zip Code	Social Security #

I am aware that federal law provides for imprisonment and/or fines for false statements or use of false documents in connection with the completion of this form.	I attest, under penalty of perjury, that I am (check one of the following): ☐ A citizen or national of the United States ☐ A Lawful Permanent Resident (Alien # A_____) ☐ An alien authorized to work until ___/___/___ (Alien # or Admission #) _____
Employee's Signature	Date (month/day/year)

Preparer and/or Translator Certification. *(To be completed and signed if Section 1 is prepared by a person other than the employee.) I attest, under penalty of perjury, that I have assisted in the completion of this form and that to the best of my knowledge the information is true and correct.*

Preparer's/Translator's Signature	Print Name
Address (Street Name and Number, City, State, Zip Code)	Date (month/day/year)

Section 2. Employer Review and Verification. To be completed and signed by employer. Examine one document from List A OR examine one document from List B and one from List C, as listed on the reverse of this form, and record the title, number and expiration date, if any, of the document(s)

List A	OR	List B	AND	List C
Document title: _____		_____		_____
Issuing authority: _____		_____		_____
Document #: _____		_____		_____
Expiration Date (if any): ___/___/___		___/___/___		___/___/___
Document #: _____				
Expiration Date (if any): ___/___/___				

CERTIFICATION - I attest, under penalty of perjury, that I have examined the document(s) presented by the above-named employee, that the above-listed document(s) appear to be genuine and to relate to the employee named, that the employee began employment on *(month/day/year)* ___/___/___ and that to the best of my knowledge the employee is eligible to work in the United States. (State employment agencies may omit the date the employee began employment.)

Signature of Employer or Authorized Representative	Print Name	Title
Business or Organization Name	Address (Street Name and Number, City, State, Zip Code)	Date (month/day/year)

Section 3. Updating and Reverification. To be completed and signed by employer.

A. New Name (if applicable)	B. Date of rehire (month/day/year) (if applicable)

C. If employee's previous grant of work authorization has expired, provide the information below for the document that establishes current employment eligibility.

Document Title: _____   Document #: _____   Expiration Date (if any): ___/___/___

I attest, under penalty of perjury, that to the best of my knowledge, this employee is eligible to work in the United States, and if the employee presented document(s), the document(s) I have examined appear to be genuine and to relate to the individual.

Signature of Employer or Authorized Representative	Date (month/day/year)

Form I-9 (Rev. 11-21-91)N Page 2

Form **4070** (Rev. June 1999) Department of the Treasury Internal Revenue Service	**Employee's Report of Tips to Employer** ▶ For Paperwork Reduction Act Notice, see back of form.	OMB No. 1545-0065
Employee's name and address		Social security number
Employer's name and address (include establishment name, if different)		**1** Cash tips received
		2 Credit card tips received
		3 Tips paid out
Month or shorter period in which tips were received from_____ , _____ , to _____ ,		**4** Net tips (lines **1** + **2** - **3**)
Signature		Date

Form 4070.

Federal tax withholding tables.

Tables for Percentage Method of Withholding
(For Wages Paid in 2001)

TABLE 1– WEEKLY Payroll Period

(a) SINGLE person (including head of household)–

If the amount of wages (after subtracting withholding allowances) is: Not over $51 . . . . . $0

Over–	But not over–	The amount of income tax to withhold is:	of excess over–
$51	—$552	. . 15%	—51
$552	—$1,196	. . $75.15 plus 28%	—552
$1,196	—$2,662	. . $255.47 plus 31%	—1,196
$2,662	—$5,750	. . $709.93 plus 36%	—2,662
$5,750	. . . . .	. . $1,821.61 plus 39.6%	—5,750

(b) MARRIED person–

If the amount of wages (after subtracting withholding allowances) is: Not over $124 . . . . . $0

Over–	But not over–	The amount of income tax to withhold is:	of excess over–
$124	—$960	. . 15%	—$124
$960	—$2,023	. . $125.40 plus 28%	—$960
$2,023	—$3,292	. . $423.04 plus 31%	—$2,023
$3,292	—$5,809	. . $816.43 plus 36%	—$3,292
$5,809	. . . . .	. . $1,722.55 plus 39.6%	—$5,809

TABLE 2– BIWEEKLY Payroll Period

(a) SINGLE person (including head of household)–

If the amount of wages (after subtracting withholding allowances) is: Not over $102 . . . . $0

Over–	But not over–	The amount of income tax to withhold is:	of excess over–
$102	—$1,104	. . 15%	—$102
$1,104	—$2,392	. . $150.30 plus 28%	—$1,104
$2,392	—$5,323	. . $510.94 plus 31%	—$2,392
$5,323	—$11,500	. . $1,419.55 plus 36%	—$5,323
$11,500	. . . . .	. . $3,643.27 plus 39.6%	—$11,500

(b) MARRIED person–

If the amount of wages (after subtracting withholding allowances) is: Not over $248 . . . . $0

Over–	But not over–	The amount of income tax to withhold is:	of excess over–
$248	—$1,919	. . 15%	—$248
$1,919	—$4,046	. . $250.65 plus 28%	—$1,919
$4,046	—$6,585	. . $846.21 plus 31%	—$4,046
$6,585	—$11,617	. . $1,633.30 plus 36%	—$6,585
$11,617	. . . . .	. . $3,444.82 plus 39.6%	—$11,617

TABLE 3– SEMIMONTHLY Payroll Period

(a) SINGLE person (including head of household)–

If the amount of wages (after subtracting withholding allowances) is: Not over $110 . . . . $0

Over–	But not over–	The amount of income tax to withhold is:	of excess over–
$110	—$1,196	. . 15%	—$110
$1,196	—$2,592	. . $162.90 plus 28%	—$1,196
$2,592	—$5,767	. . $553.78 plus 31%	—$2,592
$5,767	—$12,458	. . $1,538.03 plus 36%	—$5,767
$12,458	. . . . .	. . $3,946.79 plus 39.6%	—$12,458

(b) MARRIED person–

If the amount of wages (after subtracting withholding allowances) is: Not over $269 . . . . $0

Over–	But not over–	The amount of income tax to withhold is:	of excess over–
$269	—$2,079	. . 15%	—$269
$2,079	—$4,383	. . $271.50 plus 28%	—$2,079
$4,383	—$7,133	. . $916.62 plus 31%	—$4,383
$7,133	—$12,585	. . $1,769.12 plus 36%	—$7,133
$12,585	. . . . .	. . $3,731.84 plus 39.6%	—$12,585

TABLE 4– MONTHLY Payroll Period

(a) SINGLE person (including head of household)–

If the amount of wages (after subtracting withholding allowances) is: Not over $221 . . . . $0

Over–	But not over–	The amount of income tax to withhold is:	of excess over–
$221	—$2,392	. . 15%	—$221
$2,392	—$5,183	. . $325.65 plus 28%	—$2,392
$5,183	—$11,533	. . $1,107.13 plus 31%	—$5,183
$11,533	—$24,917	. . $3,075.63 plus 36%	—$11,533
$24,917	. . . . .	. . $7,893.87 plus 39.6%	—$24,917

(b) MARRIED person–

If the amount of wages (after subtracting withholding allowances) is: Not over $538 . . . . $0

Over–	But not over–	The amount of income tax to withhold is:	of excess over–
$538	—$4,158	. . 15%	—$538
$4,158	—$8,767	. . $543.00 plus 28%	—$4,158
$8,767	—$14,267	. . $1,833.52 plus 31%	—$8,767
$14,267	—$25,171	. . $3,538.52 plus 36%	—$14,267
$25,171	. . . . .	. . $7,463.96 plus 39.6%	—$25,171

Federal tax with-holding tables.

MARRIED Persons—BIWEEKLY Payroll Period
(For Wages Paid in 2001)

At least	But less than	0	1	2	3	4	5	6	7	8	9	10
\$1,380	\$1,400	171	155	138	121	104	88	71	54	37	21	4
1,400	1,420	174	158	141	124	107	91	74	57	40	24	7
1,420	1,440	177	161	144	127	110	94	77	60	43	27	10
1,440	1,460	180	164	147	130	113	97	80	63	46	30	13
1,460	1,480	183	167	150	133	116	100	83	66	49	33	16
1,480	1,500	186	170	153	136	119	103	86	69	52	36	19
1,500	1,520	189	173	156	139	122	106	89	72	55	39	22
1,520	1,540	192	176	159	142	125	109	92	75	58	42	25
1,540	1,560	195	179	162	145	128	112	95	78	61	45	28
1,560	1,580	198	182	165	148	131	115	98	81	64	48	31
1,580	1,600	201	185	168	151	134	118	101	84	67	51	34
1,600	1,620	204	188	171	154	137	121	104	87	70	54	37
1,620	1,640	207	191	174	157	140	124	107	90	73	57	40
1,640	1,660	210	194	177	160	143	127	110	93	76	60	43
1,660	1,680	213	197	180	163	146	130	113	96	79	63	46
1,680	1,700	216	200	183	166	149	133	116	99	82	66	49
1,700	1,720	219	203	186	169	152	136	119	102	85	69	52
1,720	1,740	222	206	189	172	155	139	122	105	88	72	55
1,740	1,760	225	209	192	175	158	142	125	108	91	75	58
1,760	1,780	228	212	195	178	161	145	128	111	94	78	61
1,780	1,800	231	215	198	181	164	148	131	114	97	81	64
1,800	1,820	234	218	201	184	167	151	134	117	100	84	67
1,820	1,840	237	221	204	187	170	154	137	120	103	87	70
1,840	1,860	240	224	207	190	173	157	140	123	106	90	73
1,860	1,880	243	227	210	193	176	160	143	126	109	93	76
1,880	1,900	246	230	213	196	179	163	146	129	112	96	79
1,900	1,920	249	233	216	199	182	166	149	132	115	99	82
1,920	1,940	254	236	219	202	185	169	152	135	118	102	85
1,940	1,960	259	239	222	205	188	172	155	138	121	105	88
1,960	1,980	265	242	225	208	191	175	158	141	124	108	91
1,980	2,000	270	245	228	211	194	178	161	144	127	111	94
2,000	2,020	276	248	231	214	197	181	164	147	130	114	97
2,020	2,040	282	251	234	217	200	184	167	150	133	117	100
2,040	2,060	287	256	237	220	203	187	170	153	136	120	103
2,060	2,080	293	262	240	223	206	190	173	156	139	123	106
2,080	2,100	298	267	243	226	209	193	176	159	142	126	109
2,100	2,120	304	273	246	229	212	196	179	162	145	129	112
2,120	2,140	310	278	249	232	215	199	182	165	148	132	115
2,140	2,160	315	284	253	235	218	202	185	168	151	135	118
2,160	2,180	321	290	258	238	221	205	188	171	154	138	121
2,180	2,200	326	295	264	241	224	208	191	174	157	141	124
2,200	2,220	332	301	270	244	227	211	194	177	160	144	127
2,220	2,240	338	306	275	247	230	214	197	180	163	147	130
2,240	2,260	343	312	281	250	233	217	200	183	166	150	133
2,260	2,280	349	318	286	255	236	220	203	186	169	153	136
2,280	2,300	354	323	292	261	239	223	206	189	172	156	139
2,300	2,320	360	329	298	266	242	226	209	192	175	159	142
2,320	2,340	366	334	303	272	245	229	212	195	178	162	145
2,340	2,360	371	340	309	278	248	232	215	198	181	165	148
2,360	2,380	377	346	314	283	252	235	218	201	184	168	151
2,380	2,400	382	351	320	289	258	238	221	204	187	171	154
2,400	2,420	388	357	326	294	263	241	224	207	190	174	157
2,420	2,440	394	362	331	300	269	244	227	210	193	177	160
2,440	2,460	399	368	337	306	274	247	230	213	196	180	163
2,460	2,480	405	374	342	311	280	250	233	216	199	183	166
2,480	2,500	410	379	348	317	286	254	236	219	202	186	169
2,500	2,520	416	385	354	322	291	260	239	222	205	189	172
2,520	2,540	422	390	359	328	297	266	242	225	208	192	175
2,540	2,560	427	396	365	334	302	271	245	228	211	195	178
2,560	2,580	433	402	370	339	308	277	248	231	214	198	181
2,580	2,600	438	407	376	345	314	282	251	234	217	201	184
2,600	2,620	444	413	382	350	319	288	257	237	220	204	187
2,620	2,640	450	418	387	356	325	294	262	240	223	207	190
2,640	2,660	455	424	393	362	330	299	268	243	226	210	193
2,660	2,680	461	430	398	367	336	305	274	246	229	213	196

If the wages are— / *And the number of withholding allowances claimed is—* / *The amount of income tax to be withheld is—*

\$2,680 and over   Use Table 2(b) for a **MARRIED person** on page 34. Also see the instructions on page 32.

Form 8109-B.

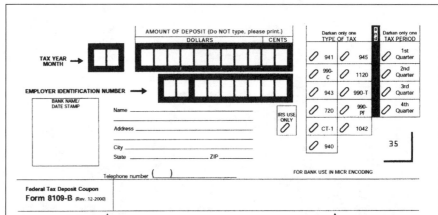

Federal Tax Deposit Coupon
Form 8109-B (Rev. 12-2000)

↑ SEPARATE ALONG THIS LINE AND SUBMIT TO DEPOSITARY WITH PAYMENT ↑ OMB NO. 1545-0257

Note: *Except for the name, address, and telephone number, entries must be made in pencil.* **Use soft lead** *(for example, a #2 pencil) so that the entries can be read more accurately by optical scanning equipment. The name, address, and telephone number may be completed other than by hand.* **You cannot use photocopies of the coupons to make your deposits.** *Do not staple, tape, or fold the coupons.*

Purpose of form. Use Form 8109-B to make a tax deposit **only** in the following two situations:

1. You have not yet received your resupply of preprinted deposit coupons (Form 8109); or

2. You are a new entity and have already been assigned an employer identification number (EIN), but you have not received your initial supply of preprinted deposit coupons (Form 8109).

Note: *If you do not receive your resupply of deposit coupons and a deposit is due or you do not receive your initial supply within 5–6 weeks of receipt of your EIN, call 1-800-829-1040.*

Exceptions. If you have applied for an EIN, have not received it, and a deposit must be made, **do not** use Form 8109-B. Instead, send your payment to the IRS address where you file your return. Make your check or money order payable to the United States Treasury and show on it your name (as shown on **Form SS-4,** Application for Employer Identification Number), address, kind of tax, period covered, and date you applied for an EIN. **Do not** use Form 8109-B to deposit delinquent taxes assessed by the IRS. Pay those taxes directly to the IRS. See **Circular E,** Employer's Tax Guide, for information on depositing by electronic funds transfer.

How to complete the form. Enter your name as shown on your return or other IRS correspondence, address, and EIN in the spaces provided. If you are required to file a Form 1120, 990-C, 990-PF (with net investment income), 990-T, or 2438, enter the month in which your tax year ends in the **TAX YEAR MONTH** boxes. For example, if your tax year ends in January, enter 01; if it ends in December, enter 12. Make your entries for EIN and tax year month (if applicable) as specified in **Amount of deposit** below. Darken one box each in the TYPE OF TAX and TAX PERIOD columns as explained below.

Amount of deposit. Enter the amount of the deposit in the space provided. Enter the amount legibly, forming the characters as shown below:

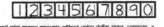

Hand print money amounts without using dollar signs, commas, a decimal point, or leading zeros. If the deposit is for whole dollars only, enter "00" in the CENTS boxes. For example, a deposit of $7,635.22 would be entered like this:

Types of Tax

Form 941	—Employer's Quarterly Federal Tax Return (includes Forms **941-M, 941-PR,** and **941-SS**)
Form 943	—Employer's Annual Return for Agricultural Employers
Form 945	—Annual Return of Withheld Federal Income Tax
Form 720	—Quarterly Federal Excise Tax Return
Form CT-1	—Employer's Annual Railroad Retirement Tax Return
Form 940	—Employer's Annual Federal Unemployment (FUTA) Tax Return (includes Forms **940-EZ** and **940-PR**)
Form 1120	—Corporation Income Tax Return (includes **Form 1120** series of returns and Form **2438**)
Form 990-C	—Farmers' Cooperative Association Income Tax Return
Form 990-T	—Exempt Organization Business Income Tax Return
Form 990-PF	—Return of Private Foundation or Section 4947(a)(1) Nonexempt Charitable Trust Treated as a Private Foundation
Form 1042	—Annual Withholding Tax Return for U.S. Source Income of Foreign Persons

Marking the Proper Tax Period

Payroll taxes and withholding. For Forms 941, 940, 943, 945, CT-1, and 1042 if your liability was incurred during:

- January 1 through March 31, darken the 1st quarter box
- April 1 through June 30, darken the 2nd quarter box
- July 1 through September 30, darken the 3rd quarter box
- October 1 through December 31, darken the 4th quarter box

Note: *If the liability was incurred during one quarter and deposited in another quarter, darken the box for the quarter in which the tax liability was incurred. For example, if the liability was incurred in March and deposited in April, darken the 1st quarter box.*

Excise taxes. For Form 720, follow the instructions above for Forms 941, 940, etc. For Form 990-PF, with net investment income, follow the instructions below for Form 1120, 990-C, etc.

Income Taxes (Form 1120, 990-C, 990-T, and 2438). To make a deposit for the current tax year for any quarter, **darken only the 1st quarter box.** This applies to estimated income tax payments.

Example 1. If your tax year ends on December 31, 2001, and a deposit for 2001 is being made between January 1 and December 31, 2001, darken the 1st quarter box.

Example 2. If your tax year ends on June 30, 2001, and a deposit for that fiscal year is being made between July 1, 2000, and June 30, 2001, darken the 1st quarter box.

To make a deposit for the prior tax year, **darken only the 4th quarter box.** This includes:

- Deposits of balance due shown on the return (Forms 1120, 990-C, 990-T, and 990-PF).

- Deposits of balance due shown on **Form 7004,** Application for Automatic Extension of Time To File Corporation Income Tax Return (be sure to darken the 1120 or 990-C box as appropriate).

(Continued on back of page.)

Department of the Treasury
Internal Revenue Service

Cat. No. 61042S

Form **8109-B** (Rev. 12-2000)

Form **941**
(Rev. January 1996)
Department of the Treasury
Internal Revenue Service (O)

4141

Employer's Quarterly Federal Tax Return
▶ See separate instructions for information on completing this return.
Please type or print.

Enter state code for state in which deposits made . ▶ [ ]
(see page 3 of instructions).

Name (as distinguished from trade name)

Trade name, if any

Address (number and street)

Date quarter ended

Employer identification number

City, state, and ZIP code

OMB No. 1545-0029

T
FF
FD
FP
I
T

If address is different from prior return, check here ▶ [ ]

IRS Use

1 1 1 1 1 1 1 1 1   2   3 3 3 3 3   4 4 4

5 5 5   6   7   8 8 8 8 8   9 9 9   10 10 10 10 10 10 10 10 10 10

If you do not have to file returns in the future, check here ▶ [ ] and enter date final wages paid ▶
If you are a seasonal employer, see **Seasonal employers** on page 1 of the instructions and check here ▶ [ ]

1 Number of employees (except household) employed in the pay period that includes March 12th ▶
2 Total wages and tips, plus other compensation . . . . | **2**
3 Total income tax withheld from wages, tips, and sick pay . . . . | **3**
4 Adjustment of withheld income tax for preceding quarters of calendar year . . . . . | **4**

5 Adjusted total of income tax withheld (line 3 as adjusted by line 4—see instructions) . . | **5**
6a Taxable social security wages . . . . | $ × 12.4% (.124) = | **6a**
  b Taxable social security tips . . . . | $ × 12.4% (.124) = | **6b**
7 Taxable Medicare wages and tips . . . . . | $ × 2.9% (.029) = | **7**
8 Total social security and Medicare taxes (add lines 6a, 6b, and 7). Check here if wages are not subject to social security and/or Medicare tax . . . . ▶ [ ] | **8**
9 Adjustment of social security and Medicare taxes (see instructions for required explanation)
  Sick Pay $ _____ ± Fractions of Cents $ _____ ± Other $ _____ = | **9**
10 Adjusted total of social security and Medicare taxes (line 8 as adjusted by line 9—see instructions) . . . . | **10**

11 **Total taxes** (add lines 5 and 10) . . . . | **11**

12 Advance earned income credit (EIC) payments made to employees, if any . . . . . . | **12**
13 Net taxes (subtract line 12 from line 11). **This should equal line 17, column (d) below** (or line D of Schedule B (Form 941)) . . . . | **13**

14 Total deposits for quarter, including overpayment applied from a prior quarter . . . . . | **14**

15 **Balance due** (subtract line 14 from line 13). See instructions . . . . | **15**
16 **Overpayment,** if line 14 is more than line 13, enter excess here ▶ $ _____
  and check if to be: [ ] Applied to next return OR [ ] Refunded.
  • **All filers:** If line 13 is less than $500, you need not complete line 17 or Schedule B.
  • **Semiweekly schedule depositors:** Complete Schedule B and check here . . . . ▶ [ ]
  • **Monthly schedule depositors:** Complete line 17, columns (a) through (d), and check here. . . . . ▶ [ ]

17	Monthly Summary of Federal Tax Liability.		
(a) First month liability	(b) Second month liability	(c) Third month liability	(d) Total liability for quarter

Sign Here
Under penalties of perjury, I declare that I have examined this return, including accompanying schedules and statements, and to the best of my knowledge and belief, it is true, correct, and complete.

Signature ▶   Print Your Name and Title ▶   Date ▶

For Paperwork Reduction Act Notice, see page 1 of separate instructions.   Cat. No. 17001Z   Form **941** (Rev. 1-96)

Form 941 Quarterly Federal Report.

Form 940 Annual Federal Unemployment Report.

Form 940

Department of the Treasury
Internal Revenue Service (99)

Employer's Annual Federal Unemployment (FUTA) Tax Return

▶ **See separate Instructions for Form 940 for information on completing this form.**

OMB No. 1545-0028

2000

T	
FF	
FD	
FP	
I	
T	

Name (as distinguished from trade name)   Calendar year

Trade name, if any

Address and ZIP code   Employer identification number

A Are you required to pay unemployment contributions to only one state? (If "No," skip questions B and C.) . ☐ Yes ☐ No

B Did you pay all state unemployment contributions by January 31, 2001? ((1) If you deposited your total FUTA tax when due, check "Yes" if you paid all state unemployment contributions by February 12, 2001. (2) If a 0% experience rate is granted, check "Yes." (3) If "No," skip question C.) . . . . ☐ Yes ☐ No

C Were all wages that were taxable for FUTA tax also taxable for your state's unemployment tax? . . . . . ☐ Yes ☐ No

If you answered "No" to any of these questions, you must file Form 940. If you answered "Yes" to all the questions, you may file Form 940-EZ, which is a simplified version of Form 940. (Successor employers see **Special credit for successor employers** on page 3 of the instructions.) You can get Form 940-EZ by calling 1-800-TAX-FORM (1-800-829-3676) or from the IRS Web Site at **www.irs.gov.**

If you will not have to file returns in the future, check here (see **Who Must File** in separate instructions), **and complete and sign the return** . . . . ▶ ☐

If this is an Amended Return, check here. . . . . ▶ ☐

Part I   Computation of Taxable Wages

1	Total payments (including payments shown on lines 2 and 3) during the calendar year for services of employees	**1**	
2	Exempt payments. (Explain all exempt payments, attaching additional sheets if necessary.) ▶	**2**	
3	Payments of more than $7,000 for services. Enter only amounts over the first $7,000 paid to each employee. (See separate instructions.) Do not include any exempt payments from line 2. The $7,000 amount is the Federal wage base. Your state wage base may be different. **Do not use your state wage limitation**	**3**	
4	Total exempt payments (add lines 2 and 3)	**4**	
5	**Total taxable wages** (subtract line 4 from line 1) . . . . ▶	**5**	

Be sure to complete both sides of this form, and sign in the space provided on the back.
For Privacy Act and Paperwork Reduction Act Notice, see separate instructions.   Cat. No. 11234O   Form **940** (2000)

DETACH HERE

Form 940-V

Department of the Treasury
Internal Revenue Service

Form 940 Payment Voucher

Use this voucher only when making a payment with your return.

OMB No. 1545-0028

2000

Complete boxes 1, 2, 3, and 4. Do not send cash, and do not staple your payment to this voucher. Make your check or money order payable to the **"United States Treasury"**. Be sure to enter your employer identification number, "Form 940", and "2000" on your payment.

1 Enter the first four letters of your last name (business name if partnership or corporation).	**2** Enter your employer identification number.	**3** Enter the amount of your payment.
		$

Instructions for Box 1

—Individuals (sole proprietors, trusts, and estates)— Enter the first four letters of your last name.

—Corporations and partnerships—Enter the first four characters of your business name (omit "The" if followed by more than one word).

4 Enter your business name (individual name for sole proprietors)

Enter your address

Enter your city, state, and ZIP code

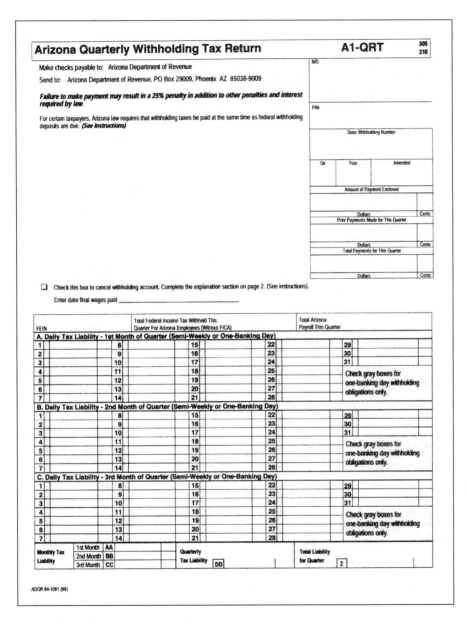

*Form A-1 State
Quarterly Report
(Arizona) (page 2).*

<u>Form A1-QRT Page 2</u>

If this is an amended return, complete the following information:

1. Total liability for quarter from section Z on page 1 of the amended return.	1	
2. Total liability for quarter (section Z) previously reported on Form A1-QRT.	2	
3. If the amount on line 2 is greater than the amount on line 1, enter the difference here. This is the amount of tax overpaid.	3	
4. If the amount on line 1 is greater than the amount on line 2, enter the difference here. This is the amount of tax underpaid.	4	

NOTE: If this amended return is being filed for a quarter in a prior year, attach an amended Form A1-R and the state copies of federal Forms W-2c for the prior year.

Explain why an amended return is being filed:

_____

_____

_____

_____

_____

_____

_____

_____

_____

Reason for cancellation of employer's withholding account (check the applicable box):

☐ 1. Reorganization or change in business entity (example: from corporation to partnership)
☐ 2. Business sold
☐ 3. Business stopped paying wages and will not have any employees in the future
☐ 4. Business permanently closed
☐ 5. Business has only leased or temporary agency employees
☐ 6. Other (specify reason) _____

_____

Under penalties of perjury, I declare that I have examined this return and to the best of my knowledge and belief, it is a true, complete and correct return.

Please Sign Here

Signature	Date	( ) Business telephone number

Paid Preparer's Use Only

Preparer's signature	Date	( ) Business telephone number
Firm's name (or preparer's, if self-employed)		Preparer's EIN or SSN or PTIN
Firm's address		ZIP code

ADOR 64-1061 (99)

State Quarterly Unemployment Report (Arizona).

FORM INCOMPLETE. DO NOT FILE.

ARIZONA DEPARTMENT OF ECONOMIC SECURITY
PO BOX 52027
PHOENIX, AZ 85072-2027

REPORT UC-018 (02/2000) PAGE 1

ARIZONA ACCOUNT NUMBER   0

CALENDAR QUARTER ENDING

TO AVOID PENALTY MAIL BY

FEDERAL ID NO.

C0000000000001 9   0000

USE BLACK INK ONLY

UNEMPLOYMENT TAX AND WAGE REPORT

Telephone (602) 248-9354

A. NUMBER OF EMPLOYEES -
Report for each month, the number of full and part-time covered workers who worked during or received pay subject to UI Taxes for the payroll period which includes the 12th of the month.

C. WAGE SUMMARY - Computation of payment due.
(See instructions for assistance)

1. **TOTAL WAGES PAID IN QUARTER**
   From Section B. Wage Listing

2. **SUBTRACT EXCESS WAGES**
   Cannot exceed Line 1 - see instructions

3. **TAXABLE WAGES PAID**
   Up to $7000 per Employee - Line 1 minus line 2

4. **TAX DUE**
   Line 3 × Tax Rate of   %
   The decimal equivalent =   .

5. **ADD INTEREST DUE**
   1% of Tax Due for each month payment is late

6. **ADD PENALTY FOR LATE REPORT**
   0.10% of Line 1 ($35 min / $200 max)

B. WAGES -
List all employees in Social Security Number order, or alphabetically by last name. Please use white paper in the same format for additional employees. If you have ten or more employees, consider reporting via magnetic media. Ask for "Arizona Magnetic Media Reporting" (PAU-430). We support diskette, tape, and cartridge media.

7. **TOTAL PAYMENT DUE**
   Check Payable to DES-Unemployment Tax

8. **AMOUNT PAID**

LIEN MAY BE FILED WITHOUT FURTHER NOTICE ON DELINQUENT TAXES.

1. Employee Social Security Number	2. Employee Name *(Last, First)*	3. Total Wages Paid in Quarter
	TOTAL WAGES THIS PAGE	
	TOTAL WAGES ALL PAGES	

Signature: _____

Title: _____

Date: _____

Prepared by: _____

Telephone: _____

PHOTO COPY FOR YOUR RECORDS

STF AZ30792F.1

SCHEDULE C
(Form 1040)

Department of the Treasury
Internal Revenue Service   (99)

Profit or Loss From Business
(Sole Proprietorship)

▶ Partnerships, joint ventures, etc., must file Form 1065 or Form 1065-B.

▶ Attach to Form 1040 or Form 1041.   ▶ See Instructions for Schedule C (Form 1040).

OMB No. 1545-0074

2000

Attachment
Sequence No. **09**

Name of proprietor

Social security number (SSN)

A Principal business or profession, including product or service (see page C-1 of the instructions)

B Enter code from pages C-7 & 8
▶

C Business name. If no separate business name, leave blank.

D Employer ID number (EIN), if any

E Business address (including suite or room no.) ▶
City, town or post office, state, and ZIP code

F Accounting method: (1) ☐ Cash   (2) ☐ Accrual   (3) ☐ Other (specify) ▶ _____

G Did you "materially participate" in the operation of this business during 2000? If "No," see page C-2 for limit on losses . ☐ Yes ☐ No

H If you started or acquired this business during 2000, check here . . . . ▶ ☐

Part I Income

1	Gross receipts or sales. **Caution.** If this income was reported to you on Form W-2 and the "Statutory employee" box on that form was checked, see page C-2 and check here . . . . . . ▶ ☐	**1**	
2	Returns and allowances	**2**	
3	Subtract line 2 from line 1	**3**	
4	Cost of goods sold (from line 42 on page 2)	**4**	
5	**Gross profit.** Subtract line 4 from line 3	**5**	
6	Other income, including Federal and state gasoline or fuel tax credit or refund (see page C-2) . . .	**6**	
7	**Gross income.** Add lines 5 and 6 . . . . ▶	**7**	

Part II Expenses. Enter expenses for business use of your home **only** on line 30.

8	Advertising	**8**	19 Pension and profit-sharing plans	**19**	
9	Bad debts from sales or services (see page C-3) . .	**9**	20 Rent or lease (see page C-4):		
			a Vehicles, machinery, and equipment .	**20a**	
10	Car and truck expenses (see page C-3)	**10**	b Other business property . .	**20b**	
11	Commissions and fees . .	**11**	21 Repairs and maintenance . .	**21**	
12	Depletion	**12**	22 Supplies (not included in Part III) .	**22**	
13	Depreciation and section 179 expense deduction (not included in Part III) (see page C-3) . .	**13**	23 Taxes and licenses	**23**	
			24 Travel, meals, and entertainment:		
			a Travel	**24a**	
14	Employee benefit programs (other than on line 19) . . .	**14**	b Meals and entertainment		
15	Insurance (other than health) .	**15**	c Enter nondeduct-ible amount included on line 24b (see page C-5)		
16	Interest:				
a	Mortgage (paid to banks, etc.) .	**16a**	d Subtract line 24c from line 24b .	**24d**	
b	Other	**16b**	25 Utilities	**25**	
17	Legal and professional services	**17**	26 Wages (less employment credits) .	**26**	
18	Office expense	**18**	27 Other expenses (from line 48 on page 2)	**27**	
28	**Total expenses** before expenses for business use of home. Add lines 8 through 27 in columns ▶			**28**	

29	Tentative profit (loss). Subtract line 28 from line 7	**29**	
30	Expenses for business use of your home. Attach **Form 8829**	**30**	
31	**Net profit or (loss).** Subtract line 30 from line 29.		
	• If a profit, enter on **Form 1040, line 12,** and **also** on **Schedule SE, line 2** (statutory employees, see page C-5). Estates and trusts, enter on Form 1041, line 3.	**31**	
	• If a loss, you **must** go to line 32.		
32	If you have a loss, check the box that describes your investment in this activity (see page C-5).		
	• If you checked 32a, enter the loss on **Form 1040, line 12,** and **also** on **Schedule SE, line 2** (statutory employees, see page C-5). Estates and trusts, enter on Form 1041, line 3.	**32a** ☐ All investment is at risk.	
	• If you checked 32b, you **must** attach **Form 6198.**	**32b** ☐ Some investment is not at risk.	

For Paperwork Reduction Act Notice, see Form 1040 instructions.   Cat. No. 11334P   **Schedule C (Form 1040) 2000**

Schedule C (Form 1040) 2000
Page **2**

Part III   Cost of Goods Sold (see page C-6)

33 Method(s) used to value closing inventory: **a** ☐ Cost   **b** ☐ Lower of cost or market   **c** ☐ Other (attach explanation)

34 Was there any change in determining quantities, costs, or valuations between opening and closing inventory? If "Yes," attach explanation . . . . ☐ **Yes** ☐ **No**

35 Inventory at beginning of year. If different from last year's closing inventory, attach explanation . . | **35** |

36 Purchases less cost of items withdrawn for personal use . . . . | **36** |

37 Cost of labor. Do not include any amounts paid to yourself . . . . | **37** |

38 Materials and supplies . . . . | **38** |

39 Other costs . . . . | **39** |

40 Add lines 35 through 39 . . . . | **40** |

41 Inventory at end of year . . . . | **41** |

42 **Cost of goods sold.** Subtract line 41 from line 40. Enter the result here and on page 1, line 4 . . | **42** |

Part IV   Information on Your Vehicle. Complete this part **only** if you are claiming car or truck expenses on line 10 and are not required to file Form 4562 for this business. See the instructions for line 13 on page C-3 to find out if you must file.

43 When did you place your vehicle in service for business purposes? (month, day, year) ▶ ___/___/___ .

44 Of the total number of miles you drove your vehicle during 2000, enter the number of miles you used your vehicle for:

a Business _____ **b** Commuting _____ **c** Other _____

45 Do you (or your spouse) have another vehicle available for personal use?. . . . . ☐ **Yes** ☐ **No**

46 Was your vehicle available for use during off-duty hours? . . . . ☐ **Yes** ☐ **No**

47a Do you have evidence to support your deduction? . . . . ☐ **Yes** ☐ **No**

  b If "Yes," is the evidence written? . . . . ☐ **Yes** ☐ **No**

Part V   Other Expenses. List below business expenses not included on lines 8–26 or line 30.

48 **Total other expenses.** Enter here and on page 1, line 27 . . . . | **48** |

Schedule C (Form 1040) 2000

Schedule C—Profit or Loss from Business (page 2).

Schedule SE—
Self-Employment
Tax.

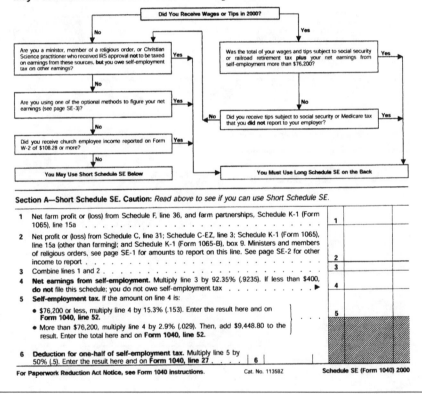

SCHEDULE SE
(Form 1040)

Department of the Treasury
Internal Revenue Service (99)

Self-Employment Tax

▶ See Instructions for Schedule SE (Form 1040).

▶ **Attach to Form 1040.**

20\ 00

Attachment
Sequence No. **17**

Name of person with **self-employment** income (as shown on Form 1040)

Social security number of person
with **self-employment** income ▶

Who Must File Schedule SE

You must file Schedule SE if:

- You had net earnings from self-employment from **other than** church employee income (line 4 of Short Schedule SE or line 4c of Long Schedule SE) of $400 or more **or**
- You had church employee income of $108.28 or more. Income from services you performed as a minister or a member of a religious order **is not** church employee income. See page SE-1.

Note. Even if you had a loss or a small amount of income from self-employment, it may be to your benefit to file Schedule SE and use either "optional method" in Part II of Long Schedule SE. See page SE-3.

Exception. If your only self-employment income was from earnings as a minister, member of a religious order, or Christian Science practitioner **and** you filed Form 4361 and received IRS approval not to be taxed on those earnings, **do not** file Schedule SE. Instead, write "Exempt–Form 4361" on Form 1040, line 52.

May I Use Short Schedule SE or Must I Use Long Schedule SE?

Did You Receive Wages or Tips in 2000?

No → Are you a minister, member of a religious order, or Christian Science practitioner who received IRS approval **not** to be taxed on earnings from these sources, **but** you owe self-employment tax on other earnings? — Yes →

No ↓

Are you using one of the optional methods to figure your net earnings (see page SE-3)? — Yes →

No ↓

Did you receive church employee income reported on Form W-2 of $108.28 or more? — Yes →

No ↓

Yes → Was the total of your wages and tips subject to social security or railroad retirement tax **plus** your net earnings from self-employment more than $76,200? — Yes →

No ↓

Did you receive tips subject to social security or Medicare tax that you **did not** report to your employer? — Yes →

No →

You May Use Short Schedule SE Below

You Must Use Long Schedule SE on the Back

Section A—Short Schedule SE. Caution: *Read above to see if you can use Short Schedule SE.*

1	Net farm profit or (loss) from Schedule F, line 36, and farm partnerships, Schedule K-1 (Form 1065), line 15a	**1**
2	Net profit or (loss) from Schedule C, line 31; Schedule C-EZ, line 3; Schedule K-1 (Form 1065), line 15a (other than farming); and Schedule K-1 (Form 1065-B), box 9. Ministers and members of religious orders, see page SE-1 for amounts to report on this line. See page SE-2 for other income to report	**2**
3	Combine lines 1 and 2	**3**
4	**Net earnings from self-employment.** Multiply line 3 by 92.35% (.9235). If less than $400, **do not** file this schedule; you do not owe self-employment tax . . . . ▶	**4**
5	**Self-employment tax.** If the amount on line 4 is: • $76,200 or less, multiply line 4 by 15.3% (.153). Enter the result here and on **Form 1040, line 52.** • More than $76,200, multiply line 4 by 2.9% (.029). Then, add $9,448.80 to the result. Enter the total here and on **Form 1040, line 52.**	**5**
6	**Deduction for one-half of self-employment tax.** Multiply line 5 by 50% (.5). Enter the result here and on **Form 1040, line 27**	**6**

For Paperwork Reduction Act Notice, see Form 1040 instructions.

Cat. No. 11358Z

Schedule SE (Form 1040) 2000

Schedule SE (Form 1040) 2000 — Attachment Sequence No. **17** — Page **2**

Name of person with **self-employment** income (as shown on Form 1040)	Social security number of person with **self-employment** income ▶

Section B—Long Schedule SE

Part I   Self-Employment Tax

Note. If your only income subject to self-employment tax is **church employee income,** skip lines 1 through 4b. Enter -0- on line 4c and go to line 5a. Income from services you performed as a minister or a member of a religious order **is not** church employee income. See page SE-1.

A If you are a minister, member of a religious order, or Christian Science practitioner **and** you filed Form 4361, but you had $400 or more of **other** net earnings from self-employment, check here and continue with Part I . . . . . ▶ ☐

1	Net farm profit or (loss) from Schedule F, line 36, and farm partnerships, Schedule K-1 (Form 1065), line 15a. **Note.** Skip this line if you use the farm optional method. See page SE-3 . .	**1**	
2	Net profit or (loss) from Schedule C, line 31; Schedule C-EZ, line 3; Schedule K-1 (Form 1065), line 15a (other than farming); and Schedule K-1 (Form 1065-B), box 9. Ministers and members of religious orders, see page SE-1 for amounts to report on this line. See page SE-2 for other income to report. **Note.** Skip this line if you use the nonfarm optional method. See page SE-3.	**2**	
3	Combine lines 1 and 2	**3**	
4a	If line 3 is more than zero, multiply line 3 by 92.35% (.9235). Otherwise, enter amount from line 3	**4a**	
b	If you elect one or both of the optional methods, enter the total of lines 15 and 17 here . .	**4b**	
c	Combine lines 4a and 4b. If less than $400, **do not** file this schedule; you do not owe self-employment tax. **Exception.** If less than $400 and you had church **employee income,** enter -0- and continue ▶	**4c**	
5a	Enter your **church employee income** from Form W-2. **Caution:** See page SE-1 for definition of church employee income.	**5a**	
b	Multiply line 5a by 92.35% (.9235). If less than $100, enter -0- .	**5b**	
6	**Net earnings from self-employment.** Add lines 4c and 5b . . .	**6**	
7	Maximum amount of combined wages and self-employment earnings subject to social security tax or the 6.2% portion of the 7.65% railroad retirement (tier 1) tax for 2000	**7**	76,200 00
8a	Total social security wages and tips (total of boxes 3 and 7 on Form(s) W-2) and railroad retirement (tier 1) compensation .	**8a**	
b	Unreported tips subject to social security tax (from Form 4137, line 9)	**8b**	
c	Add lines 8a and 8b	**8c**	
9	Subtract line 8c from line 7. If zero or less, enter -0- here and on line 10 and go to line 11 . ▶	**9**	
10	Multiply the **smaller** of line 6 or line 9 by 12.4% (.124)	**10**	
11	Multiply line 6 by 2.9% (.029)	**11**	
12	**Self-employment tax.** Add lines 10 and 11. Enter here and on **Form 1040, line 52**	**12**	
13	**Deduction for one-half of self-employment tax.** Multiply line 12 by 50% (.5). Enter the result here and on **Form 1040, line 27**	**13**	

Part II   Optional Methods To Figure Net Earnings (See page SE-3.)

Farm Optional Method. You may use this method **only** if:
• Your gross farm income[1] was not more than $2,400 **or**
• Your net farm profits[2] were less than $1,733.

14	Maximum income for optional methods	**14**	1,600 00
15	Enter the **smaller** of: two-thirds (⅔) of gross farm income[1] (not less than zero) **or** $1,600. Also include this amount on line 4b above	**15**	

Nonfarm Optional Method. You may use this method **only** if:
• Your net nonfarm profits[3] were less than $1,733 and also less than 72.189% of your gross nonfarm income[4] **and**
• You had net earnings from self-employment of at least $400 in 2 of the prior 3 years.
Caution: You may use this method no more than five times.

16	Subtract line 15 from line 14	**16**	
17	Enter the **smaller** of: two-thirds (⅔) of gross nonfarm income[4] (not less than zero) **or** the amount on line 16. Also include this amount on line 4b above	**17**	

[1]From Sch. F, line 11, and Sch. K-1 (Form 1065), line 15b.   [3]From Sch. C, line 31; Sch. C-EZ, line 3; Sch. K-1 (Form 1065), line 15a; and Sch. K-1 (Form 1065-B), box 9.
[2]From Sch. F, line 36, and Sch. K-1 (Form 1065), line 15a.   [4]From Sch. C, line 7; Sch. C-EZ, line 1; Sch. K-1 (Form 1065), line 15c; and Sch. K-1 (Form 1065-B), box 9.

Schedule SE **(Form 1040) 2000**

Schedule ES—
Estimated Tax
Worksheet.

Making Payments by Check or Money Order Using the Payment Voucher

There is a separate payment voucher for each due date. The due date is shown in the upper right corner. Please be sure you use the voucher with the correct due date for each payment you make. Complete and send in the voucher **only** if you are making a payment by check or money order. To complete the voucher:

• Type or print your name, address, and SSN in the space provided on the voucher. If filing a joint voucher, also enter your spouse's name and SSN. List the names and SSNs in the same order on the joint voucher as you will list them on your joint return. If you and your spouse plan to file separate returns, file separate vouchers instead of a joint voucher.

• Enter on the payment line of the voucher only the amount you are sending in by check or money order. When making payments of estimated tax, be sure to take into account any 1999 overpayment that you choose to credit against your 2000 tax, but **do not** include the overpayment amount on the payment line.

(continued on page 5)

2000 Estimated Tax Worksheet (keep for your records)

1	Enter amount of adjusted gross income you expect in 2000 (see instructions)	1
2	• If you plan to itemize deductions, enter the estimated total of your itemized deductions. **Caution:** *If line 1 above is over $128,950 ($64,475 if married filing separately), your deduction may be reduced. See Pub. 505 for details.* • If you do not plan to itemize deductions, see **Standard deduction for 2000** on page 2, and enter your standard deduction here.	2
3	Subtract line 2 from line 1	3
4	Exemptions. Multiply $2,800 by the number of personal exemptions. If you can be claimed as a dependent on another person's 2000 return, your personal exemption is not allowed. **Caution:** *See Pub. 505 to figure the amount to enter if line 1 above is over: $193,400 if married filing jointly or qualifying widow(er); $161,150 if head of household; $128,950 if single; or $96,700 if married filing separately*	4
5	Subtract line 4 from line 3	5
6	**Tax.** Figure your tax on the amount on line 5 by using the **2000 Tax Rate Schedules** on page 2. **Caution:** *If you have a net capital gain, see Pub. 505 to figure the tax*	6
7	Alternative minimum tax from Form 6251	7
8	Add lines 6 and 7. Also include any tax from Forms 4972 and 8814 and any recapture of the education credits (see instructions)	8
9	Credits (see instructions). Do not include any income tax withholding on this line	9
10	Subtract line 9 from line 8. Enter the result, but not less than zero	10
11	Self-employment tax (see instructions). Estimate of 2000 net earnings from self-employment $_____ ; if **$76,200 or less**, multiply the amount by 15.3%; if **more than $76,200**, multiply the amount by 2.9%, add $9,448.80 to the result, and enter the total. **Caution:** *If you also have wages subject to social security tax, see Pub. 505 to figure the amount to enter* . .	11
12	Other taxes (see instructions)	12
13a	Add lines 10 through 12	13a
b	Earned income credit, additional child tax credit, and credit from Form 4136	13b
c	Subtract line 13b from line 13a. Enter the result, but not less than zero. **THIS IS YOUR TOTAL 2000 ESTIMATED TAX** . . . . ▶	13c
14a	Multiply line 13c by 90% (66⅔% for farmers and fishermen) . . .	14a	
b	Enter the tax shown on your 1999 tax return (108.6% of that amount if you are not a farmer or fisherman and the adjusted gross income shown on line 34 of that return is more than $150,000 or, if married filing separately for 2000, more than $75,000)	14b	
c	Enter the **smaller** of line 14a or 14b. **THIS IS YOUR REQUIRED ANNUAL PAYMENT TO AVOID A PENALTY** . . . . ▶	14c
	Caution: *Generally, if you do not prepay (through income tax withholding and estimated tax payments) at least the amount on line 14c, you may owe a penalty for not paying enough estimated tax. To avoid a penalty, make sure your estimate on line 13c is as accurate as possible. Even if you pay the required annual payment, you may still owe tax when you file your return. If you prefer, you may pay the amount shown on line 13c. For more details, see Pub. 505.*	
15	Income tax withheld and estimated to be withheld during 2000 (including income tax withholding on pensions, annuities, certain deferred income, etc.)	15
16	Subtract line 15 from line 14c. (**Note:** *If zero or less, or line 13c minus line 15 is less than $1,000, stop here. You are not required to make estimated tax payments.*)	16
17	If the first payment you are required to make is due April 17, 2000, enter ¼ of line 16 (minus any 1999 overpayment that you are applying to this installment) here, and on your payment voucher(s) if you are paying by check or money order. (**Note:** *Household employers, see instructions.*) . .	17

Page 4

1099–MISC.

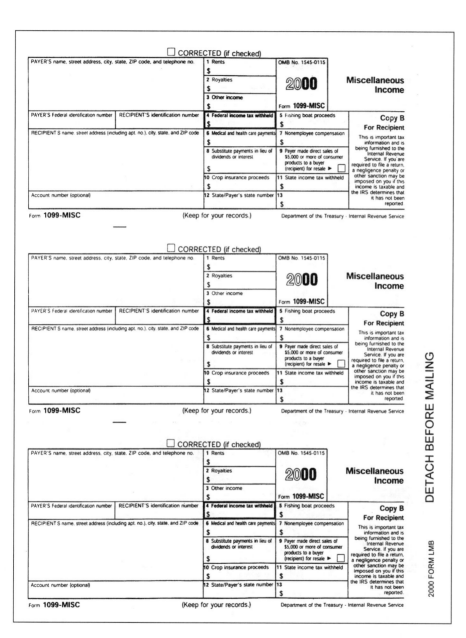

1096 Transmittal for 1099 Reports.

DO NOT STAPLE 6969

Form **1096**		**Annual Summary and Transmittal of U.S. Information Returns**	OMB No. 1545-0108
Department of the Treasury Internal Revenue Service			**2000**

ATTACH IRS LABEL HERE

FILER'S name

Street address (including room or suite number)

City, state, and ZIP code

If you are not using a preprinted label, enter in box 1 or 2 below the identification number you used as the filer on the information returns being transmitted. Do not fill in both boxes 1 and 2.	Name of person to contact if the IRS needs more information	**For Official Use Only**
	Telephone number ( )	

1 Employer identification number	2 Social security number	3 Total number of forms	4 Federal income tax withheld $	5 Total amount reported with this Form 1096 $

Enter an "X" in only one box below to indicate the type of form being filed. If this is your FINAL return, enter an "X" here .... ▶ ☐

W-2G 32	1098 81	1098-E 84	1098-T 83	1099-A 80	1099-B 79	1099-C 85	1099-DIV 91	1099-G 86	1099-INT 92	1099-LTC 93	1099-MISC 95	1099-MSA 94	1099-OID 96
☐	☐	☐	☐	☐	☐	☐	☐	☐	☐	☐	☐	☐	☐

1099-PATR 97	1099-R 98	1099-S 75	5498 28	5498-MSA 27
☐	☐	☐	☐	☐

Please return this entire page to the Internal Revenue Service. Photocopies are NOT acceptable.

Under penalties of perjury, I declare that I have examined this return and accompanying documents, and, to the best of my knowledge and belief, they are true, correct, and complete.

Signature ▶   Title ▶   Date ▶

Instructions

Purpose of form. Use this form to transmit paper Forms 1099, 1098, 5498, and W-2G to the Internal Revenue Service. (See **Where To File** on the back.) DO NOT USE FORM 1096 TO TRANSMIT MAGNETIC MEDIA. See **Form 4804**, Transmittal of Information Returns Reported Magnetically/Electronically.

Use of preprinted label. If you received a preprinted label from the IRS with Package 1099, place the label in the name and address area of this form inside the brackets. Make any necessary changes to your name and address on the label. However, do not use the label if the taxpayer identification number (TIN) shown is incorrect. **Do not prepare your own label. Use only the IRS-prepared label that came with your Package 1099.**

If you are not using a preprinted label, enter the filer's name, address (including room, suite, or other unit number), and TIN in the spaces provided on the form.

Filer. The name, address, and TIN of the filer on this form must be the same as those you enter in the upper left area of Form 1099, 1098, 5498, or W-2G. A filer includes a payer, a recipient of mortgage interest payments (including points) or student loan interest, an educational institution, a broker, a barter exchange, a creditor, a person reporting real estate transactions, a trustee or issuer of any individual retirement arrangement or a medical savings account (MSA) (including a Medicare+Choice MSA), and a lender who acquires an interest in secured property or who has reason to know that the property has been abandoned.

Transmitting to the IRS. Send the forms in a flat mailing (not folded). Group the forms by form number and transmit each group with a **separate** Form 1096. For example, if you must file both Forms 1098 and 1099-A, complete one Form 1096 to transmit your Forms 1098 and another Form 1096 to transmit your Forms 1099-A. You need not submit original and corrected returns separately. **Do not** send a form (1099, 5498, etc.) containing summary (subtotal) information with Form 1096. Summary information for the group of forms being sent is entered only in boxes 3, 4, and 5 of Form 1096.

Box 1 or 2. Complete only if you are not using a preprinted IRS label. Individuals not in a trade or business must enter their social security number (SSN) in box 2; sole proprietors and all others must enter their employer identification number (EIN) in box 1. However, sole proprietors who do not have an EIN must enter their SSN in box 2.

Box 3. Enter the number of forms you are transmitting with this Form 1096. Do not include blank or voided forms or the Form 1096 in your total. Enter the number of correctly completed forms, not the number of pages, being transmitted. For example, if you send one page of three-to-a-page Forms 5498 with a Form 1096 and you have correctly completed two Forms 5498 on that page, enter "2" in box 3 of Form 1096.

Box 4. Enter the total Federal income tax withheld shown on the forms being transmitted with this Form 1096.

For more information and the Privacy Act and Paperwork Reduction Act Notice, see the 2000 General Instructions for Forms 1099, 1098, 5498, and W-2G.

41-1628081   Form **1096** (2000)

DETACH BEFORE MAILING

2000 FORM L1096

Accounting Terms, Resources, and Further Reading

ACCOUNTING TERMS

account   A specific place within an accounting system used to record and hold financial data.

Accounts Payable   The account set up to record Expenses that are owed but not yet paid out.

Accounts Receivable   The account set up to record Income on sales or services that will be collected at a later date.

accrual basis   Recognizing Income on sales or services that has not yet been collected, and recognizing Expenses that have not yet been paid out. This method puts Accounts Payable and Accounts Receivable into use.

amortization   The process by which the value of intangible business Assets is reduced and written off the books.

Asset   Something of value that is owned by a business.

Balance Sheet   The financial report that presents the year-to-date values of Assets, Liabilities, and Equity.

bottom line   The net profit or loss.

capital   Cash or something of value that is invested in an enterprise.

cash basis   The method of accounting that recognizes only the revenue that has actually been received and the Expenses that have actually been paid out.

Cash Disbursements Journal   The place in an accounting system where outgoing payments are recorded.

Cash Receipts Journal   The place in an accounting system where incoming revenue is recorded.

Chart of Accounts   The listing of accounts established to record financial data.

credit   An offset to a debit.

debit   An offset to a credit.

depreciation   The reduction in value of an asset.

entry   The method by which financial information is recorded.

Equity   The value that is retained.

financial statements   Reports that present the financial condition of a business.

General Journal Entry   An adjustment made to accounts in the General Ledger.

General Ledger   The place in an accounting system that holds all the accounts and the entries that have been posted to them.

Gross Profit   The amount of Income remaining after direct costs have been deducted from the revenue generated by sales or services.

Income Statement   Another term for the Profit and Loss Statement.

Liabilities   Debts or Expenses.

net loss   The amount that exceeds the Income from sales or services after costs and Expenses have been deducted.

net profit   The amount of Income remaining after direct costs and Expenses have been deducted from the revenue generated by sales or services.

Profit and Loss Statement   The report that presents the Income and Expenses of a business enterprise.

retained earnings   The amount of profit or loss that is carried over from month to month and year to year.

Trial Balance   A report that lists all the accounts in the General Ledger, with their year-to-date balances.

RESOURCES

Your state's Society of Certified Public Accountants can recommend professional accountants to handle more complex accounting duties and tax issues.

The Internal Revenue Service offers a number of tax assistance and information programs for individuals and small businesses.

You can access the IRS's Internet Web site 24 hours a day, 7 days a week, at www.irs.gov to download forms, instructions, and publications; see answers to frequently asked tax questions, and figure your withholding allowances by using the site's W-4 calculator.

IRS forms and publications can also be obtained by calling 1-800-829-3676. You can listen to prerecorded messages on tax topics by calling 1-800-829-4477.

Contact your state for state tax information, forms, and publications. Many states have Web sites that provide these services as well.

FURTHER READING

The following books will provide more information on the topics that you studied in this text:

Aslett, Don. *The Office Clutter Cure: How to Get Out from Under It All*. USA: Marsh Creek Press, April, 1995.

Hemphill, Barbara. *Taming the Paper Tiger at Work*. USA: Kiplinger Books, October, 1998.

Horngren, Charles T. *Cost Accounting: A Managerial Emphasis*. USA: Prentice Hall, July, 1999.

Horngren, Charles T. et al. *Introduction to Management Accounting*. USA: Prentice Hall, August, 1998.

Tracey, John A. *How to Read a Financial Report*. USA: John Wiley & Sons, February, 1999.

Viale, J. David. *Basics of Inventory Management: From Warehouse to Distribution Center*. USA: Crisp Publications, January, 1997.

Appendix D

Answers to "Hour's Up!" Quizzes

Hour 1

1. b
2. a
3. b
4. b
5. d
6. a
7. b
8. b
9. b
10. a

Hour 2

1. b
2. c
3. d
4. a
5. b
6. a
7. a
8. c
9. a
10. a

Hour 3

1. a
2. a
3. a
4. b
5. b
6. a
7. b
8. c
9. a
10. c

Hour 4

1. a
2. a
3. b
4. d
5. a
6. a
7. b
8. b
9. c
10. b

Hour 5

1. a
2. d
3. b
4. b
5. a
6. c
7. b
8. a
9. a
10. b

Hour 6

1. a
2. a
3. b
4. b
5. a
6. c
7. a
8. b
9. a
10. a

Hour 7

1. a
2. b
3. a
4. a
5. a
6. b
7. b
8. b
9. b
10. b

Hour 8

1. b
2. a
3. b
4. c
5. a
6. b
7. b
8. a
9. c
10. b

Hour 9

1. b
2. a
3. c
4. a
5. b
6. a
7. a
8. b
9. a
10. c

Hour 10

1. b
2. a
3. b
4. c
5. a
6. a
7. a
8. d
9. b
10. b

Hour 11

1. a
2. b
3. a
4. b
5. c
6. b
7. b
8. a
9. b
10. a

Hour 12

1. c
2. a
3. b
4. b
5. a
6. b
7. a
8. c
9. c
10. b

Hour 13

1. a
2. b
3. a
4. b
5. b
6. c
7. a
8. b
9. b
10. b

Hour 14

1. c
2. b
3. b
4. d
5. a
6. b
7. b
8. a
9. b
10. a

Hour 15

1. a
2. a
3. c
4. a
5. a
6. b
7. d
8. a
9. b
10. c

Hour 16

1. c
2. b
3. a
4. b
5. c
6. b
7. b
8. b
9. b
10. a

Hour 17

1. a
2. b
3. a
4. b
5. b
6. c
7. a
8. b
9. a
10. b

Hour 18

1. b
2. a
3. c
4. c
5. b
6. b
7. a
8. b
9. b
10. c

HOUR 19

1. c
2. a
3. b
4. a
5. a
6. b
7. a
8. a
9. a
10. d

HOUR 20

1. b
2. a
3. c
4. b
5. d
6. a
7. a
8. a
9. a
10. a

HOUR 21

1. b
2. a
3. c
4. a
5. b
6. a
7. a
8. b
9. a
10. c

HOUR 22

1. a
2. a
3. b
4. a
5. c
6. b
7. a
8. a
9. c
10. b

HOUR 23

1. a
2. a
3. c
4. b
5. b
6. b
7. b
8. a
9. a
10. b

HOUR 24

1. a
2. a
3. c
4. b
5. d
6. a
7. a
8. b
9. a
10. c

Index

depreciable assets,
7-9
Equipment, 8
Furniture and
Fixtures, 8
Inventory, 6-7
Land, 7
Leasehold
Improvements, 8
Organization Costs, 8
Other Assets, 9
Vehicles, 8
Auto Expenses
accounts, 19

B

Balance Sheets, 5-6,
245-247
Assets accounts, 6-9
Accounts
Receivable, 6
Accumulated
Depreciation, 7-8
Amortization
(Organization
Costs), 9
Building, 7
Cash in Checking,
6
Cash in Savings, 6
Cash on Hand, 6
current versus
long-term assets,
6

depreciable assets,
7-9
Equipment, 8
Furniture and
Fixtures, 8
Inventory, 6-7
Land, 7
Leasehold
Improvements, 8
Organization
Costs, 8
Other Assets, 9
Vehicles, 8
Equity accounts,
11-13
Capital, 11
Common Stock,
11
Drawing, 11
Retained Earnings,
11
Liabilities accounts, 9
Accounts Payable,
9
Accrued Expenses,
10
Accrued Payroll
Taxes, 10
Credit Cards
Payable, 10
Loans Payable, 10
long-term versus
short-term liabili-
ties, 9-10
Sales Tax
Collected, 10

utilizing as a manag-
ing tool, 249
balancing
Accounts Receivable,
192-195
accrual accounts,
199-200
bank accounts,
221-225
bank accounts, 221-225
Bank Service Charges
accounts, 20
*Basics of Inventory
Management: From
Warehouse to
Distribution* (Viale), 86
bottom line, 253
Building accounts, 7
businesses
checking accounts,
107-110
taxes, 176-177,
268-269

C

calculations, interest,
99-102
Capital accounts, 11
cash basis accounting
systems, 4
Cash Disbursements
Journals, 199
balancing accrual
accounts, 199-200

H-I

hiring employees, 136-137

I-9 forms, 138
Income accounts, 16
Income Taxes accounts, 21
Interest Income, 16
Other Income, 16
Sale of Fixed Assets, 17
Sale of Goods or Services, 16
Sales Discounts, 16
Sales Returns and Allowances, 16
Insurance accounts
Employee Group accounts, 20
General accounts, 20
Officers Life accounts, 20
interest
calculations and adjustments, 99-102
Interest Expense accounts, 20
Interest Income accounts, 16
inventory
additions and subtractions, 80-86

control methods
perpetual inventory, 85
specific identification, 84-85
FIFO (first in, first out), 85
Inventory accounts, 6-7
LIFO (last in, first out), 85

J-K

journals
Cash Disbursements Journals, 199
balancing accrual accounts, 199-200
petty cash funds, 202-207
tax payments, 200-201
Temporary Distribution account postings, 207
Cash Receipts Journals, 181
cash/credit transactions, 188-189
current month and year-to-date financial data, 181-188

posting cash receipts and sales to the General Ledger, 190
General Journal Entries, 225
Payroll Journals, 211

L

Land accounts, 7
last in, first out (LIFO), 85
Leasehold Improvements accounts, 8
ledgers
employee, 167-168
general, 4-5
account setup, 25-26
accounting periods, 26-27
adding accounts, 45-46
bank reconciliation postings, 226-230
cash receipts and sales postings, 190
debit and credit accounts, 28-30
eliminating accounts, 47-48